Library and Information Science in China

Bibliographies and Indexes in Library and Information Science

English-Language Dictionaries, 1604-1900
Robert Keating O'Neill, compiler

Government Information: Education and Research, 1928-1986
John Richardson, Jr.

Library and Information Science in China

An Annotated Bibliography

Compiled by
Karen T. Wei

Foreword by Michael Gorman

Bibliographies and Indexes in Library and Information Science, Number 3

Greenwood Press
New York • Westport, Connecticut • London

Library of Congress Cataloging-in-Publication Data

Wei, Karen T.
Library and information science in China : an annotated bibliography / compiled by Karen T. Wei ; foreword by Michael Gorman.
p. cm. — (Bibliographies and indexes in library and information science, ISSN 0742-6879 ; no. 3)
Includes indexes
ISBN 0-313-25548-2 (lib. bdg. : alk. paper)
1. Library science—China—Bibliography. 2. Information science—China—Bibliography. 3. Libraries—China—Bibliography.
I. Title. II. Series.
Z845.C5W45 1988
016.02'0951—dc19 88-17767

British Library Cataloguing in Publication Data is available.

Library of Congress Catalog Card Number: 88-17767
ISBN: 0-313-25548-2
ISSN: 0742-6879

First published in 1988

Greenwood Press, Inc.
88 Post Road West, Westport, Connecticut 06881

Printed in the United States of America

The paper used in this book complies with the Permanent Paper Standard issued by the National Information Standards Organization (Z39.48-1984).

10 9 8 7 6 5 4 3 2 1

Contents

Foreword

I welcome the opportunity to write the foreword to my colleague Professor Wei's latest book. She brings a deep knowledge of modern bibliography (as demonstrated in her earlier Women in China) and an expertise in area studies librarianship to bear on the literature of librarianship in China. This research guide has an impressive scope, covering all of the twentieth century and the latter years of the nineteenth century. Using this annotated bibliography the researcher will find a compilation of all the important sources regarding library and information science in China as well as many of the lesser known citations. The emphasis of Professor Wei's Library and Information Science in China is literature written in English, although the guide also includes citations to important items in Western European and Asian languages. I have found the arrangement of the material to be especially helpful and the grouping of citations useful in identifying topics and correlating information. Professor Wei's annotations are thorough and analytical and will assist the scholar in distinguishing between relevant and marginal reference items.

The great purpose of librarianship is that of preserving and disseminating the records of culture and scholarship. Works such as the present volume carry on that great purpose in an exemplary manner. The result is a unique and indispensable tool for the beginning researcher and the advanced scholar alike. I commend Professor Wei and recommend her book to all with an interest in the world of international librarianship.

Michael Gorman
Director of the General Services Department
University of Illinois at Urbana-Champaign Library

Preface

This book is designed to serve as a research guide to library and information science in China and to meet the needs of scholars, researchers, librarians, and library school students in their search for sources in the field. Although there are a few small bibliographies in the field, this compilation represents the most comprehensive and up-to-date work, covering a longer time period and larger geographical areas than other bibliographies.

More than two years have passed since the conception and eventual publication of this work. During this period, my graduate student assistants and I thoroughly searched major catalogs, indexes, abstracts, and bibliographies on library and information science, Chinese and Asian studies, and social science studies. Wilsonline and ERIC databases were also consulted. Data were gathered, selected, verified, annotated, and classified into the present form in this book of nearly 1,000 citations.

The present work consists mainly of English-language materials and titles of great importance in Chinese, French, German, and Japanese literature. Any comments and suggestions from users would be highly appreciated.

I am greatly indebted to the faculty and staff of the University of Illinois Library for their support during the long process of compiling this guide. I am particularly grateful to the financial support I received from the Research and Publications Committee of the University Library.

I would also like to extend my thanks to the librarians at the Asian Library, Library and Information Science Library, and the interlibrary loan services; to Professors Michael Gorman, William S. Wong, Patricia Stenstrom, and

Priscilla Yu for their generous assistance and advice; and to Gina Chu and Hung-ying Hsü for their diligent work in the initial collection of data. My thanks are also due to Alex Pan for his assistance in using the computer to generate this work and to Lisa Boise for her assistance in producing the final manuscript from a laser printer.

Finally, I would like to thank my family members for their support and encouragement. Without their understanding and cooperation this book would not have reached fruition.

Karen T. Wei
Chinese Librarian
University of Illinois at Urbana-Champaign Library

Introduction

Library and Information Science in China is an annotated bibliography covering literature from the late nineteenth century to early 1987. This work encompasses approximately one hundred years of work in the field, though the emphasis is on twentieth-century publications. Although not intended to be exhaustive, this volume contains substantial information concerning the subject.

Included in the bibliography are books, chapters or sections of books, journal articles, conference papers, master's theses, doctoral dissertations, and documents from the ERIC database. The annotations are based on the library collection of the University of Illinois at Urbana-Champaign and on materials made accessible through interlibrary loan services. Over 96% of the citations are annotated with full bibliographical information. Some items not available for examination are cited according to the published sources.

The bibliography consists of nearly 1,000 entries. The majority are in English. However, important foreign titles in Chinese, French, German, and Japanese are selectively included. For foreign titles to be included in this bibliography, they had to be relevant to the subject, indexed in the major library literatures, have English translations or abstracts, and be accessible.

Organization of the Book

The book is organized according to eleven topical arrangements: Bibliography and Reference, Books and Printing, History, Types of Libraries, Technical Services Activities, Automation and Information Services, Education for Librarianship, Publishing and Trade, General Works, International Exchange and Activities, and Librarians.

Within each topic, the arrangement is alphabetical by the author's last name (or by title if the author is unknown). The annotations are based on items which have been examined by the compiler and are generally descriptive as well as analytical in nature. Thus, the reader can form reasonable judgments and make selection decisions.

Two indexes are included. The author index is an alphabetical listing of authors, co-authors, compilers, and corporate bodies as authors cited in the book. Using Library Literature as a guide, the subject index supplements the topical arrangement of the work, providing access to multiple subject entries. Every effort has been made to classify entries in the most suitable topic. Entries are cross-referenced in the subject index to ensure accessibility from different subjects. The numbers cited in both indexes refer to entry numbers rather than pages.

Content of the Book

Chapter 1 of the book includes major bibliographies and reference works in the fields of Asian Studies, Chinese Studies, and library and information science in China and Taiwan. A few short bibliographies on the subject of Chinese librarianship are also identified in this chapter. Chapter 2 includes bibliographies on books and printing in China. From a historical perspective, this section deals with the history of Chinese books, the evolution of Chinese printing, and the impact of modern technology on the current publishing industry.

Chapter 3, one of the more lengthy in the book, concerns the history of Chinese libraries and librarianship. This chapter is chronologically divided into four sections, starting with the earliest development of Chinese libraries and running through to the eve of the establishment of the People's Republic of China in 1949. During this period, the emphasis of the bibliography is placed on the traditional Chinese library development and the western influence, particularly American, on the public library movement in China during the first quarter of the twentieth century. Chinese library conditions during the destructive Sino-Japanese War of 1937-1945 are listed here as well. The next section of chapter 3 examines the period of the People's Republic of China from 1949 until the end of the Cultural Revolution in 1976. The communist ideology dominated the library operation of this period. Although the Chinese government recognized the importance of libraries in the education of Chinese people and the enormous growth of libraries in mainland China, the basic operations of libraries did not meet the needs of modern times let alone the stalemate situation of the Cultural Revolution period (1966-1976) which hindered the normal development of the libraries in China. The passing of the Mao era and the modernization of the country under new leadership allowed for advancement in the field of libraries and librarianship in China. Especially noted is the growth of international exchange activities after 1976. The personal reports of foreign librarians visiting China on arranged study tours increased dramatically during this period. A separate subsection is thus created to accommodate literature of this genre. Finally, chapter 3 covers library activities under the nationalist government of the Republic of China in Taiwan from 1945 to the present. The progress of the library movement in Taiwan is steady and enjoying the stable political circumstances and advanced technology. A few articles covering overlapping periods within this chapter are generally classified according to the earlier period unless the latter period is stressed.

Chapter 4 lists entries concerning types of libraries according to the following categories: National, College and University, Public, Special, School/Children's Libraries, and Archives. Citations that involve both types of libraries and functions of libraries, such as acquisition work of a national library, are placed under National Libraries; the subject index allows accessibility through "acquisitions."

Chapter 5--Technical Services Activities--comprises two sections: Cataloging and Classification and Chinese Collections and Acquisitions. Many of the entries in this chapter are closely related to chapter 6 which concerns automation and information services of modern libraries in China. Therefore, the use of the subject index is extremely important in locating desirable materials in both chapters.

Librarianship is the theme of chapter 7. Both the formal education for librarians in the classroom setting and informal education (such as in-service training, workshops, on-the-job instruction) under a professional librarian are included in this chapter. The book trade and publishing industry in China and Taiwan are the focus of chapter 8. Current publishing conditions, future trends, publishers, and various exhibits and displays leading toward the signing of book trade between China and other countries are included in this section. Chapter 9 consists of citations not easily categorized in any of the other chapters. Such topics as copyright legislation, library associations, and research in librarianship are listed here.

The last chapters, International Exchange and Activities and Librarians, include bibliographies on international exchange of publications and personnel and the librarian's life and career in the field of library and information science in China respectively.

Cross-reference

The Wade-Giles romanization system is used in the text when Chinese personal, geographic, and corporate bodies are involved. However, both Wade-Giles and Pinyin romanization systems are used in entries according to their original citations. It is understood that in the absence of Chinese characters it is difficult to determine original names in order to consistently use one form of transliteration. As a result, cross-references are made in the index sections whenever possible to ensure that readers have all the possible avenues needed to locate an item. Cross-references are also made in the text when a reference is made to other bibliographic entries in the book.

The citations contain full bibliographic description of the items. Standard information is supplied to all entries. When an ERIC document is cited, the ERIC document number is provided in parenthesis, i.e. (ED 123 456).

1

Bibliography and Reference

1. ALA World Encyclopedia of Library and Information Services, edited by Robert Wedgeworth. 2nd ed. Chicago: American Library Association, 1986. 895 pp.

   Containing 85% new or revised contributions as well as a 43% increase over the original, this second edition of the encyclopedia is divided into four parts: (1) the library in society; (2) the library as an institution; (3) theory and practice of librarianship; and (4) education and research. It includes articles on the People's Republic of China and the Republic of China (Taiwan) regarding their history, various types of libraries, and the library profession. It also contains biographical information on famous librarians in these two Chinas.

2. Berton, Peter, and Wu, Eugene. Contemporary China: A Research Guide. Stanford: Hoover Institution on War, Revolution, and Peace, Stanford University, 1967. 695 pp.

   This bibliography provides the most significant bibliographic and reference works, selected documentary compilations, and a listing of series, dissertations, and theses on contemporary China. There is a section on library science under subject bibliographies.

3. Bibliography of Asian Studies, 1941-. Ann Arbor: Association for Asian Studies. Annual.

   This annual, previously issued as part of the Journal of Asian Studies, provides a comprehensive listing of publications in Western languages on Asian countries. Entries are geographically arranged and then classified by subject. "Library and Information Sciences" is listed under each geographic unit and subarranged by archives, bibliography, cataloging, libraries and information centers, manuscripts, and reference. There is an author index, but no annotations. Cumulations are available as described in #12.

4. A Bibliography of the History of the Chinese Book and Calligraphy: List of Catalogued Books. Vancouver: Asian Studies Division, University of British Columbia Library, 1970. 21, 19 leaves.

   This annotated bibliography includes only holdings on the history of Chinese books and calligraphy in the Asian Studies Division of the University of British Columbia Library. The section on the history of Chinese books includes entries on paper, materials, and instruments for writing, printing, and binding Chinese books.

5. Chin, Elise Y. S. L., and Lo, Karl K. "Serials from the People's Republic of China, 1966-76: A Guide." The Serials Librarian 2 (1): 31-48 (Fall 1977).

   This paper provides brief historical background on publishing and distributing Chinese serials, examines problems dealing with Chinese serials, presents suggestions on how to acquire the current limited number of titles, and offers some speculations concerning the near future. It includes two listings: (1) People's Republic of China Serials Available to United States Libraries, 1966-1976, and (2) Aids and Translations of People's Republic of China Serials.

6. "China." In Major Libraries of the World: A Selective Guide, edited by Colin Steele, pp. 51-58. New York: Bowker, 1976.

   This is a listing of six libraries in Nanking, Peking, and Shanghai that includes information on each library's address, history, special collections, exhibition areas, hours, admission, parking, classification, catalogs, and services.

7. "China (People's Republic)." In World Guide to Library Schools and Training Courses in Documentation, 2nd ed., pp. 123-126. London: Clive Bingley, 1981.

   This lists three institutes which offer library science training in China. The information includes each institute's name and address, status, programs, admission requirements, and curricula.

8. "China, People's Republic of." In A Handbook of Comparative Librarianship, 3rd ed., rev. and enl., edited by M. MacKee, pp. 493-498. London: Clive Bingley, 1983.

Over 100 reference sources relating to libraries and librarianship in China are listed. Entries include books, articles, yearbooks, etc. There are no annotations.

9. China Press and Publishing Directory. Editor-in-chief: Gao Guo-Gan; executive editor, Wu Ren-yong. Peking: Modern Press; London: Longman Group Limited, 1985. 360 pp.

This directory is the first to provide a full and systematic introduction to all the publishing houses and major book-distribution enterprises in China. It also gives detailed information on Chinese newspapers and periodicals that have worldwide distribution. It lists 2,353 entries, including 296 in the Publishers Section, 375 in the Booksellers Section, and 1,682 in the Newspapers and Periodicals Section. For each entry in the first two sections, it provides such information as the name of the publisher in English and Chinese, address, telephone and cable numbers, and date of founding. For the Newspapers and Periodicals Section, it gives the title in English and Chinese, frequency of publication, founding date and evolution, names of the editorial board and publisher, address, and telephone number.

10. "China, Republic of (Taiwan)." In A Handbook of Comparative Librarianship, 3rd ed., rev. and enl., edited by M. MacKee, pp. 499-500. London: Clive Bingley, 1983.

Over fifty reference sources related to libraries and librarianship in Taiwan are listed. Entries include books, articles, yearbooks, etc. There are no annotations.

11. Chiu, A. Kaiming. "Bibliography of the Works of Dr. A. K'aiming Ch'iu." Harvard Journal of Asiatic Studies 25: 16-18 (1964-1965).

A listing of fifty publications by Dr. Kaiming Chiu, a prominent Chinese librarian, on various subjects is provided. About half of his works concern library and information science in China.

12. Cumulative Bibliography of Asian Studies. Boston: G. K. Hall, 1969-1973.

This is a cumulation of the Bibliography of Asian Studies. Currently there are four cumulations: Author Bibliography, 1941-65, 4 vols.; Author Bibliography, 1966-70, 3 vols.; Subject Bibliography,

1941-65, 4 vols.; Subject Bibliography, 1966-70, 3 vols.

13. Directory of Chinese Libraries, edited by Wang Enguang, Wu Renyong, and Xie Wanruo. Peking: China Academic Publishers, 1982. 427 pp.

Consisting of approximately 700 major libraries in the People's Republic of China, this directory is the first of its kind ever published. It includes information on each library's founding date, address, phone number, holdings, scope, special features, exchange programs, librarians, and publications. The entries are grouped by types of libraries and are written in both Chinese and English.

14. Encyclopedia of Library and Information Science, edited by Allen Kent, Harold Lancour, and Jay E. Daily. New York: Marcel Dekker, 1968- 35 vols. and Supplement, v. 36-

Presenting a comprehensive coverage of the broad field of modern librarianship, this title integrates library and information science with an emphasis on depth of treatment. It is arranged in one straight alphabet, providing cross-references from one heading to another. The last two volumes (vols. 34 and 35) contain a detailed analytical index. Information concerning Chinese libraries is accessible by using the index.

15. International Guide to Library and Information Science Education, edited by Josephine Riss Fang and Paul Nauta, with the assistance of Anna J. Fang. Munich: K. G. Saur, 1985. 537 pp.

The section on China includes thirty-one entries on higher education institutions which offer library science education in China, including Taiwan. The entries are arranged alphabetically according to the name of the institution. Each entry includes the name, address, head, programs, physical resources, founding date, administrative structure, sources of finance, teaching staff, continuing education, professional status, and a note regarding the library science education program of the institution.

16. International Library Directory; A World Directory of Libraries. London: A. P. Wales Organizations, 1963-1970.

Including sections on "China (People's Republic of China)" and "Taiwan (Formosa)," this directory lists international libraries alphabetically by city. Each entry gives information on the name, address, type of library, and collection size. Although some of the information is out of date, other sources are still useful.

17. Ju, William C., comp. A Union List of Chinese Periodicals in Universities and Colleges in Taiwan. San Francisco: Chinese Materials Center, 1975. 580 pp.

Containing a list of 2,487 Chinese periodicals found in libraries in Taiwan, this work is arranged alphabetically by title, and cross-references are given for title changes. Each entry includes the following information: title, frequency of publication, date of the first issue, date of cessation, description, and location of the title.

18. Lee, Lucy Te-chu. English-Chinese Terminology of Library and Information Science. Taipei: Han Mei Book Publishing Company, 1985. 418 pp.

This dictionary contains more than 6,000 terminologies in library and information science with fourteen appendixes, including the Wade-Giles system of romanization, general abbreviations, special signs, Western chronological tables of Chinese dynasties, codes of publishers in the Taiwan area, and codes of library and information centers in the Taiwan area.

19. Leung, Patricia Wai-ching. "Libraries and Librarianship in the People's Republic of China: An Annotated Bibliography, 1960-1975, with a Selection of Earlier Writings." M.A. thesis, School of Library Science, Kent State University, 1976. 40 leaves.

Consisting of 113 entries of books, periodicals, articles, encyclopedias, newspapers, translated essays, and theses, this annotated bibliography provides a comprehensive list of materials available for the study of library development in Communist China between 1960 and 1975. The entries are arranged in chronological order by date of publication and then by author or title. It includes an author-subject index.

20. Li, Heng. Dictionary of Library and Information Sciences. English-Chinese/Chinese-English. Munich and New York: K. G. Saur, 1984. 327 pp.

This is the first bilingual dictionary of library and information sciences, with a bilingual index, that uses the Chinese phonetic alphabet. It has more than 1,800 terms with definitions which are arranged on a word-by-word basis. It provides an index in Chinese phonetic alphabetical order to serve as a Chinese-English dictionary.

21. Li, Tze-chung. "A Quarter Century of Reference Books in the Republic of China." International Library Review 6 (3): 321-339 (July 1974).

Divided into two parts, this paper reviews the production of reference books in Taiwan since 1949 and presents a list of some sixty useful and significant reference books published in the last quarter-century. The list is grouped under five categories: general works, social sciences, humanities, history and area studies, and science and technology.

22. Library and Information Science Abstracts, vol. 1, 1969- London: Library Association, 1969-

This reference work abstracts articles on library and information science from more than 500 titles of journals in approximately sixty countries and supplies an English-language abstract of source documents. It provides comprehensive name and alphabetical subject indexes. It is also available for online searching via Lockheed Dialog and Derwent-SDC Orbit systems. It supersedes Library Science Abstracts (vol. 1-19, January/March 1950--October/December 1968).

23. Library Literature, 1933- New York: H. W. Wilson, 1933-

This is an author and subject index to materials on library and information science. It indexes books, articles, pamphlets, non-print materials, and library school theses in the field. All entries are arranged in one alphabetical list according to the Library of Congress filing rules.

24. Library of Congress. Science and Technology Division. Mainland China Organizations of Higher Learning in Science and Technology and Their Publications: A Selected Guide, compiled by Chi Wang. Washington, D. C.: Library of Congress, 1961. [New York: AMS, 1974] 104 pp.

This guide identifies and describes scientific organizations and publications of Mainland China in order to serve the needs of librarians, scientists, educators, and government officials. The guide includes a section on libraries with the following information: official name of the library in romanization, official name in Chinese characters, official name in English translation, location or address, founding date, officials, research activities and facilities, size and types of collections, and principal publications.

25. Lin, Cheng-huang. "Bibliographic Control in the Republic of China." _Journal of Educational Media and Library Sciences_ 22 (1): 65-90 (Autumn 1984).

This article reviews various bibliographies and indexes, such as national and commercial bibliographies, union catalogs, selected bibliographies, periodicals, government documents, and non-print materials, compiled in Taiwan after 1911. It also points out the pressing need for bibliographical control in Taiwan and the ways to remedy the situation. The text is in Chinese, with an abstract in English.

26. Lin, Sharon Chien, and Leung, Martha C. _Chinese Libraries and Librarianship: An Annotated Bibliography_. Oak Park, IL: Chinese Culture Service, 1986. 99 pp.

Covering the period from 1936 to 1984, this annotated bibliography lists 550 citations on library and information science, books, publishing, documentation, and archives published both inside and outside China. Organized under nine major topics, it primarily contains materials in English, including books, dissertations, theses, pamphlets, articles, journals, conference proceedings, and newspapers. Approximately 75% of the citations are annotated, with an author/title index.

27. Lin, Sharon Chien. "Chinese Serial Publications on Librarianship: An Annotated List." _Serials Review_ 11 (1): 7-20 (Spring 1985).

This is an annotated list of Chinese library science journals published by professional societies, library schools, individual libraries, and commercial agencies at the provincial level and above. The entries are arranged in chronological order. Each entry includes the Chinese title, a romanized title, an original English title, volume number, dates, frequency of publication, place of publication, and the publisher.

28. Ling, Scott K. _Bibliography of Chinese Humanities: 1941-1972; Studies on Chinese Philosophy, Religion, History, Geography, Biography, Art, and Language and Literature_. Taipei: The Liberal Arts Press, 1975. 645 pp.

Including books, periodicals, articles, theses, and dissertations, this bibliography of Chinese humanities contains publications written in various languages which appeared between the years 1941 and 1972. All materials are classified according to subject. The section on "Bibliography, Books and Libraries, Reference, Museums, Printing" contains thirty-two pages of bibliographies relating to the library field. There are no annotations.

29. Liu, J. B., comp. and ed. Resources on the History of Chinese Books and Printing. Hong Kong: Lung Men Press, 1974. 803 pp.

This volume is a collection of sixty-three articles pertaining to the history of Chinese books and printing published in various scholarly journals, with original bibliographic information included. It contains only articles written by Chinese and published after 1912. Some typical topics include the Chinese script and writing, the study of oracle-shell and ox-bone inscriptions, the study of bronze and stone-drum inscriptions, wooden tablets, the evolution of Chinese book formats, Chinese bibliography, the classification of Chinese books, the invention of paper and printing, and the Chinese encyclopedia. The text is in Chinese, with a list of articles in English.

30. Lowe, C. H. Notable Books on Chinese Studies: A Selected, Annotated, and Subject Divided Bibliographic Guide Compiled and Edited, with Introductory Essays. Taipei: China Printing, Ltd., 1978. 228 pp.

This book contains two chapters which are of interest to library and information science professionals: Chapter 6, "Chinese Contributions to Library Science"; and Chapter 7, "Chinese Librarians and Intercultural Cooperation." The former summarizes biographies and the records of some vanguards in librarianship contributed by senior Chinese librarians. The latter lists fifty-seven books, doctoral dissertations, and master's theses produced by Chinese librarians since 1925 to show the nature and scope of their research and writings.

31. Ma, John T. Elementary Chinese for American Librarians: A Simple Manual. Hanover, NH: Oriental Society, 1968. 38 pp.

Designed for librarians who do not read Chinese to help them cope with the rapid growth of Chinese language acquisitions in many libraries, this basic manual provides information on: where to find essential bibliographical data in a Chinese publication, how to use a Chinese dictionary, and how to convert the new Chinese alphabet into the Wade-Giles romanization. It also provides a basic vocabulary for identifying or translating Chinese bibliographical data. It appends the most frequently used Chinese characters.

32. Nunn, G. Raymond. Asian Libraries and Librarianship: An Annotated Bibliography of Selected Books and Periodicals, and a Draft Syllabus. Metuchen, NJ: Scarecrow, 1973. 137 pp.

This is an annotated bibliography on Asian libraries and librarianship. Chapter IV, "East Asia," contains a section on China (pp. 66-74). Divided into China, Hong Kong, and Taiwan, the citations include materials on publishing, libraries, university libraries, special libraries, public libraries, cataloging and classification, and the national library.

33. Quarterly Bulletin of Chinese Bibliography, vol. 1-4, 1934-1937; Series 2, v. 1- 1940- Shanghai: The Chinese National Committee on Intellectual Cooperation.

Devoted to Chinese national bibliography, this Bulletin features articles and reviews on Chinese bibliography, bibliography with annotations, notes and news of the Chinese publishing industry, and selection publication in both Chinese and foreign languages. It is published in both Chinese and English editions.

34. Su, Meng-fen. "Current Library Science Journals in China." The Serials Librarian 9 (2): 93-106 (Winter 1984).

This paper reviews the current state of library science journals published in Mainland China, outlines their characteristics, and identifies the problems of obtaining information for such a study. The second half of the paper consists of a partially annotated bibliography of current Chinese library science journals.

35. Survey and Research Corporation. Directory of Selected Scientific Institutions in Mainland China. Stanford: Hoover Institution Press, 1970. 469 pp.

Providing information on 490 selected research and development institutions, this directory details each institution's location, year of establishment, structure, facilities, nature of work, major activities, publications, and biographical sketches of key scientific or administrative personnel. It also has an introduction, which describes the organization and management of scientific research in Mainland China, and a user's guide for handy reference.

36. Swannack-Nunn, Susan. Directory of Research Institutes in the People's Republic of China, executive editor, Nicholas H. Ludlow. Washington, D. C.: National Council for U. S.-China Trade, 1977. 3 vols. in 4.

37. Tsien, Tsuen-hsuin, and Cheng, James K. M. China: An Annotated Bibliography of Bibliographies. Boston: G. K. Hall, 1978. 604 pp.

Over 2,500 bibliographies concerning China, published up to 1977, are listed in this reference work. The entries are arranged in two main parts: (1) general and special bibliographies; and (2) subject bibliographies. Of particular interest to Chinese librarians is the section on "Bibliographies on Librarianship."

38. Tsien, Tsuen-hsuin, and Wu, K. T. Chinese Library Resources: A Syllabus. Mimeo ed. Chicago: Institute for Far Eastern Librarianship, Graduate Library School, University of Chicago, 1969.

This includes four works: (1) Tsien's "Chinese Library Resources;" (2) "Chinese Library Systems: A Syllabus," by A. Kaiming Chiu; (3) "A Guide to Reference and Source Materials for Chinese Studies," by Tsien and Weiying Wan; and (4) "Terminology of Chinese Books," by Tsien (#106). An excellent bibliography follows each lecture, which is designed for library school students. The lectures center on the evaluation of Chinese books before printing, the development of printing, publishing and trade, and the development of library and library resources in Chinese Studies.

39. Wolff, Ernst, with the assistance of Corcoran, Maureen. Chinese Studies: A Bibliographic Manual. San Francisco: Chinese Materials Center, 1981. 152 pp.

Containing information on Chinese bibliographies and references, this manual has a section on the history of printing and book classification in China which should be of particular interest to librarians.

40. Wolff, Ernst. "Recent Bibliographic Sources on Mainland China." Journal of Library and Information Science 4 (2): 91-105 (October 1978).

Presented at the Annual Conference of the Association for Asian Studies in Chicago in 1978, this paper reviews the bibliographic situation in Mainland China from 1970 to 1977. It provides an exhaustive listing of all research aids in Communist China during the period and gives a rough outline of the publications. An extensive bibliography is appended.

41. Wong, Vi-lien. "Libraries in China: A Selected Annotated Bibliography." Bulletin of Bibliography 15 (8): 147-148 (September/December 1935); 15 (9): 168-169 (January/April 1936); 15 (10): 191-193 (May/August 1936).

This is an annotated bibliography of books, pamphlets, periodicals, and newspaper articles, covering all aspects of the library in China from the earliest times to 1935. The entries are arranged by large topics presented in an historical sequence. Under each topic, the entries are arranged alphabetically by author or title. A descriptive sentence, paragraph, content note, or quotation is provided for each entry.

42. World Guide to Libraries = Internationales Bibliotheks-Handbuch, 7th ed., edited by Helga Lengenfelder. Munich and New York: K. G. Saur, 1986. 1,203 pp.

Comprising 35,871 libraries in 165 countries, this newest edition of the title lists general research (national, federal, or state) libraries; main university and college libraries; school, professional school, and public libraries with holdings of more than 30,000 volumes; and special libraries with holdings of more than 5,000 volumes. It is arranged alphabetically by country and then by type of library. The section on China includes "China, People's Republic" (pp. 131-136) and "China, Republic" (pp. 136-139).

43. The World of Learning, 37th ed. London: Europa Publications, 1987. 1,933 pp.

This newest edition of the title includes the latest possible information concerning the entries, which are listed alphabetically by country and then by type of organization. The section on China includes "People's Republic of China" (pp. 297-310) and "China (Taiwan)" (pp. 311-316). The information concerning the libraries includes the name of the library, address, holdings, and the director's name.

44. Yuan, T'ung-li. China in Western Literature. New Haven, CT: Far Eastern Publications, Yale University, 1958. 802 pp.

This is a scholarly work which records virtually all books concerning China; published monographs in English, French, and German between 1921 and 1957. It includes 18,000 works with no annotations. There is a section on "Bibliography and Reference" which contains citations concerning libraries as well as printing and paper in China.

2

Books and Printing

45. Batts, Grover, and McDonough, John. "Manuscript Displays Papers Relating to Celestial Empire." Library of Congress Information Bulletin 38 (2): 12 (January 12, 1979).

This short article describes a display of a variety of manuscripts relating to American interest in the Celestial Empire, the China of the Manchus, which are in the Manuscript Division of the Library of Congress.

46. Brown, Yu-ying. "Pictorial Printing in Chinese Books: Three Examples from the Seventeenth Century." British Library Journal 4 (2): 187-195 (Autumn 1978).

Brown provides descriptive notes on the art of book illustration which reached a state of perfection and diversity in China between 1570 and 1670. He gives detailed information on three items which the Department of Oriental Manuscripts and Printed Books of the British Library purchased recently: a copy of the 1610 edition of P'i-p'a-chi (Romance of the Lute); a 1638 edition of Ch'u-tz'u shu-chu (Elegies of the State of Ch'u); and a 1669 edition of Ling-yen-ko kung-ch'en t'u-hsiang (an album of portraits of twenty-four officials meritorious in the founding of the T'ang Dynasty, 618-906 A.D.).

47. Bullen, Henry Lewis. "Histories of Printing and Paper in China and Japan." Far Eastern Review, pp. 195-197 (October 1915).

This is a brief, illustrated sketch of the histories of printing and paper in China and Japan from ancient times to the early twentieth century.

48. Carter, Thomas Francis. The Invention of Printing in China and Its Spread Westward, 2nd ed., rev. by L. Carrington Goodrich. New York: Ronald Press, 1955. 293 pp.

Gathering and correlating source materials from different ages and different parts of the world, this book investigates the truth that printing was a Chinese invention. It is divided into four parts, with information on the background of printing in China, block printing in China, the westward course of block printing, and printing with movable type. It contains a good bibliography.

49. Chan, Lois Mai. "The Burning of the Books in China, 213 B. C." Journal of Library History 7 (2): 101-108 (April 1972).

Chan accounts an early incident, the burning of books, carried out by imperial edict in China in the year 213 B.C. She provides the historical and intellectual background of the event and argues that it was Li Ssu, the Grand Councillor of Ch'in Shih-Huang-ti, who proposed the burning and executed it by an imperial decree. Politically dangerous books, such as history, poetry, and philosophy, suffered the most while all technical books were spared. The event has occupied a special place in the history of censorship in the world.

50. Chang, Pi-teh. "The Evolution of Block Printing in Successive Dynasties." West and East 10 (5): 6-9 (May 1965); 10 (6): 8-11 (June 1965).

The author first traces the history and background of the invention and evolution of block printing in China from the Sui Dynasty down to the Ch'ing Dynasty, approximately twelve centuries. He then discusses in detail the invention and development of movable-type printing from the Sung Dynasty to the Ch'ing Dynasty, approximately eight centuries. Although the art form is highly respected and influential throughout the world, it can no longer fulfill the modern mission of fast production and low cost.

51. Chang, Raymond. "The Renaissance of Book Arts in the Ming Period." Journal of Library History 16 (3): 501-508 (Summer 1981).

The article traces the history of printing in China from 202 B.C. to the Ming period when the era of large-scale printing with movable copper types began. It also discusses the outstanding features of printing in this period.

52. Chang, Te-chang. "Geographical Distribution of Bookprinting Trade in the Ch'ing Dynasty and Its Cultural Significances." Asian Culture Quarterly 3 (3): 65-71 (Autumn 1975).

Chang explores the relationship between the traditional bookprinting trade in Ch'ing Dynasty and the high level of cultural achievement in the lower Yangtze region and the southeastern coastal provinces of Fukien and Kwangtung. He also outlines characteristics common to these areas for their contribution to bookprinting trade in Ch'ing China.

53. Chen, Paul T. H. "Introduction to the Study of the Development of Chinese Books of Different Ages." Monthly List of Chinese Books 5 (11/12): 1-10 (November/December 1964).

As head of the Acquisition Department of the National Central Library, the author gave a lecture on the occasion of the exhibition of Chinese classics held at the Library in 1964. He traced the development of Chinese books in six sections which corresponded to the exhibition: inscriptions on the oracle bones, bronze inscription, rubbings from stone tablets, manuscripts, woodblock printing, and maps.

54. Cheng, Chao-sheng. "Books and Libraries." Journal of Educational Media and Library Sciences 20 (4): 363-373 (Summer 1983).

This paper traces the origin and evolution of writing materials, the physical format of books, and their features. It then discusses the beginning of the library and outlines the functions of a library in modern society, with emphasis on library development in China. The text is in Chinese, with an abstract in English.

55. Chi, Pingfeng. "The Programs for Reproducing and Preserving Twentieth-Century Chinese Publications at the Center for Chinese Research Materials in Washington, D.C." Committee on East Asian Libraries Bulletin No. 70/71: 43-48 (February/June 1983).

This describes the founding of the Center for Chinese Research Materials and outlines its tasks, its reproduction and preservation programs, and two special projects: the government gazettes project and the Chinese newspapers project.

56. "Chinese Books and Bookmakers." Book-lore 3: 133-134 (1885/1886).

This article examines the destruction of books by Emperor Ch'in Shih Huang and the subsequent search for old books and the preparation of new copies of all works found. The government's promotion of literature has encouraged bookmakers to publish useful books, twenty or fifty printed in succession in uniform shape.

57. "Chinese Communist Leader Burns the Books." Library Journal 75 (17): 1609 (October 1, 1950).

This is a note on an editorial in The New York Times reporting that Chairman Mao ordered the burning of books considered reactionary in 1950.

58. Chuang, Lien. "The Development of Ancient Book Editions as Revealed by the Exhibition of Rare Books." West and East 11 (4): 10-11 (April 1966); 11 (5): 8-10 (May 1966).

By examining the rare books of the National Library of Peking brought back from the U.S. Library of Congress, the author traces the history and evolution of ancient book editions in China. The exhibit of this collection contains more than 2,800 kinds of rarities, including the earliest Sung editions, the earliest butterfly-binding books, the most valuable manuscripts of Yung-lo Ta-tien, the rarest topographical records of the Ming Dynasty, and many existing sole copies. The author centers his discussion on methods of printing and bookbinding, and on the rarest of Chinese rare books.

59. Creel, Herrlee Glessner. Studies in Early Chinese Culture. Washington, D.C.: American Council of Learned Societies, 1938. 266 pp.

Although this book is concerned with early Chinese culture, it contains a full treatment of the evolution of both writing and the book in ancient China during the Shang period, approximately twelfth century B.C.

60. Daland, Judson. "The Evolution of Modern Printing and the Discovery of Movable Metal Type by the Chinese and Koreans in the Fourteenth Century." Journal of the Franklin Institute 212 (2): 209-234 (August 1931).

The author examines the sequence of events in the evolution of modern printing, including seals, rubbings, wooden blocks, clay, copper, and bronze movable type. He states that the Chinese discovery of movable metal type printing was the result of their need to reproduce sacred writings. Over the years, improvements were made in casting, matrices, and composing, as well as in other aids to typography and methods for rapidly securing many impressions. The Chinese also discovered printer's ink and paper, which made printing possible.

61. Dobson, W. A. C. H. "Authenticating and Dating Archaic Chinese Texts." T'oung Pao 53 (4/5): 233-242 (1967).

62. Fosdick, Sidney O. "Chinese Book Publishing During the Sung Dynasty (A.D. 960-1279): A Partial Translation of Istoriia Kitaiskoi Pechatnoi Knigi Sunskoi Epokhi by Konstantin Konstantinovich Flug with Added Notes and an Introduction." M.A. thesis, University of Chicago, 1968. 153 pp.

Flug's book on the history of printing in Sung China, published in 1959, is considered an outstanding work of Soviet scholarship in Chinese bibliography and Sung history. Fosdick's thesis introduces Flug and his writings, summarizes Flug's monograph on Sung printing, comments on the contribution of his work, and notes the methods of translation. The author intended this as a contribution to the understanding of the early history of printing and book publishing in China as well as the impact of this art upon Chinese intellectual life during the Sung period.

63. Gimm, Martin. "The Book in China." In The Book Through Five Thousand Years, edited by Hendrik D. L. Vervliet, pp. 109-128. London and New York: Phaidon, 1972.

This is a lengthy, illustrated article on the development of the Chinese book. It chronicles the early history of woodblock printing from the Five Dynasties, through the Sung, Yüan, Ming, and Ch'ing Dynasties.

64. Goodrich, L. Carrington. "The Development of Printing in China and Its Effects on the Renaissance under the Sung Dynasty (960-1279)." Journal of the Hong Kong Branch of the Royal Asiatic Society 3: 36-43 (1963).

The article traces the history of the development of printing in Sung China, 960-1279, including the demand for printing and the main ingredients and technical processes of printing. The second half of the article discusses libraries during the Sung period. It also explores the palace collection, school libraries, and private collections.

65. Goodrich, L. Carrington. The Literary Inquisition of Ch'ien-lung. 2nd ed. New York: Paragon Book Reprint Corporation, 1966. 275 pp.

This is a study of censorship during the Ch'ing Dynasty. Using case studies, it examines the political setting for censorship, book burnings prior to 1772, and the inquisition.

66. Hayes, James. "Popular Culture in Late Ch'ing China: Printed Books and Manuscripts from the Hong Kong Region." Journal of the Hong Kong Library Association No. 7: 57-72 (1983).

Based on materials collected in Hong Kong, the article reviews categories of printed Chinese books and manuscripts relating to the popular culture of late imperial and early republican China, 1870-1930. It emphasizes specialists on social etiquette and family and community occasions, as well as the importance of hand-written village handbooks as source materials on popular culture in the Hong Kong region.

67. Hummel, Arthur W. "The Development of the Book in China." Journal of the American Oriental Society 61: 71-76 (1941).

A presidential address delivered at the American Oriental Society's Annual Meeting in Chicago in 1941, this article sketches the history of the book in China for the past three thousand years. It describes the transformation of the Chinese book as it developed from the wooden or bamboo slip to the silk or paper scroll, the folded album, and the paged book of modern times.

68. Hummel, Arthur W. "Movable Type Printing in China: A Brief Survey." Library of Congress Quarterly Journal of Current Acquisitions 1 (2): 18-24 (October/December 1943).

This is a scholarly and informative article on the art of movable-type printing in China, based on an analysis of collections in the Library of Congress.

69. Jametel, M. Maurice. "Some Chinese Book-lore." Book-lore 3: 63-64 (1885-1886).

Based on the author's visit to China, this article provides a glimpse of the old-book world of China. It examines both the producer and purchaser, with a special focus on the character of the collector.

70. Kanda, Nobuo. "Present State of Preservation of Manchu Literature." In Memoirs of the Research Department of the Toyo Bunko, vol. 26, pp. 63-95. Tokyo: Toyo Bunko, 1968.

Based on on-the-spot surveys of Manchu literature at various American and West European libraries and universities, and at the Academia Sinica and the Palace Museum in Taiwan, the article describes the present state of the preservation of Manchu literature and recent publications on it. The author points out the need for a union catalog of Manchu literature on a worldwide scale.

71. Kecskes, Lily Chia-jen. "Chinese Ink and Inkmaking." Printing History 8 (1): 3-12 (1986).

Kecskes gives an account of the historical background of inkmaking in China, the technical aspects and artistic value of the Chinese language, and the Chinese love of ink, a prerequisite for printing. She also traces the use of ink as far back as the Shang-Yin Dynasty (around twelfth century B.C.) and discusses the process of making ink and collecting it.

72. Kecskes, Lily Chia-jen. "Study of Chinese Inkmaking: Historical, Technical and Aesthetic." M.A. thesis, University of Chicago, 1981. 102 pp.

73. Koopman, Harry Lyman. "The Chinese Book." Printing Art 16 (6): 449-453 (February 1911).

The author depicts exactly what the Chinese book-form is. Using illustrations, he describes the paper, print, and binding. He also discusses, from an occidental point of view, the chief defects of Chinese books.

74. Laufer, Berthold. Paper and Printing in Ancient China. New York: Burt Franklin, 1973. 33 pp.

This was prepared as a lecture for the members of the Caxton Club of Chicago, and was read before them by the author on March 29, 1930. It traces the history of Chinese books before the invention of paper by Ts'ai Lun in 105 A.D. and discusses Chinese books after the invention of printing.

75. Li, Meng-jinn. "Book Disasters in China" (in Chinese). Journal of the Hong Kong Library Association 5: 77-87 (1980).

76. Lin, Pin-shiang. "The Development of Movable Types in China: A Survey." Journal of Educational Media and Library Sciences 22 (4): 376-396 (Summer 1985).

This article is an extensive survey of the methods used in producing the various types of movable-type printing (i.e., glued mud, wood engraving, copper, tin, lead, etc.) since Pi Sheng's invention of movable type in the Northern Sung Dynasty. It describes chronologically the results of these experiments down to the Ch'ing Dynasty. The text is in Chinese, with an abstract in English.

77. Liu, Kuo-chun. "Ancient Chinese Book Production." Chinese Literature No. 5: 72-77 (1962).

Using illustrations, this article traces the history of Chinese book production in three stages: the use of bamboo strips and wooden tablets, scrolls, and leaves bound together.

78. Liu, Kuo-chun. "Paper-Making and Printing: Two Great Contributions of the Chinese People to World Culture." People's China No. 12: 19-27 (June 16, 1954).

This article concentrates on the inventions of paper, printing, and movable type in China. It traces the origin and development of papermaking to Tsai Lun of the Han Dynasty in 105 A.D., describes the invention of printing at the beginning of the seventh century, and discusses the invention of printing with movable type by Pi Sheng in the middle of the eleventh century.

79. Liu, Kuo-chun. Story of the Chinese Book. Peking: Foreign Languages Press, 1958. 87 pp.

Divided into seven chapters, this work is the story of the evolution of the Chinese book: (1) oracle bone inscription, bronze and stone inscriptions; (2) writings on bamboo strips, wooden boards, and silk; (3) the invention of paper and the scroll system; (4) block-printing; (5) movable-type printing; (6) books after the invention of printing; and (7) modern books.

80. Lo, Chin-tang. The Evolution of Chinese Books. Taipei: National Historical Museum, 1958. 56, 102 pp.

This book is an historical account of the development of Chinese books from ancient times to the end of the Ch'ing Dynasty. It includes illustrations. The text is in both English and Chinese.

81. Lowe, C. H. "Books and Printing in China, before Gutenberg." Chinese Culture 20 (2): 111-123 (June 1979).

Surveying books and printing in China, this article traces the beginning of Chinese writing, examines some ancient Chinese books, and discusses the invention of paper in China and how printing came about. It details the controversy over whether Feng Tao (881-954

A.D.) invented printing in China. It also mentions the first printed book in China and first block-printed specimens in Japan.

82. Mann, Charles William. "Block Printing." In Encyclopedia of Library and Information Science, vol. 2, edited by Allen Kent and Harold Lancour, pp. 638-644. New York: Marcel Dekker, 1969.

This article provides a general description of block printing in the world, with emphasis on the early development of Chinese block printing and its influence in other parts of the world.

83. Martinique, Edward. "The Binding and Preservation of Chinese Double-Leaved Books." The Library Quarterly 43 (3): 227-236 (July 1976).

This paper discusses the making of Chinese stitch-bound books and their protective covers. It also describes some of the methods the Chinese use to preserve books, including the use of chemical preservatives and insect repellents, well-planned bookroom arrangements, and skillful techniques. It points out that as a result of these methods, the Chinese double-leaved books remain one of the most successful forms of book preservation in the world.

84. Martinique, Edward. Chinese Traditional Bookbinding: A Study of Its Evolution and Techniques. Taipei: Chinese Materials Center, 1983. 87 pp.

Examining the evolution of Chinese bookbinding from the T'ang Dynasty to the early twentieth century, this book discusses the arrangement of earlier books, the roll book, and the stitched binding. It also explores in detail the construction, materials, and methods used to protect and preserve Chinese double-leaved books.

85. Martinique, Edward. "Preserving Rare Books in Taiwan." Committee on East Asian Libraries Bulletin No. 62: 38-44 (June 1980).

This article reports the author's observations on the preservation of rare books at four of the larger academic and cultural institutions in Taiwan. It describes in detail the processes and techniques practiced in Taiwan, particularly in the control of conditions, the repair of individual works, and the dissemination of the contents.

86. Miller, Constance R. "Inquiry into the Technical and Cultural Pre-requisites for the Invention of Printing

in China and the West." M.L.S. thesis, University of Chicago, 1975. 68 pp.

87. Miller, Constance R. Technical and Cultural Prerequisites for the Invention of Printing in China and the West. San Francisco: Chinese Materials Center, 1983. 79 pp.

This study attempts to provide a new perspective on the origin of printing in the West and to compare a productive (China) and a non-productive (Europe) environment for the rapid development of block printing. It compares the materials available, techniques used, demand for reproduction, and system of writing which affect the invention of printing in China in the eighth century and the West until the fifteenth century.

88. Nordstrand, Ove K. "Chinese Double-Leaved Books and Their Restoration." Libri 17 (2): 104-130 (1967).

The author traces the history of Chinese double-leaved books and provides detailed information, with illustrations, on the preparation and restoration of these books. He hopes that the article will help curators to restore correctly the Chinese double-leaved books in their custody. He appends recipes for preparing the paste used in restoration.

89. Peake, Cyrus H. "Additional Notes and Bibliography on the History of Printing in the Far East." Gutenberg Jahrbuch 14: 57-61 (1939).

This is the author's comments and bibliographical notes on the history of printing in the Far East. It examines titles about Chinese printing and provides short descriptive annotations and additional notes.

90. Peake, Cyrus H. "The Origin and Development of Printing in China in the Light of Recent Research." Gutenberg Jahrbuch, 1935, pp. 9-17. Mainz: Verlag der Gutenberg Gesellschaft, 1935.

This article adds material concerning the origin and development of printing and the invention of ink, discusses whether China first used movable metal type other than that made from tin, and corrects some errors found in Carter's Invention of Printing in China and Its Spread Westward (#48). The author consults more recent studies carried out by Chinese, Japanese, and Western scholars and compares these materials.

91. Poon, Ming-sun. "Books and Printing in Sung China (960-1279)." Ph.D. dissertation, University of Chicago, 1979. 560 pp.

Based on a collection of Sung imprints and a search of contemporary records mentioning books, scholarship, and printing during that period, this study recounts the history of books and printing in Sung China. It also investigates the geography of printing, its political and legal aspects, its relationship to scholarship and education, the role of the government as printer, the activities of private and trade printing, and some technical features of Sung books.

92. Poon, Ming-sun. "The Printer's Colophon in Sung China, 960-1279." *The Library Quarterly* 43 (1): 39-52 (January 1973).

By examining thirty sample colophons contained in books printed during the Sung Dynasty in China, the author traces the origin and development of colophons, elaborates on their contents and use, and notes the artistic aspects of colophons. By using both objective and subjective methods, the author discovers the regional and chronological patterns exhibited by colophons during the period.

93. Roy, Kuldip Kumar. "Earliest Forms of Libraries in China." *Library History Review* 1 (2): 43-83 (June 1974).

This lengthy article traces the early history of libraries in China. It describes in detail the development of materials for the recording of knowledge in China, including the oracle bones, bronze vessels, stone books, bamboo, wood, silk, and paper. Among other things, it points out that woodblock printing, movable type printing, color printing, illustrations and woodblock prints, and paged volume bindings have all contributed to the development of modern Chinese libraries.

94. Shaffr, Robert. "Words for 'Printing Block' and the Origin of Printing." *Journal of American Oriental Society* 80 (4): 328-329 (1960).

Challenging the traditional belief that printing originated in China, the author hypothesizes that printing was invented in Tibet. He urges Oriental libraries to collect old editions or editions from the oldest print blocks so that researchers can seriously reexamine the origin of printing.

95. Shaw, Shiow-jyu Lu. The Imperial Printing of Early Ch'ing China, 1644-1805. Taipei: Chinese Materials Center, 1983. 88 pp.

This study is the author's M.A. thesis (#96), completed at the Graduate Library School of the University of Chicago in 1974. It explores the emergence and flourishing of imperial printing and provides the history, organization, and function of the Imperial Printing Office at the Wu-ying Palace. It also examines in detail the format, printing types, paper, labor and material, number of sets of each printing, storage, and distribution of the "palace edition." Finally, it gives an assessment of its significance in and contribution to the overall history of Chinese printing.

96. Shaw, Shiow-jyu Lu. "Official Printing in Early Ch'ing China, 1644-1805." M.A. thesis, University of Chicago, 1974.

97. Shih, Hsio-yen. "On Ming Dynasty Book Illustration." M.A. thesis, University of Chicago, 1958.

98. Shih, Nancy Shu-hua. "A Critical Bibliographical Essay about the History of Printing in China during the Ming Dynasty (1368-1644 A.D.)" Unpublished Master's Report, Palmer Graduate Library School, Long Island University, 1970. 100 pp.

This study researches a limited number of books and articles which examine printing during the Ming Dynasty. The essay is based on seventeen selected items which are available in large research libraries in New York City. It also includes a checklist of selected Ming Dynasty titles and their locations in New York City. A comparative evaluation of the books and articles and the conclusions of the study are found in Chapter 5.

99. Sun, Ts'ung-t'ien. "Bookman's Manual." Harvard Journal of Asiatic Studies 14 (1/2): 215-260 (1951).

This is a translation of Ts'ang-shu chi-yao, Sun's notes on book collecting over the years, by Achielles Fang. Sun discusses in great detail the essential points pertaining to book collecting: acquisition, discrimination, copying, collation, binding, cataloging, preservation, and sunning.

100. Swingle, Walter T. "Chinese Books and Libraries." American Library Association Bulletin 11 (4): 121-124 (July 1917).

This article introduces block printing, movable type, and some of the famous Chinese encyclopedias. It also provides comments on Chinese libraries and some of the large Chinese collections at home and abroad.

101. Swingle, Walter T. "Chinese Books: Their Character and Value and Their Place in the Western Library." In Essays Offered to Herbert Putnam by His Colleagues and Friends on His Thirtieth Anniversary as Librarian of Congress, 5 April 1929, edited by William Warner Bishop and Andrew Keogh, pp. 429-444. Freeport, NY: Books for Libraries Press, 1967.

This article traces the development of the Chinese library and the invention of paper and printing in ancient China. It concentrates on the birth of printing, the advantage of block printing in China, the compilation of encyclopedias, collections of reprints, the use of Chinese books in the Western world, and the influence of the examination system. It also recognizes Dr. Putnam's contribution to building the greatest Chinese library in the Western world at the Library of Congress.

102. Tsien, Tsuen-hsuin. "China, True Birthplace of Paper, Printing, and Movable Type." The UNESCO Courier 25: 4-11 (December 1972).

This is an historical account of papermaking, woodblock printing, and movable type in China and their spread to other parts of the world. It includes illustrations.

103. Tsien, Tsuen-hsuin. "The Pre-Printing Records of China: A Study of the Development of Early Chinese Inscriptions and Books." Ph.D. dissertation, Graduate Library School, University of Chicago, 1957. 302 pp.

Presenting a thorough investigation of the development of early Chinese records, this dissertation reconstructs from available evidence a general picture of Chinese written records from about 1400 B.C. to about 700 A.D. The study is organized according to the different types of materials most commonly used during successive periods, with emphasis on the development of the physical properties of early inscriptions and books. The study is based primarily on various field reports of archaeological excavations, photographic reproductions of objects and inscriptions, interpretations, and critical studies by scholars in various disciplines.

104. Tsien, Tsuen-hsuin. "Raw Materials for Old Papermaking in China." Journal of the American

Oriental Society 93 (4): 510-519 (October/December 1973).

Tsien explores some of the raw materials most commonly used in papermaking in China. He carefully traces the nature and preparation of the fibers, as well as the origin and extent of their use, in documenting the long history of Chinese hand papermaking throughout the centuries.

105. Tsien, Tsuen-hsuin. "A Study of the Book Knife in Han China (206 B.C.-220 A.D.)." Chinese Culture 12 (1): 87-101 (March 1971).

Originally written in Chinese and translated into English by John H. Winkelman, the article examines book knives and discusses several specific points in light of existent evidence. It also explores the functions and forms of the book knife used in the Han Dynasty.

106. Tsien, Tsuen-hsuin. Terminology of Chinese Books: A Draft. Chicago: Department of Far Eastern Languages and Civilizations, University of Chicago, 1969. 12 leaves.

The author provides definition concerning Chinese books under the following categories: authorship, text, format, materials, imprints, production, and collecting.

107. Tsien, Tsuen-hsuin. Written on Bamboo and Silk: The Beginnings of Chinese Books and Inscriptions. Chicago: University of Chicago Press, 1962. 233 pp.

This book traces the origin and evolution of all kinds of written records produced in ancient China from about 1400 B.C. to about 700 A.D. It places special emphasis on the origin of inscriptions and books and on the development of such physical aspects as materials, format, and technology. It includes an excellent bibliography.

108. Wang, Basil. "The History of Rare Chinese Books." Free China Review 13 (4): 29-35 (April 1963).

This is a glimpse of the legacy of ancient Chinese civilization embodied in books. It traces the history of rare Chinese books from 400 B.C. to the Ming Dynasty (1368-1644). It also introduces some famous sole copies at the National Central Library and the National Palace and Central Museums.

109. Wang, Yi-t'ung. "The Origins of Chinese Books: A Review Article." Pacific Affairs 37 (4): 436-439 (Winter 1964/1965).

This is a book review of Tsuen-hsuin Tsien's Written on Bamboo and Silk: The Beginnings of Chinese Books and Inscriptions (University of Chicago Press, 1962, #107). According to Wang, this book is the first successful and exhaustive treatment of how the Chinese strove to produce, transmit, and preserve their written records. Wang summarizes the new discoveries as well as major contributions of the book under the subtitles mentioned in the book.

110. Winkelman, John H. "Scholarship and Society in China: A Bibliographical Review." Journal of Education for Librarianship 13 (3): 169-175 (Winter 1973).

Presenting a bibliographical review of works on Chinese scholarship and books, this article describes selected works in the following categories: general works, pursuit of scholarship, production and distribution of books, conservation of books, classification and cataloging systems, Chinese libraries, and bibliographies.

111. Wolff, Ernst. "Chinese Printing." In Encyclopedia of Library and Information Science, vol. 24, edited by Allen Kent, Harold Lancour, and Jay E. Daily, pp. 76-87. New York: Marcel Dekker, 1978.

Tracing the history of Chinese printing, this article discusses four factors that contributed to the invention of printing in China: (1) the early use of seals; (2) the use of charms and amulets by Buddhists and Taoists; (3) the carving of stone inscriptions and the technique of obtaining rubbings from them; and (4) the rising demand for "religious" literature.

112. Wong, William Sheh. "Anatomy of a Chinese Book." Library Scene 9 (4): 36-37 (December 1980).

This article intends to provide a brief but kaleidoscopic glimpse into the physical aspects of a traditional Chinese book. Using illustrations, it explains some important terms of Chinese bibliography to familiarize readers with the literary works of an ancient culture.

113. Wong, William Sheh. "Pan Pen Hsüeh and Chinese Rare Book Librarians." Journal of Library History 18 (2): 178-189 (Spring 1983).

This article traces the significant historical developments and major problems of the Pan pen hsüeh, the traditional Chinese study of editions, including the development of woodblock printing and the origin and evolution of printed texts. It also discusses requirements for personnel training.

114. Wong, William Sheh. "Rarity in Books, a Traditional Chinese Approach to Appreciation." Libri 32 (4): 278-283 (December 1982).

Discussing traditional Chinese criteria for determining the "rarity" of editions, this paper points out the difference between Western notions of rarity and the Chinese concept of rarity. To Chinese, age is secondary in importance to textual accuracy and completeness. The year 1644, the last year of the Ming Dynasty, constitutes the cut-off date for automatically categorizing an edition as rare.

115. Wu, K. T. "The Chinese Book: Its Evolution and Development." T'ien Hsia Monthly 3 (1): 25-33 (August 1936).

Based on a survey of the physical structure of Chinese books, the article traces the development and evolution of the material and appearance of the Chinese book. It investigates the use of oracle bones and shells, bamboo strips and wooden tablets, silk and stain, and paper to analyze the evolution of books in China.

116. Wu, K. T. "Chinese Printing under Four Alien Dynasties (916-1368 A.D.)." Harvard Journal of Asiatic Studies 13 (3/4): 447-523 (December 1950).

This lengthy article reviews the highlights, characteristics, accomplishments, and typical publications of the four alien dynasties in China--the Liao, Hsi-hsia, Chin, and the Mongols--from the tenth century to the latter part of the fourteenth century. The author maintains that there is no doubt that these heterogeneous people contributed, through the Chinese under their rule, to the extension and improvement of the art of Chinese printing.

117. Wu, K. T. "Colour Printing in the Ming Dynasty." T'ien Hsia Monthly 11 (1): 30-44 (August 1940).

This article examines the development of a new printing technique in the Ming Dynasty, 1368-1644. The technique, known in Chinese as T'ao-pan, introduced color printing by woodcuts. The paper discusses the technique in three fields: color illustrations, colored maps, and texts with punctuation and comments in color.

118. Wu, K. T. "The Development of Printing in China." T'ien Hsia Monthly 3 (2): 137-160 (September 1936).

This is a continuation of the author's previous work, "The Chinese Book: Its Evolution and Development" (#115). Wu examines in chronological order a few of the most important theories regarding the development of printing in China. He presents documentary evidence from literary sources and explores extant relics as well as archaeological discoveries to prove that the art of printing existed and possibly originated in the T'ang Dynasty. He outlines the evolution from rubbings or impressions from stones, woodblocks, and movable types.

119. Wu, K. T. "The Development of Typography in China during the Nineteenth Century." The Library Quarterly 22 (3): 288-301 (July 1952).

This article first highlights the development of typography in China up to the introduction of Western methods during the nineteenth century. It then proceeds to detail the Chinese development of typography, with missionary assistance, during the nineteenth century. It outlines the stages which have led to its present status and explores various problems.

120. Wu, K. T. "Illustrations in Sung Printing." Quarterly Journal of the Library of Congress 28 (3): 173-195 (1971).

Wu reviews a few of the typical and best known illustrated books of the Sung Dynasty. The works described demonstrate the innovations of Sung artisans who experimented and opened up a new vista of artistic expression. The works examined include Buddhist deities, landscapes, and Sung life (biographies, archaeology, science, and amusement).

121. Wu, K. T. "Ming Printing and Printers." Harvard Journal of Asiatic Studies 7: 203-260 (1942-43).

This authoritative article explores why Ming printing flourished and discusses the four distinct achievements of the dynasty: colored printing, illustration by woodcut, the application of copper movable type, and woodcut facsimiles of the earliest editions. It includes a bibliography for further reading.

122. Wu, K. T. "Scholarship, Book Production and Libraries in China, 618-1644." Ph.D. dissertation, Graduate Library School, University of Chicago, 1944. 290 pp.

This dissertation explores the development of Chinese scholarship, book production, and libraries from the T'ang Dynasty to the end of the Ming Dynasty, 618-1644, with a special focus on the libraries. The distinctive features of scholarship and book production in each period are examined for their impact on cultural life in general and libraries in particular.

3

History

I. CHINA, PRE-1949

123. Au, Chih-chun Tien. "American Impact on Modern Chinese Library Development." M.A. thesis, Graduate Library School, University of Chicago, 1964. 114 leaves.

Primarily based on articles in library science journals and monographs published in China and the U.S., the study surveys modern Chinese library development from the turn of the century to 1945, with special emphasis on American influence. It examines the U.S. contribution to Chinese professional librarianship, the American role in establishing modern Chinese libraries, and American techniques of processing library materials.

124. Axon, W. E. A. "Notes on Chinese Libraries I and II." Library Journal 5 (1): 6-10 (January 1880); 5 (2): 35-37 (February 1880).

This two-part article describes the development of libraries in China and some of the great collections in Chinese history up to the late Ch'ing Dynasty.

125. Bostwick, Arthur E. "China: Not Literate but Literary." Bookman 64 (1): 24-30 (September 1926).

Based on the author's two-month journey through the country, this article provides general observations on libraries in China. It comments specifically on the problem of illiteracy, copyright treaties, the Mass Education Movement, the Thousand Character Plan, library buildings, and public libraries.

126. Bostwick, Arthur E. "China's Libraries." The Nation 124 (3216): 208 (February 23, 1927).

This is a general overview of Chinese libraries by the author, who was sent to China in 1924 as a delegate of the American Library Association. He surveyed the libraries of the country and advised them regarding their extension and improvement. He recommended two features which should be adopted in China: free access to the libraries and home use of books.

127. Bostwick, Arthur E. "Libraries in China." Library Journal 50: 895-898 (November 1, 1925).

As an official delegate of the American Library Association, Bostwick visited China in 1925 to inspect Chinese libraries and to make recommendations for their improvement and extension. He comments on their library collections, closed stacks, limited circulation, and card catalogs.

128. Bostwick, Arthur E. "The Library Situation in China." Public Libraries 30: 318-319 (1925).

As a delegate of the American Library Association invited by the Chinese Association for the Advancement of Education, Bostwick talks about his mission to China to investigate library conditions there and to advise them regarding their progress.

129. Bostwick, Arthur E. "Reports of Arthur E. Bostwick's Mission to China as A.L.A. Delegate." American Library Association Bulletin 20 (2): 35-48 (February 1926).

The article consists of three reports: the first was presented to the Executive Board of the American Library Association; the second and the third were presented to the Library Association of China and the National Association for the Advancement of Education. The reports are findings of current library conditions in China based on a visit by the author as an American Library Association delegate. They include suggestions on how to address some of the problems.

130. Brown, Charles H. "China News: A Request from China." Library Journal 69: 691 (September 1, 1944).

This is a news item about a request from T. L. Yuan, librarian of the National Library of Peking and chairman of the Executive Board of the Library Association of China, for copies of the latest reports of university and research libraries and his announcement of the appointment of an Advisory Committee and a Committee of Selection of Publications for the thirteen libraries cooperating in the purchase-pool for Chinese publications.

131. Brown, Charles H. "Implementation of the China Program." Library Journal 69: 238-241 (March 15, 1944).

Based on "A Proposed Cultural Program for Sino-American Relations Involving Libraries," this outlines steps to be taken to rebuild Chinese libraries after World War II. The American Library Association Committee on the Orient and Southwest Pacific urges American libraries to give all the assistance to China that they possibly can.

132. Chiang, Fu-tsung. "A Historical Sketch of Chinese Libraries." Philobiblon 2 (2): 1-6 (March 1948).

Dividing the history into three periods, this article traces the development of Chinese libraries as follows: (1) the sanctuary period, when the public had absolutely no access; (2) the transitional period, which comes between the time ancient libraries were totally closed to the public and when modern libraries were at the service of all; and (3) developments after 1925, when the Library Association of China was founded and libraries modeled on Western prototypes with Western equipment sprang up.

133. Chiang, Fu-tsung. "Modern Chinese Libraries under Sino-American Cooperation." Chinese Culture 3 (1): 140-154 (October 1960).

Chiang sketches the history of the modern Chinese library from the late Ch'ing Dynasty until the republican government moved to Taiwan. He discusses the creation of the library school by Mary Elizabeth Wood, the establishment of modern libraries in the early twentieth century, and their development from the Sino-Japanese War until 1960 under Sino-American cooperation.

134. "China." Library Journal 69: 249 (March 15, 1944).

This is an editorial forum on T. L. Yuan's story of war-torn Chinese libraries (#213), which appears in the same issue, and on Charles H. Brown's practical approach to aiding them during and after the war (#131).

135. "China Receives Books." Library Journal 71 (9): 662-663 (May 1, 1946).

This is a copy of a report to the State Department from the Cultural Attaché of the American Embassy at Chungking, China on the status of the delivery of books selected and purchased in 1945 by the American

Library Association under a grant from the Department to libraries in the Chengtu area.

136. "China's Libraries Appeal for Aid." Wilson Bulletin for Librarians 12 (7): 460 (March 1938).

The chairman of the Library Association of China presents his appeal for aid to rebuild over thirty-five national and private universities, cultural institutions, libraries, and laboratories which were destroyed or dispersed by the Japanese invasion.

137. "Chinese Libraries." American Library Association Bulletin 20 (2): 19-20 (February 1926).

Reporting on information received by Dr. A. E. Bostwick, this article concerns the decision made by the China Foundation on Education and Culture to fund a national library in Peking, six other libraries in various parts of the country, and four popular branch libraries in Peking.

138. "Chinese Library Progress." Libraries 31 (3): 128 (March 1926).

This reports on information received by Dr. A. E. Bostwick, the American Library Association's representative to China in 1925, concerning plans for the new Metropolitan Library in Peking. The promotion of public libraries in China is well-recognized.

139. Chiu, A. Kaiming. "Chief Events in the Chinese Library World, 1933-1934." Library Journal 59 (16): 698-701 (September 15, 1934).

The major events in the Chinese library field during the year 1933-34 are chronicled. It particularly focuses on the Annual Conference of the Library Association of China, a report on the growth of Chinese libraries, new library buildings and plans for a new building, activities of some of the large libraries, publications of rare books, and the establishment of Chinese libraries abroad.

140. Chiu, A. Kaiming. "China." In Popular Libraries of the World, edited by Arthur E. Bostwick, pp. 52-62. Chicago: American Library Association, 1933.

Presenting an account of the Chinese popular library movement of the early twentieth century, this article describes seven types of libraries: national libraries; provincial libraries; county and city public libraries; popular libraries, reading rooms, and people's educational centers; children's and primary school libraries; school and college libraries; and society and governmental bureau libraries. It also summarizes statistics on the growth of various types of libraries in China from 1925 to 1931.

141. Chiu, A. Kaiming, and Kwei, John Chih-ber. "Libraries in China." American Library Association Bulletin 20: 194-196 (1926).

Tracing the history of libraries in China since 1905, when many provincial libraries were established, this article describes public, school and college, and society and special libraries. It also mentions the training of librarians, library organizations, and library publications.

142. Chiu, A. Kaiming. "Modern Library Movement in China." In Libraries in China, pp. 1-17. Peking: Library Association of China, 1935.

Divided into four periods, this survey of the modern library movement in China reports on the status of libraries before the advent of modern public libraries; the beginning of modern public libraries, 1905-16; the second period of the development of public libraries, 1917-26; and the development of public libraries under the Nanking government, 1927. It also presents seven types of libraries in China at the present and statistics on their growth.

143. Chiu, A. Kaiming. "Report on Library Conditions in China." IFLA Publications 5: 100-106 (1933).

Information on current library activities and recent statistics on library conditions in China is provided. Among the chief activities are the publication of Ssu K'u Chuan Shu, the development of plans for erecting a big building for the National Central Library, the establishment of the first Sino-International Library at Geneva, and the reconstruction of the Commercial Press Library destroyed by the Japanese. It presents four tables of statistics of libraries and book production in China, based on official and unofficial sources.

144. Clapp, V. W. "Visit to China." Library of Congress Information Bulletin, pp. 7-11 (March 2-8, 1948).

This describes the author's visit to major libraries in Nanking, Peking, and Shanghai in 1948 to make arrangements for the acquisition of books, official publications, etc.

145. Danton, J. Periam. "Books for China." Library Journal 63 (17): 714 (October 1, 1938).

Authorized by the Executive Board of the American Library Association, this is an appeal to every library in the U.S. for any duplicate material to be sent to cultural institutions in China, whose buildings and equipment were destroyed by the Japanese invasion.

146. Danton, J. Periam. "Have You Helped?" American Library Association Bulletin 32 (13): 1046 (December 1938).

This is a report on the American Library Association's campaign for books for China, where libraries were partially or wholly destroyed as a result of the Japanese invasion. As chairman of the Committee on International Relations in charge of the operation, Danton encourages assistance in this venture in international library cooperation.

147. Danton, J. Periam. "More Books for China." Library Journal 64 (10): 386 (May 15, 1939).

Danton, chairman of the American Library Association Committee on International Relations, appeals to the U.S. libraries to donate duplicates to Chinese libraries, which were destroyed by the Sino-Japanese war.

148. Doo, Ding U. "A Librarian in Wartime." American Library Association Bulletin 38 (1): 4-5 (January 1944).

This describes the evacuation of library materials during World War II. Although most were lost, some 50,000 volumes were transferred to a safe place.

149. Douglas, R. K. "Chinese Libraries." In Transaction Proceedings, vol. 6, pp. 40-44. London: Library Association, 1983.

A brief sketch of modern libraries in China during the Ch'ing Dynasty is presented. It describes two types of libraries: the imperial and official libraries and the libraries belonging to private individuals. It also explores some of the most noteworthy collections in the Peking area.

150. Evans, Tony. "China, the Inscrutable Phoenix: Libraries from Pre-Ming to Post-Mao." Aslib Proceedings 37 (10): 381-394 (October 1985).

Presented as the Aslib Eighteenth Annual Lecture in London in 1985, this paper provides an historical overview of library development in China during the last few hundred years of very high-level professional activity. It discusses in detail the general aspects and current problems of libraries, including library collection, budgets, acquisitions, technical processing and automation, reader services, staffing, and professional education. It also describes the Institute of Scientific and Technical Information of China, the national information center on science and technology, and outlines its principal tasks. It briefly notes the library building situation and future programs in China.

151. "First Library on Wheels." Library Journal 51 (3): 132 (February 1, 1926).

This is a news item on an earthenware statuette of an ancient ox-cart, the representation of "the earliest traveling library in the world," which was presented to the American Library Association by the Library Association of China. It also mentions the use of the remitted Boxer Indemnity Fund for library purposes.

152. Gaskill, Gussie Esther. "China's Postwar Libraries." Far Eastern Survey 18 (6): 68-70 (March 23, 1949).

Surveying post-war libraries in China, this article concludes that the larger libraries suffered minimal losses while the libraries of many small institutions suffered relatively greater losses. It maintains that most libraries need more money for books, buildings, and staff, as well as mutual assistance between the U.S. and China.

153. Goodrich, L. Carrington. "The Development of Chinese Libraries under the Ch'ing Dynasty, 1644-1911, by Cheuk-woon Taam." Pacific Affairs 9 (1): 116-118 (March 1936).

This is a review of Taam's book devoted to the imperial, provincial, monastic, and private libraries during the Ch'ing Dynasty, which was published by the Commercial Press in Shanghai in 1935 (#187). Goodrich points out some carelessness in detail and urges readers to check Taam's statements against the book's useful bibliography.

154. Gunton, Denis. "Chinese Libraries under the Ch'ing Dynasty." The Library World 64 (746): 40-41 (August 1962).

The Development of Chinese Libraries under the Ch'ing Dynasty, 1644-1911 by Cheuk-woon Taam (Shanghai: Commercial Press, 1935) is reviewed. For an annotation of this book, see the entry under Taam, Cheuk-woon (#187).

155. Herbert, P. A. "From Shuku to Tushuguan: An Historical Overview of the Organisation and Function of Libraries in China." Papers on Far Eastern History (Canberra) 22: 93-121 (September 1980).

This paper provides an overview of the organization and function of libraries in China and an assessment of the situation of libraries before 1949. The development of the library from imperial shuku, a place for storing books with limited use, to tushukuan, the library as a tool for mass education, has been slow and long. The term shuku was dropped in favor of tushukuan, the library, in the Republican Period.

156. "How Libraries Have Grown Up in China." The China Press (May 9, 1926).

While presenting a chronological survey of the development of Chinese libraries since 2357 B.C., this article also describes the Oriental Library of Shanghai, established and maintained by the Commercial Press and opened to the public on May 2, 1926.

157. Hsiao, Tsai-yu. "A Project for Reestablishing Libraries in China after the War." China Institute Bulletin 8 (11/12): 1-4 (September/October 1943).

A program submitted to the China Institute for establishing libraries in China after the war is described. The project involved three types of activities: (1) microfilming out-of-print publications; (2) collecting current and available publications; and (3) planning a photographic service laboratory. The article provides a detailed outline of procedures for undertaking the project.

158. Hu, Tienshe. "Appeal for China." Wilson Library Bulletin 13 (2): [160] (October 1938).

On behalf of the Library Association of China, the author wrote this letter informing the U.S. population about the destruction of books and libraries in China because of the Japanese invasion. He appeals for donations of books dealing with scientific, artistic, or literary subjects.

159. Kan, Lai-bing. "The Organization and Treatment of Libraries in the Ming and Ching Dynasties" (in Chinese with English summary). Ph.D. dissertation, Hong Kong University, 1968. 2 vols.

160. Kuo, P. W. "The Evolution of the Chinese Library and Its Relation to Chinese Culture." American Library Association Bulletin 20 (10): 189-194 (October 1926).

Presented at the Fiftieth Anniversary Conference of the American Library Association in Atlantic City in 1926, the article traces the history of the development of Chinese books and libraries from ancient times to the present. It also discusses factors influencing the development of the library movement in China.

161. Kwei, John Chih-ber. "China's Library Heritage." China Critic 1 (23): 448-451 (November 1, 1928).

This article offers an historical sketch of the development of libraries and classification schemes in China from the earliest time to the establishment of the great Ssu Ku Imperial Library in 1772.

162. Kwei, John Chih-ber. "China's Stone Libraries." Library Journal 53 (6): 247-249 (March 15, 1928).

Using illustrations, Kwei traces the history of stone libraries in China from the eighteenth century B.C. to 1791. He also describes the three most famous remaining stone libraries in Sian, Peking, and Chufu.

163. Kwei, John Chih-ber. "Chinese Library and Literary Development Visualized." Library Journal 54 (10): 456 (May 15, 1929).

This table shows Chinese library and literary activities and world history, with parallels and comparisons to Chinese political history from ancient times to the early twentieth century.

164. Kwei, John Chih-ber. "Chinese Library Movement in 1933." China Weekly Review 68 (11): 430-431 (May 12, 1934).

Highlighting library activities in 1933, this article notes on the planning of a national library, the creation of the Chinese International Library at Geneva, the establishment of a new endowment, the extension of the National Central University Library, the publication of rare classics, the opening of the National Tsing Hua University Library and the Canton

Municipal Library. It also comments on the Chinese Library Association Conference.

165. Kwei, John Chih-ber. "Chinese Modern Library Movement." China Weekly Review 46: 77-78 (October 10, 1928).

Sketching the modern library movement in China, this article notes some general tendencies which are already apparent. It also mentions the importance of social education, the thirty years of work contributed by Mary Elizabeth Wood, eminent scholars' visit to China, and Dr. A. E. Bostwick's help.

166. Kwei, John Chih-ber. "Evolution of the Chinese Library." Chinese Students' Monthly 23 (3): 41-43 (January 1928).

This is an historical overview of the evolution of Chinese methods of recording thought, from knotted cords to the printing of books. The second half of the paper explores the development of libraries from ancient days to the first quarter of the twentieth century.

167. Kwei, John Chih-ber. "An Historical Survey of Chinese Libraries." M.A. thesis, School of Library Services, Columbia University, 1928. 44 leaves.

Aiming to provide an historical survey of Chinese libraries and to trace the development of methods of recording thought, this thesis explores the evolution of the library idea, introduces stone libraries, discusses imperial library development from 2800 B.C. to the Ch'ing Dynasty, and describes the modern library movement.

168. Kwei, John Chih-ber. "History of Chinese Libraries." Librarian and Book World 18 (9): 326-328 (May 1929).

Same as Kwei's "Chinese Library and Literary Development Visualized." See annotation #163.

169. Kwei, John Chih-ber. "Library Conditions in China." Chinese Students' Monthly 22 (2): 45-46 (December 1926).

Examining the present conditions of libraries in China, the author divides the libraries into four types: public libraries, college and university libraries, society and special libraries, and the Chinese Library Association.

170. Kwei, John Chih-ber. "A Short Sketch of Chinese Library Development." Library Journal 51 (22): 111-114 (December 15, 1926).

Dividing the history into three periods, this article outlines the development of Chinese libraries as follows: (1) the era before Confucius, up to 190 B.C.; (2) the period beginning in 190 B.C. and ending with the succession of Kwang Hsu in 1875 A.D.; and (3) the reform movement of 1898 to the present day.

171. Kwei, John Chih-ber. "The Story of China's 'Four Libraries.'" China Weekly Review 36: 142 (April 10, 1926).

This short article describes the Ssu K'u Chuan Shu, or the Complete Set of the Four Libraries. The "libraries" mean libraries of the classics, history, philosophy, and miscellany. It explains why it was compiled under the Manchu rule instead of any other time. It also notes the compiling process and the personnel involved in producing this 36,000 volume work.

172. "Library Notes from China." Public Libraries 25 (9): 523 (1920).

These are three short notes on Boone University's conferring an honorary degree of Master of Arts to Mary E. Wood, founder and librarian of the Boone University Library; the Wushi Public Library; and an appeal for library volunteers.

173. Lo, Yiu-chung. Library Development in China, 1905-1949. London: Library Association, 1972. 274 pp.

174. Lu, Ho-sheng. "Studies on the Major Repositories of Hang Books." Journal of Educational Media and Library Sciences 20 (3): 281-291 (Spring 1983).

This article describes in detail the nature and collections of three leading libraries in the Han Dynasty (202 B.C.-220 A.D.). These libraries are: Shih Ch'ü Ko, Lan T'ai, and Tung Kuan. The text is in Chinese, with an abstract in English.

175. "Mary Elizabeth Wood Foundation." Library Journal 58 (8): 368-370 (April 15, 1933).

While showing the significance and progress of the library movement in China, this letter also appeals for aid to the Foundation for endowing the Boone Library School.

176. "Next Steps in Chinese Library Development." Library Journal 50 (19): 908 (November 1925).

This summarizes a report on Chinese library development presented by Dr. Bostwick to the National Association for the Advancement of Education and to the Library Association of China. It outlines ways in which China might obtain free public libraries on the American plan. It also lists libraries which have already made books accessible to the public.

177. "A Notable Library." Washington Library Association Bulletin 2 (2): 10 (April 1906).

The ancient Imperial Library in Mukden is noted, with emphasis on its holdings.

178. Oguro, Koji. "The Imperial Library at the Beginning of the Northern Sung China" (in Japanese). Annals of Japan Society of Library Science 29 (4): 167-180 (December 1983).

179. "Oil for the Lamps of China." Library Association Record 41 (8): 405-405 (August 1939).

The destruction of Chinese libraries as a result of the Japanese invasion is reported. It also appeals to British libraries to join American libraries in donating books and periodicals to help reconstruct Chinese libraries.

180. Pélissier, Roger. Les Bibliothèques en Chine. Paris: Mouton, 1971. 366 pp.

This book investigates Chinese library development from 1898 to 1945 and examines in detail the impact of tradition, politics, economics, and cultural movements. It includes statistical information on various aspects of Chinese libraries and a biographical sketch of fifty-seven Chinese librarians. The text is in French.

181. Putnam, Herbert. "Chinese Libraries Appeal for Help." American Library Association Bulletin 32 (6): 403-404 (June 1938).

Putnam, who is the Librarian of Congress, conveys a message from China asking that gifts of any printed materials be sent to China to aid the libraries which suffered so much depletion during the Japanese invasion.

182. "A Report on the Distribution of Books Donated by Institutions in U.S.A." Philobiblon 2 (1): 63-74 (September 1947).

Submitted by the Shanghai Forwarding and Clearing Office, organized by the Ministry of Education in September 1947, this report lists various types of materials that were donated and their recipients. It notes that the Office expressed gratitude on behalf of Chinese learned bodies to the American donors for their generosity and goodwill in supplying the needed books for war-torn China.

183. Schultheis, Frederic D. "Chinese Libraries and the Sino-Japanese Conflict." PNLA Quarterly 3 (2): 106-108 (January 1939).

Returning to the U.S. after spending three years as librarian of the College of Chinese Studies in Peking, the author describes the library conditions during the Japanese invasion. The National Library of Peking, the Library of the Palace Museum, and many of the finest collections in Shanghai, Soochow, Hangchow, and Nanking were destroyed or damaged. He points out that rebuilding the collections became the most eminent task for Chinese educators.

184. Seng, Samuel T. Y. "Can the American Library System Be Adapted to China?" Library Journal 41 (6): 384-389 (June 1916).

The library in China is the main subject of this paper in which the author traces the history of old Chinese libraries and libraries of the present. He also reviews the classification of books in Chinese libraries, discusses various aids for cataloging and filing, and tries to find out how the American system can be advantageously adapted as well as how the Boone University Library can be used as a model of the American library in China.

185. Seng, Samuel T. Y. "My Impressions of Chinese Libraries." Library Journal 59 (11): 456-459 (June 1, 1934).

This is a report of a survey of over thirty Chinese libraries in more than ten cities, which Seng undertook in behalf of the Chinese National Library Association. Noting the progress that has been made in library development, Seng also outlines the forces that prevent library growth in China.

186. Soong, Chien-cheng. "The Modern Library Movement in China." Journal of Educational Media and Library Sciences 20 (1): 65-93 (Autumn 1982).

This paper traces the collection of books in ancient China from four sources: official, private, school, and temple. It describes in detail the rise of the library system from the Opium War in the mid-nineteenth century to the early twentieth century. It also discusses the Western impact on the library system in China. The text is in Chinese, with an abstract in English.

187. Taam, Cheuk-woon. The Development of Chinese Libraries under the Ch'ing Dynasty, 1644-1911. Ph.D. dissertation, Graduate Library School, University of Chicago, 1933. Private edition distributed by the University of Chicago Libraries, 1935. 107 pp.

Divided into five chapters, this dissertation aims to provide a comprehensive account of Chinese library development under the Ch'ing Dynasty, when the library achieved its greatest importance. It describes outstanding library developments, such as the printing of books and the compilation of catalogs. It also mentions important events in connection with the development of Chinese libraries.

188. Tai, T. C. "A Brief Sketch of Chinese Libraries." Library Journal 44 (7): 423-429 (July 1919). Also in Public Libraries 24: 37-40 (1919).

Dividing Chinese history into six periods, the author provides an excellent historical account of Chinese libraries from 2697 B.C. to the early twentieth century. He provides details on the library development and special features of each period.

189. Tai, T. C. "Libraries Aid in Educating China." Special Libraries 12 (1): 30-31 (February 1921).

Tai discusses the library situation in China, pointing out that since 1914 students returning from an education in American library schools were the main force in the successful development of Chinese libraries.

190. Tai, T. C. "Library Movement in China." Librarian and Book World 15 (10): 364-369 (1923). Also in Bulletin on Chinese Education 2 (3): 1-20 (1923).

Reviewing the situation of Chinese libraries, this article examines the modern library movement in China from 1915 to 1923. Topics included in the discussion are the attitude of government, classes of libraries (public, traveling, college, society, and special libraries), library schools, library meetings, and American library school graduates.

191. Tai, T. C. "Modern Library Development and Its Relation to Scholarship." Chinese Social and Political Science Review 11 (1): 124-141 (1927).

With emphasis on China, this article explores the relationship between the historical development of the library and scholarship of the world. It discusses two factors contributing to the development of modern libraries in China: the democratic ideal in education and the spirit of research. It maintains that although the relationship between the library and scholarship was passive and static, the library in the future can be a dynamic force in the betterment of society and culture as well as in molding man with scholarly achievement.

192. Tai, T. C. "Present Library Conditions in China." Public Libraries 24 (2): 37-40 (February 1919).

Examining a few so-called "leading libraries," this article roughly classifies them into three types: society, college, and public libraries. It also provides statistics on a few well-known public libraries in four provinces: Chihli, Shangtung, Kiangsu, and Chekiang.

193. Wang, Hsiu-chin. "Popular Library Movement in China in the Last Thirty Years." Master's thesis, University of Washington, 1952. 84 leaves.

The study presents a comprehensive account of the popular library movement in China between 1905 and 1945. It provides historical background on old-type libraries and examines the factors which spurred the beginning of the popular library movement (from 1905 to 1926) and the library laws promulgated during this period. It also investigates the development of the movement and the establishment of various kinds of libraries (from 1927 to 1937) and describes the library conditions in wartime (1938-45). Finally, it discusses the problems confronting Chinese libraries and measures taken.

194. Wang, Sing-wu. "A Brief Sketch of the Development of Modern Libraries in China." Library Culture 3 (4): 74-103 (October 1961).

Attempting to give a description of the development of Chinese modern libraries, this article is divided into eight sections. It discusses the following topics: status of old libraries, the modern library movement, Chinese libraries during the second Sino-Japanese War (1937-45), types of libraries in China and their growth, libraries in Taiwan, classification and cataloging, training for librarianship, and the Library Association of China.

195. Wead, Katherine H. "Impressions of Chinese Libraries." American Library Association Bulletin 16 (1): 197-200 (1922).

This reports on the author's impressions of Chinese libraries, including provincial and public libraries in various cities. It also briefly mentions the Boone Library and the Boone Library School established by Mary E. Wood.

196. Winkelman, John H. "The Imperial Library in Southern Sung China (1127-1279)." Ph.D. dissertation, University of Chicago, 1968. 175 pp.

The study tries to determine the manner in which the Imperial Library carried out the function of preserving written records of the Southern Sung Dynasty, primarily during the second and third quarter of the twelfth century. It discusses three aspects of the Imperial Library: (1) administration and personnel; (2) reconstitution of the book collections; and (3) the operation of the Imperial Library.

197. Winkelman, John H. "The Imperial Library in Southern Sung China, 1127-1279." The Library Quarterly 39 (4): 299-317 (October 1969).

An abridged version of the author's dissertation of the same title, this piece concentrates on the buildings and grounds, personnel, reconstruction of the collections, and preparation and use of the collections in the Imperial Library during the Southern Sung Dynasty (1127-1279).

198. Winkelman, John H. "The Imperial [Library] in Southern Sung China: Outline of a Lecture." NTU Library Science Circular No. 8: 1-3 (December 1968).

This is a lecture outline which gives an introduction to the quarters of the Southern Sung Imperial Library and its administration, personnel, reconstitution of the book collections, and operation of the Imperial Library. It also notes problems for future research.

199. Wong, Vi-lien. "Libraries and Book-Collecting in China from the Epoch of the Five Dynasties to the End of Ch'ing." T'ien Hsia Monthly 8: 327-343 (1939).

The paper is a continuation of K. T. Wu's article, "Libraries and Book-Collecting in China Before the Invention of Printing" (#205). The present work traces the history of libraries and book collecting during 1,500 years, from the epoch of the Five Dynasties to the end of the Ch'ing Dynasty (907-1911). Wong states that during this period the libraries concentrated on the preservation of the books rather than on their actual use. The patronage of the ruling houses and the devotion to literary works by the masses helped save many of the valuable books, but the importance of popularizing the idea of libraries was not recognized.

200. Wong, Vi-lien. "Library Chronicle." T'ien Hsia Monthly 6 (4): 369-376 (April 1938).

The rise of the modern library movement in China is chronicled. It also describes the general conditions and problems of libraries, with emphasis on the library buildings, collections, personnel, and funds.

201. Wong, William Sheh. "The Development of Archives and Libraries in China: An Historical Account." Libri 26 (2): 140-155 (June 1976).

Discussing archives and libraries in China from an historical perspective, this article outlines their development from ancient times to the Republican Period, ending in 1945 when a portion of the national collection was removed to Taiwan. It includes valuable notes.

202. Wood, Mary Elizabeth. The Boxer Indemnity and the Library Movement in China. Hankow: Central China Post, [1924]. 38 pp.

This is a collection of official documents pertaining to the Boxer Indemnity and public libraries in China. The documents include a petition drawn up by the Chinese to the President of the United States; a resolution passed by the National Association for the Advancement of Education; and the statement of Mary Elizabeth Wood, Boone University, Wuchang, China, from the hearings held before the Foreign Affairs Committee, U.S. House of Representatives.

203. Wood, Mary Elizabeth. "Recent Library Development in China." American Library Association Bulletin 18: 178-182 (1924).

This is an account of the recent progress made by Chinese libraries and the various factors contributing to the success of such a library movement during the early twentieth century.

204. Wu, K. T. "The Development of Modern Libraries in China." *China Weekly Review* 47: 236-237 (January 5, 1929).

This article presents an overview of library development in modern China. Discussion topics include types of libraries, buildings, the library movement and its organization, the Boxer Indemnity Fund, library education, and the attitude of educational authorities toward library movements. It also mentions some specific problems and a proposal for a national system of libraries in China.

205. Wu, K. T. "Libraries and Book-Collecting in China Before the Invention of Printing." *T'ien Hsia Monthly* 5 (3): 237-260 (October 1937).

Based on various dynastic histories, catalogs of national collections, and other literature, this paper presents a kaleidoscopic review of the collection of Chinese books before the invention of printing. It surveys the formation, destruction, and rebuilding of libraries and collection of books from the beginning of Chinese history until the end of the T'ang Dynasty. The author points out that although Chinese books and libraries have experienced several major catastrophes, the conscientious effort of different monarchs helped preserve and transcribe an enormous number of literary works.

206. Wu, K. T. "Library Progress in China." *Library Journal* 61 (22): 950-953 (December 15, 1936).

Surveying the highlights of the modern library movement in China, the author furnishes some idea of the progress that has been made within the last few years. The discussion concentrates on the development and improvement of library architecture, the growth of book collections, the training of modern librarianship, the cooperation between libraries, and increased efficiency of library services.

207. Wu, Rui-lan Ku. "A Summary of the Study of Chinese Shu Yuan (Colleges at Sung, Yuan, Ming, Ching Dynasty) Library." In *Proceedings of the First Conference on Asian Library Cooperation*, edited by Tamkang College, pp. 336-344. Taipei: Tamkang College, 1974.

This study is divided into five sections: (1) introduction, which traces the origin of Shu Yuan libraries and their collections; (2) resources or books for Shu Yuan; (3) management of libraries; (4) printing; and (5) book collections in Shu Yuan libraries.

208. Yarham, E. R. "Chinese Libraries in War-time." Librarian and Book World 34 (10): 148-149 (June 1945).

Describing library conditions in China during World War II, the author reports that the Library Association of China supported plans to rehabilitate the libraries and to establish more public, school, and special research libraries after the war. He also notes that there were plans for cooperation between the libraries of China and the U.S. as well as exchanges of personnel and publications.

209. Yen, Wen-yu. "Co-operation between Libraries in China." In Libraries in China, pp. 73-89. Peking: Library Association of China, 1935.

An account of the development of cooperation between libraries in Peking is provided. It discusses the work of the national and local professional organizations, cooperative purchasing, interlibrary loans, union catalogs, and centralized cataloging.

210. Yen, Wen-yu. "Ssu K'u Ch'uan Shu, 'The Four Treasuries Library' and Its Influence upon Chinese Culture: An Historical and Critical Study." M.A. thesis, School of Library Service, Columbia University, 1932. 124 pp.

This study provides detailed information concerning the Ssu K'u Ch'uan Shu in terms of Chinese book collecting, classification, and cataloging. It presents an historical sketch of the work and its compilation and management, catalogs and indexes, and classification system. It also discusses the merits and defects of the library and its influence upon Chinese scholarship. It briefly notes the present condition of the Ssu K'u Ch'uan Shu and the failed plans for printing it.

211. Yu, Houo-Joei. "Library Progress in China in 1935." International Federation of Library Associations. Publications 8: 125-129 (1936).

Divided into two sections, this paper discusses library progress in China in 1935 and Chinese library work abroad. The first part reports on various programs carried out by national, university, and other libraries as well as publications and services provided by the library community in China in 1935. The second part notes the activities of the Bibliothèque Sino-Internationale in Geneva. It also gives a list of its publications on various subjects.

212. Yuan, T'ung-li. "Grateful for Gifts to China." American Library Association Bulletin 33 (5): 352 (May 1939).

This is a letter from T. L. Yuan, chairman of the executive board of the Library Association of China, to the American Library Association Commission on International Relations expressing gratitude for the books donated by American libraries and institutions to aid libraries in China which were destroyed by the Japanese invasion.

213. Yuan, T'ung-li. "Library Situation in China." Library Journal 69: 235-238 (March 15, 1944).

This is a detailed report on the partial or total destruction of the great majority of Chinese libraries during the Sino-Japanese War, especially between 1937 and 1943. It also outlines plans for the reorganization of Chinese libraries after World War II.

214. Yuan, T'ung-li. "The Next Twenty-five Years in the Development of Chinese Libraries." College and Research Libraries 8: 376-379 (July 1947).

Offering a blueprint for the development of Chinese libraries in the next twenty-five years, the author stresses the plan's practicality and flexibility as well as consistency and coherency. He also outlines the functions of national, provincial, and special libraries. He mentions both the salary situation for librarians and the integrated services for patrons.

II. PEOPLE'S REPUBLIC OF CHINA, 1949-1976

215. Brewer, J. G. "Libraries in China: A Comparative View." Library Association Record 70 (5): 124-127 (May 1968).

Based on secondary sources, the article presents an outline of the libraries of China which serves as a basis for a comparative study in an analysis of the historic traditions of Chinese librarianship. It points out that Western influence, particularly Russian ideology, has had a great impact on the development of Chinese libraries. It also discusses the similarities between the libraries of Communist China and those of the Soviet Union.

216. Cheng, Chi. "Libraries in China Today." Libri 9 (2): 105-110 (1959).

The article explores library conditions during the first decade of the establishment of the People's Republic of China. It provides statistics on libraries of various capacity. It also mentions the training of library professionals and publications in the library science field.

217. "Chinese Communist Library Service in the Past Decade." Union Research Service 19 (8): 105-115 (April 26, 1960); 19 (10): 130-149 (May 3, 1960).

Translated from the Peking University Journal (No. 4, 1959) in two installments, this lengthy article describes library service in Communist China from 1950 to 1960. Divided into three periods, the article highlights the progress of each period: (1) the restoration of the national economy period saw the transformation of the library service into a socialist library service and the execution of the Party's cultural and educational policy; (2) the first five-year plan period saw further renovations and steady progress in various types of libraries; and (3) the Big Leap Forward period stressed the socialist library service and progress was made in the administration of the libraries, compilation of catalogs, and editing of indexes. Emphasis on propaganda and political indoctrination was the most outstanding feature of library development during the 1950's.

218. "Chinese Libraries." Library Journal 100 (14): 1368 (August 1975).

This is a note about a report made by Josephine Riss Fang, faculty member at Simmons College, on her observations of Chinese libraries and publishing facilities while visiting China in 1974. The report appeared in The Simmons Librarian.

219. Fang, Josephine Riss. "China, People's Republic of." In ALA World Encyclopedia of Library and Information Services, edited by Robert Wedgeworth, pp. 137-139. Chicago: American Library Association, 1980.

Presenting an overview of the history of Chinese library development, this essay provides general information and statistics on the National Library of Peking, academic libraries, public libraries, school libraries, special libraries, and library associations.

220. Fang, Josephine Riss. "Chinese Libraries Carry Out Chairman Mao's Dictum: 'Serve the People.'" Wilson Library Bulletin 49 (10): 744-749 (June 1975).

An overall impression of Chinese libraries gained during the author's five-week tour in 1974 is presented. She points out that since the library is an integral part of the Chinese society, the goal of the library service is to "Serve the People." The author visited the Peking National Library, Peking University Library, The Shanghai Public Library, Futan University, Chiao Tung University, Yunnan University Library, Kwangtung Polytechnic Institute Library, and Chung-shan University Library. She discusses their collections, services, and personnel.

221. Fang, Josephine Riss. "Library Developments in the People's Republic of China." In The Bowker Annual of Library and Book Trade Information, 21st ed., edited and compiled by Madeline Miele, Roberta Moore, and Sarah Prakken, pp. 382-387. New York: Bowker, 1976.

Adapted from an article that appeared in the June 1975 issue of the Wilson Library Bulletin, which was based on a 1974 visit to China, the article reports library developments in several institutions in Peking, Sian, Shanghai, Kunming, and Kwangchow. It especially notes the impact of the National Library of Peking on cataloging and classification at all the libraries visited. (See also entry #220).

222. Goldberg, Birgitte. "Libraries and Mass Communication in the People's Republic of China." Scandinavian Public Library Quarterly 8 (2): 62-71 (1975). Also in Library Lit; The Best of 1976, edited by W. A. Katz, pp. 32-46. Metuchen, NJ: Scarecrew Press, 1977.

This is an account of a visit to China in 1974 by a Danish friendship delegation. As a librarian, the author collected material on libraries, mass communication, and the mediation of culture. She makes general observations on libraries in China and media used for mass communication, such as radio, television, newspapers, and magazines. She also mentions publishing in China.

223. Howard, Roger. "Libraries in the People's Republic of China." Assistant Librarian 67 (4): 54-57 (April 1974).

The article describes the Peking Library, which is China's national library and the largest in China, and the Capital Library in Peking. It also examines in detail the Peking University Library's history, collections, circulation, and stacks, as well as its old building and the new library being built.

224. Huang, Nancy Lai-shen. "Library Development in Communist China, 1949-1962." M.A. thesis, Graduate Library School, University of Chicago, 1964. 114 leaves.

An unpublished master's thesis, this piece attempts to analyze the role and operations of libraries in Communist China in order to understand the motivations of the library movement and its effects on the political, social, economic, and cultural lives of the Chinese people. The study includes historical background and the philosophy underlying the Chinese Communist library movement, the characteristics and roles of different types of libraries, the theories and practices of classification and cataloging systems, and library resources and reader services.

225. Kuo, Leslie T. C. "Communist China: Restoration and Expansion." Library Journal 87 (2): 4133-4136 (November 15, 1962).

This article is in a collection of papers entitled "Libraries in the Far East: An Inquiry into the State of the Library Art in Burma, Taiwan, Communist China, Korea, Indonesia, and East Pakistan," edited by Paul Bixler. Based on documents, articles, and news items from Chinese, Japanese, and Russian sources, as well as reports by foreign observers, the article traces the history of Chinese library development. It emphasizes post-war restoration and expansion after Communist China took over the mainland in 1949.

226. Kuo, Thomas C. "The State of Current Library Operation in China." Center for Chinese Research Materials Newsletter No. 20: 1-9 (April 1976).

Delivered to the Association of University Librarians at the University of Pittsburgh, this informative speech presents personal observations on the state of current library operation in China. It comments on management, personnel, technical services, public services, and library buildings at the four libraries the author visited: National Peking Library, Shanghai Library, Academia Sinica Library, and Peking University Library. A selected list of materials purchased in the People's Republic of China and Hong Kong is appended.

227. "Libraries in China." China Reconstructs 14 (1): 39 (January 1965).

This is a note on current library conditions in China. It examines public, university and school, and specialized libraries, as well as smaller libraries run by workers in trade unions, farmers in rural clubs, and urban residents.

228. Ma, John T. "Libraries in the People's Republic of China Since 1949." Wilson Library Bulletin 45 (10): 970-975 (June 1975).

The author characterizes the important features of library development since 1949 as centralization, unification, expansion, and socialization. He maintains that all the organizational, technical, fiscal, and physical changes of libraries are aimed at meeting the political and economic needs of Communist China. He particularly discusses the growth of labor union libraries, bibliographic control, catalog cards, classification schemes, and coordinating attempts.

229. Neelameghan, A. "China." In Free Book Service for All: An International Survey, edited by S. R. Ranganathan, A. Neelameghan, and A. K. Gupta, pp. 226-230. Bombay: Asia Publishing House, 1968.

Describing library development in China, this article touches upon the social forces behind it, the agencies promoting it, library legislation, the training of library personnel, library finance, and various achievements.

230. Ng, Wai-tak Alexander. "Library Development in the People's Republic of China, 1950-1960." Thesis accepted for the Fellowship of the British Library Association, 1977. 303 pp.

This thesis describes the historical background of the Chinese library, the development of different types of libraries, and how they were used as propaganda organs during the 1950's. The work is divided into eight chapters, with detailed discussions on Chinese book classification and cataloging (Chapter 5), library education and training (Chapter 6), and publishing (Chapter 7).

231. Nunn, G. Raymond. "Libraries and Publishing in Mainland China." Library Journal 91 (13): 3327-3332 (July 1966).

This is an account of the increased library services after the National Library Coordination Act was promulgated in November 1957. It describes in detail library activities in various academic libraries serving science and technology development. It examines the catalogs, classification, and bibliographic control of library collections. It also comments on government policies supporting the publishing industry and the problems of providing materials for research purposes.

232. Peng, Tao-chen. "New China's Libraries." China Reconstructs No. 5: 44-48 (September/October 1952).

Relating the growth and improvement of libraries in China since 1949, this article expounds upon such topics as regional, provincial, municipal, children's, workers', and village libraries as well as county reading rooms and the rise in readership.

233. Proett, Polly-Ann Brumley. "A History of Libraries in the People's Republic of China, including Some Aspects of College and University Library Development, 1949-1974." Ed.D. thesis, George Washington University, 1974. 221 pp.

Surveying the historical development of libraries in the People's Republic of China since 1949, this study focuses on how they have served the Communist state. It also includes an historical chronology of events relating to libraries and bookmaking since antiquity. It concludes that libraries, as an educational institution, have had a significant impact. It also outlines ways in which the growth and development of libraries were affected by educational, political, and economic conditions.

234. Rafikov, A. "In Chinese Libraries." Special Libraries 51 (10): 527-532 (December 1960). Translated from Bibliotekar' [Librarian] (Moscow) No. 9: 47-51 (September 1959).

The paper reports a visit to China in 1958 by a delegation of library workers of the Academy of Sciences of the U.S.S.R. It discusses general characteristics of scholarly and special libraries in China. It specifically discusses the following libraries: Library of the Academy of Sciences, Peking State Library, Nanking Provincial Library, Nanking University Central Library, and Shanghai City Library.

235. Richnell, D. T., and Nelson, Howard. "Libraries in the People's Republic of China: A Report of a Visit, June 1976." Journal of Librarianship 9 (1): 1-16 (January 1977).

The joint paper describes the state of development and the organization of the public and university library service of the People's Republic of China, with emphasis on the educational and political activities of librarians and on the efforts to extend the library service to the grass-roots level since 1973. It also explores access to the libraries, publishing activities, tools of bibliographic control, and the training of librarians. Major libraries such as the National Library of Peking and the Library of Academia Sinica are described in detail.

236. Sascaro, Germana. "L'activité des Bibliothèques dans la République Popularie Chinoise." Revue de la Documentation [Review of Documentation] 22 (3): 88-90 (September 1955).

Providing a general description of the current conditions in China, this essay divides libraries into the following four types: public libraries; trade union libraries and houses of culture; school libraries; and peasant lending libraries. The text is in French.

237. "Thomas C. Kuo Talks about Chinese Libraries." Committee on East Asian Libraries Newsletter No. 48: 57-60 (November 1975).

This is a translation of an extract from Ta Kung Pao, a Chinese newspaper in Hong Kong, dated September 19, 1975. It is an interview with Thomas C. Kuo following his China visit. Kuo talks about his impressions of the Peking Library and the Shanghai Library, comments on literary criticism of Shui Hu, and discusses his meeting with Ting-lung Ku, senior scholar and editor of the famous bibliographic work, Chung-kuo Ts'ung Shu Tsung Mu.

238. Ting, Lee-hsia Hsu. "Chinese Libraries and Library Education, 1949-1980: Truth and Myth in the People's Republic of China." Paper presented at the 100th Annual Conference of the American Library Association, San Francisco, California, June 29, 1981. 28 pp. (ED 214 516).

Based on available Chinese materials, this paper presents the history of Chinese libraries under the Communist regime. It analyzes the impact of the changing political, economic, and social conditions of China on library operations, the role of the library, collections, use, and development in Chinese society. The discussion is divided into four periods: (1) the young People's Republic and the First Five Year Plan, 1949-57; (2) the Second Five Year Plan and the prelude to the Cultural Revolution, 1958-65; (3) the Cultural Revolution, 1966-76; and (4) after the Cultural Revolution, 1976-80. It also outlines recent achievements and describes library education in China.

239. Ting, Lee-hsia Hsu. "Chinese Libraries during and after the Cultural Revolution." Journal of Library History 6 (2): 417-434 (Spring 1981).

This paper is based primarily on the data the author collected during her visit to libraries in China in 1978. Organized in three sections, the paper gives an account of the history of Chinese libraries in contemporary China: (1) before the Cultural Revolution, 1949-66; (2) the Cultural Revolution, 1966-76; and (3) after the Cultural Revolution, 1976-present. It also describes how the libraries are meeting the challenges of providing scientific and technological research, and what their problems are.

240. Ting, Lee-hsia Hsu. "Library Services in the People's Republic of China: A Historical Overview." The Library Quarterly 53 (2): 134-160 (April 1983).

Largely based on a review of Chinese library literature, this paper explores problems concerning the operation of Chinese libraries from 1949 to 1982. It stresses the impact of political, economic, and cultural conditions on the development of Chinese libraries. The author discusses library services in China during four periods: (1) new democracy and the First Five Year Plan, 1949-57; (2) the Great Leap Forward and the prelude to the Cultural Revolution, 1958-65; (3) the Great Proletarian Cultural Revolution, 1966-76; and (4) after the Cultural Revolution, 1976-82.

241. Wang, Chi. "Library and Publishing Activities in China: Personal Observations from a Visit to the People's Republic of China." Foreign Acquisitions Newsletter No. 38: 1-5 (Fall 1973).

Adapted from a paper delivered at the Twenty-fifth Annual Meeting of the Association for Asian Studies in 1973, the article presents a summary of the author's personal impressions of the new China, particularly its libraries and bookstores. It comments on collections, organization, staff, and international exchange programs of various libraries and presents publishing trends.

242. Wang, Chi. "Report of Visit to China, June 1-18, 1972." Library of Congress Information Bulletin 31 (39): A169-173 (September 29, 1972).

Reporting on the 1972 visit to libraries, universities, and bookstores in Canton, Hangchow, Shanghai, and Peking, this article gives information on the library's holdings, Western publication collections, classification schemes, organizational structure, and library services. It briefly mentions reading materials available in the bookstores in China.

243. Wang, Ling-ling. "The Library on the Chinese Mainland: Its Past and Present." Issues and Studies 13 (1): 91-106 (January 1977).

This article explores the development of library operations before and after the Cultural Revolution and provides an explanation of library operations under the Communist regime. It presents general conditions in public libraries, libraries in institutions of higher education, libraries of the China Science Academy, professional libraries, and labor union libraries before the revolution. It further describes library development after the Cultural Revolution by discussing rural libraries, street and alley libraries, and company headquarter libraries. Finally, it analyzes catalogs and classification systems as well as library staff and collections in the libraries of Mainland China. The author points out that little attention has been paid to the normal development of library operations, which are further restricted by policy, concept, financial stringency, and strict control of the Communist party.

244. Wang, Sing-wu. "Impressions of Chinese Libraries and the Chinese Book Market." Australian Academic and Research Libraries 5 (1): 19-24 (1974).

Based on the author's 1973 visit to five libraries and six bookshops, this report centers on the National Library of Peking, the Shanghai Library, and the Chinese book market. It describes problems of cataloging, personnel, and reader services in both libraries. It also discusses three groups of bookshops in the Peking and Shanghai areas.

245. Wang, You-mei, and Rogers, A. R. "Thirty Years of Library Development in the People's Republic of China." International Library Review 14 (4): 399-409 (October 1982).

This paper reviews the development of Chinese libraries during the past thirty years. It is divided into four sections: (1) basic information; (2) the three stages of library development (from 1949 to 1965, from 1966 to 1976, and from 1977 to the present); (3) academic libraries; and (4) the founding of the Chinese Library Association.

246. Wu, K. T. "China, Libraries in the People's Republic of." In Encyclopedia of Library and Information Science, vol. 4, edited by Allen Kent and Harold Lancour, pp. 627-646. New York: Marcel Dekker, 1970.

This article presents the historical background of Chinese libraries, with an emphasis on library development in Communist China for the first two decades. The article provides an excellent overview of library progress in two stages: the first decade saw the proliferation of libraries and library activities and the entire nation was library-conscious; the second decade was marked by a number of momentous events which adversely affected library activities. It gives information on various large libraries, including their collections, services, and activities.

III. PEOPLE'S REPUBLIC OF CHINA, 1976-PRESENT

247. Campbell, Harry. "Library Modernization in the People's Republic of China." IFLA Journal 8 (2): 225-229 (1982).

Campbell presents an account of library modernization as a background to understanding the changes and revisions that Chinese library leaders have undertaken. He also attempts to sketch a few of the highlights of the interdependence of policy and planning that is carried out between various agencies responsible for libraries of different levels. He discusses the growth of library publications and provides concrete examples of modernization in Chinese libraries.

248. Chandler, George. "The Chinese Library System." International Library Review 12 (4): 393-427 (October 1980).

This article reviews the Chinese library system. It details general principles, membership, structure, finance, and publications of the Society of Chinese Libraries. It also examines the governmental administration of libraries and describes the role, history, building, organization, staff, collections, and services of the National Library of Peking. In addition, it notes national special libraries, provincial and public libraries, and university libraries.

249. Chen, Ching-chih. "Recent Developments in Library and Information Science in China." Bulletin of the American Society for Information Science 6 (4): 10-11 (April 1980).

The author, who lectured on various information science topics in China in 1979, describes the development of Chinese libraries. She also discusses the central role played by the Institute of Scientific and Technical Information of China, international cooperation and exchange, and the role of the Council of the American Society of Information Science.

250. Ding, Zhigang. "China, People's Republic of." In ALA World Encyclopedia of Library and Information Services, 2nd ed., edited by Robert Wedgeworth, pp. 190-192. Chicago: American Library Association, 1986.

This article provides information on the history of the Chinese library and its national library, academic libraries, public libraries, school libraries, and special libraries. It also describes the library profession, the China Society of Library Science and its bulletin, and library education and training.

251. Fang, Josephine Riss. "Chinese Libraries on the New Long March: The Role of Libraries in Education in the Post-Mao Era." Leads 21 (3): 3-4 (Fall 1979).

Focusing on major developments and trends in Chinese libraries in the post-Mao era, this article presents a preliminary report of the Council on Library Resources Fellowship Study. Topics include the preparation of a National Union Catalog of Ancient Classical Books, reestablishment of the Library Association of China, formation of regional library groups, library buildings, library education and training, library management, reader services, and collection policies.

252. Fang, Josephine Riss. "Contemporary Developments in Librarianship in the People's Republic of China." International Library Review 13 (2): 211-219 (April 1981).

Based on a study trip under a fellowship from the Council on Library Resources, the paper reports developments in librarianship in contemporary China. The discussion centers on historical background, national professional organizations, library building, library education and training, management, and catalogs. It also explores the individual development of the national, academic, public, school, and special libraries.

253. Fang, Josephine Riss. "The People's Republic of China." In International Handbook of Contemporary Developments in Librarianship, edited by Miles M. Jackson, pp. 281-284. Westport, CT: Greenwood Press, 1981.

With emphasis on the post-Mao era, this article describes the development of libraries in China since 1949. It discusses national, academic, public, and special libraries. It points out that China's libraries have experienced an era of expansion, new challenges, and an awareness of the need for a worldwide exchange of information, which should contribute toward effective planning for national library and information services.

254. Fang, Josephine Riss. "The People's Republic of China, Libraries in." In Encyclopedia of Library and Information Science, vol. 22, edited by Allen Kent, Harold Lancour, and Jay E. Daily, pp. 5-34. New York: Marcel Dekker, 1977.

This lengthy article highlights some of the current trends and describes some prominent libraries in China. The major sections are: (1) the national library; (2) college and university libraries; (3) special libraries at government agencies and scientific institutions; (4) public libraries, including national, provincial, municipal, and others; (5) children's and school libraries; (6) library legislation; (7) library education; (8) library associations; and (9) publishing and mass media. A good bibliography follows.

255. Hu, Yaohui. "China's Four Modernizations and Library Service." Paper presented at the 49th Annual Conference of the International Federation of Library Associations, Munich, West Germany, August 21-27, 1983. (ED 239 635).

The relationship between the four socialist modernizations and library resources in China after the Cultural Revolution is explored. It outlines the following ways to improve library service in order to cope with China's four modernizations: (1) further develop library collections; (2) organize extensive coordination among libraries; (3) continuously improve the professional knowledge of the library staff; (4) improve the overall condition of Chinese libraries, i.e., increase space, funds, and facilities; and (5) draw useful experience from the libraries of other countries.

256. "Libraries in China Today: National Revitalization Effort." Library Journal 104 (12): 1301-1302 (June 15, 1979).

This is a staff report of Josephine Riss Fang's recent visit to China. It points out that the end of the Cultural Revolution signaled fundamental changes in policy and attitudes towards library development in the People's Republic of China. It also notes such significant changes as the steps taken towards a national network, the strengthening of the professional identity of librarianship, and the professional administrative personnel's taking charge of libraries.

257. "Library Work Needs Reform." Beijing Review 29 (28): 27 (July 14, 1986).

This article points out that since the number of libraries in China has increased drastically, libraries are in urgent need of reform. The Chinese need: (1) to reform library management and remove barriers between different departments and regions; (2) to publicize the important role libraries play in promoting the country's economic and cultural development; and (3) to grant libraries more autonomy.

258. Wang, Chi. "An Overview of Libraries in the People's Republic of China." China Exchange News 12 (3): 1-5 (September 1984).

Wang outlines the overall administrative structure of Chinese libraries and the problems they are now facing. Topics included in the discussion are: types of libraries, library management and function, library collections, library organization, library buildings and space problems, library service, international exchange activities, automation, and archives.

259. Wang, Sing-wu. "Recent Developments of Library and Information Services in China." In Essays in Commemoration of the Golden Jubilee of the Fung Ping Shan Library (1932-1982): Studies in Chinese Librarianship, Literature, Language, History and Arts, edited by Chan Ping-leung and others, pp. 1-38. Hong Kong: Fung Ping Shan Library, University of Hong Kong, 1982.

Based on personal observations, articles and reports published in Chinese newspapers and library journals, and accounts given by foreign visitors to China, the article examines recent developments of library and information services in China. It discusses various types of libraries, institutes of scientific and technical information, the organization of library materials, Chinese script and library automation, the training of librarians and information scientists, societies of library and information science, and publications on library and information science.

260. Wong, William Sheh. "Opening Up the People's Republic: Library Cooperation with China." Wilson Library Bulletin 55 (5): 336-341 (January 1981).

The paper outlines library development in the People's Republic, notes the current construction and expansion of physical facilities, and describes bibliographic control and networks as well as professional associations and library education. It also examines problems in locating Chinese publications. Finally, it suggests an exchange of visitors and materials, following the Japanese model, to further cooperation between the U.S. and China in the future.

Personal Reports

261. Barclay, John. "China: Libraries 'Serve the People.'" Australian Library Journal 27 (4): 54-63 (March 17, 1978).

Based on a 1976 study tour by members of the Sydney University China Education Society, this report presents a general overview of Chinese libraries. It provides remarks on the library network, library education, access to materials, foreign language materials, problems of translation, and classification of materials. It also highlights a representative institution and libraries of teachers colleges, universities, schools, and cadre schools.

262. Barclay, John. "The Four Modernisations Embrace Libraries in the People's Republic of China." Australian Library Journal 28 (7): 102-110 (May 4, 1979).

Reporting on the Library Association of Australia's China Library Study Tour in late 1978 and early 1979, this paper discusses the impact of the four modernizations on libraries and information services in China. It briefly describes eleven libraries in five cities the group visited, including the Peking National Library, the Library of the Chinese Academy of Science, and various university libraries, public library services, libraries for the young, and other information agencies.

263. Baskin, Judith. "NLA Delegation's Visit to China." Australian Academic and Research Libraries 12 (1): 35-40 (March 1981).

This article relates a visit to China by a delegation of four librarians from the National Library of Australia (NLA) in 1980 to discuss developments and the exchange of library materials between the NLA and the National Library of Peking. The trip included visits to various academic and public libraries in Peking, Shanghai, Hangchou, and Canton. The article points out China's need for trained librarians, automation, Western information, and closer contact between the two countries.

264. Benton, Charles. "A Beijing Journal." Bulletin of the American Society for Information Science 6 (4): 15-16 (April 1980).

The chairman of the National Commission on Libraries and Information Science (NCLIS) reports on his 1980 visit to Peking with a UNICEF delegation. He describes the structure of library systems in China and the American system and affirms the assistance of the NCLIS if China needs it.

265. Campbell, Harry. "A Letter from China: Library Science in the People's Republic." Quill and Quire 50 (6): 13-14 (June 1984).

The former chief librarian of the Toronto Public Library reports on the current state of libraries and publishing in China. He recommends inviting foreign experts to introduce comparative methods of information services and library technologies, with an eye to mechanizing and automating China's antiquated library service.

266. Chen, Chiou-sen. "Observations and Suggestions." Chinese-American Librarians Association Newsletter No. 30: 9 (June 1984).

The author, who visited several major libraries in 1983, summarizes the current status of Chinese libraries, commenting particularly on personnel, technical services, public service, and the automation network.

267. Chiu, Mrs. "Libraries in China Today." New Jersey Libraries 12 (5): 3-6 (September 1979).

These are notes on a personal visit to three libraries in China in 1978: the Peking Library, the library of the Shih-fan University in Peking, and the Lushan

Public Library in Kiangsi. She comments on their collections, personnel, stacks, and services.

268. Chou, Nelson. "China Revisited." Chinese-American Librarians Association Newsletter No. 30: 10+ (June 1984). Also in Center for Chinese Research Materials Newsletter No. 36: 2-4 (Spring 1984).

This article presents the author's observations on Chinese libraries during a 1983 visit to China through the exchange program between Chilin and Rutgers universities. He comments mainly on the manual process of card production, the shipping of printed materials, the accommodations in the reading rooms and the time schedules, closed stacks, lack of up-to-date foreign language materials, lack of subject access, and personnel policies. He also outlines seven seminars and five lectures he gave while in China.

269. Cohen, Monique. "Bibliothèques Chinoises. Printemps 1981" (in French). [Chinese Libraries. Spring 1981]. Bulletin d'Informations de l'Association des Bibliothècaires Français No. 117: 11-14 (1982).

270. Conger, Mary Jane. "Libraries, Books, and Reading in the People's Republic of China: A Traveler's Account." North Carolina Libraries 40 (3/4): 248-253 (Fall/Winter 1982).

The author, who visited a technical research reading room of a Canton factory and the library of the Shansi Teacher's Training University in 1979, provides her observations on the role of libraries, reading, and books. She comments on collection, card catalog, circulation, service, and access to libraries.

271. Fraley, Barbara. "Barbara Fraley's Visit to China." Wyoming Library Roundup 41 (1): 46-47 (Winter 1986).

Fraley describes her visit to China with a group of library and information science specialists from the U.S. in 1985. The group visited libraries in Peking, Sian, Wuhan, Nanking, and Canton. The article includes observations on the closed stacks, reading rooms, and buildings, as well as her impression of China's historical sites.

272. "IFLA Visit to the People's Republic of China." International Cataloguing 10 (3): 27 (July/September 1981).

A news item about the International Federation of Library Associations (IFLA) officers' visit to China in May at the invitation of the National Library of

Peking and the China Society of Library Science. Scheduled events included talks with officers of the China Society, visits to libraries, and formal addresses to librarians in Peking and Shanghai.

273. "Impressions on Libraries in the People's Republic of China." Chinese-American Librarians Association Midwest Chapter Newsletter, pp. 3-4 (October 1983).

This represents general observations and remarks on Chinese libraries made by two U.S. librarians, William S. Wong and Eugene Wu, who visited China on separate occasions in 1982.

274. Kathman, Michael D. "Chinese Libraries." Minnesota Libraries 27 (12): 335-336 (Winter 1984/85).

As one of about sixty librarians who went on a consultative tour to China in 1985 at the invitation of China's Society of Library Science, the author presents his personal impressions of Chinese libraries. He comments on the closed stack, classified catalog, book selection, special collections, buildings, automation and networking, as well as the infrastructural problems facing Chinese libraries.

275. Landram, Christina. "A Visit to Libraries in the People's Republic of China." The Southeastern Librarian 28 (3): 165-167 (Fall 1978).

The author, a member of the China Study Tour, reports on her visit to China, which was sponsored by the U.S.-China Peoples Friendship Association. She discusses a middle school library in Peking and the library of Chengchou University.

276. Lau, Chau-mun. "Libraries and Acquisitions in the People's Republic of China." Hawaii Library Association Journal 36: 5-11 (1979).

This paper reports on a library tour to the People's Republic of China in 1979, when fourteen librarians visited nine libraries. It includes observations on the conditions of libraries, book exchange, reader services, staff, acquisitions, and Pinyin romanization.

277. "LC Tour Reveals Growth in China's Libraries." Library Journal 110 (1): 16 (January 1985).

This is a digest of what has been reported by Warren Tsuneishi on the Library of Congress's tour to China in 1984. For more information about the tour, see

Tsuneishi, "LC Delegation Visits Chinese Libraries" (#295).

278. Lerner, Esther T. "Glimpses of Libraries and Reading in the People's Republic of China." Ohio Media Spectrum 34 (3): 42-46 (Fall 1982).

Based on information the author gained while visiting libraries in China in 1981, the article discusses the Peking National Library, school libraries, the Shanghai Public Library, library funding, children's books, and the history of reading in China.

279. Li, Tze-chung. "A New Look at Chinese Libraries." American Chinese Scholar 4: 14-16 (1982).

280. Line, Maurice B., and Smith, E. S. "British Library Staff Visit China." Interlending Review 9 (1): 29-30 (January 1981).

This is a report of a small British Library delegation's 1980 visit to Peking, Shanghai, Wuhan, and Canton, at the invitation of the Institute of Scientific and Technical Information of China. The visit was to learn about the library and information system in China, to look at possible forms of cooperation, and to examine the scope for extending the Lending Division's International Photocopy Service to China.

281. Line, Maurice B. "The Chinese Library and Information Scene: Reflections on a Visit to China in June 1980." UK Serials Group Newsletter 5: 2-6 (December 1980).

Reporting on a two-week visit to Chinese libraries in 1980, this essay comments on acquisition funds, underdeveloped services, collections, the emphasis on academic and research libraries, the interest in developing information services, card catalogs, buildings, interlibrary lending, library coordination, the Chinese Library Association, and library schools.

282. Line, Maurice B. "Visit to China, June 1980." Focus on International and Comparative Librarianship 11 (2): 15-17 (1980).

This article describes the British Library delegation's visit to China in 1980 at the invitation of the Institute of Scientific and Technical Information of China. It includes observations on Chinese libraries in Peking, Shanghai, Wuhan, and Canton. It explores the possibilities of future cooperation and extending the British Lending Library's International Photocopy Services to China.

283. Lo, Karl. "Rationed Like Rice--Information Service in the People's Republic of China." PNLA Quarterly 42 (1): 4-8+ (Fall 1977). Reprinted in Library Lit: The Best of 1978, edited by Bill Katz, pp. 83-91. Metuchen, NJ: Scarecrow Press, 1979.

The author, who visited Chinese bookstores and four of the largest libraries in China in 1977, recounts his personal impressions on the availability of various forms of information in China.

284. "Observations of Libraries and Library Operations in the PRC." Chinese-American Librarians Association Newsletter No. 31: 13+ (December 1984).

This represents a brief account of two librarians' visit to four Chinese university libraries in China between 1978 and 1983.

285. Perushek, Diane E. "Chinese Libraries by Horseback." Cornell University Library Bulletin No. 213: 1-5 (September/December 1979).

A group of East Asian librarians' visit to China in 1979 is reported. The purpose of the trip was to investigate the possibility of gifts and exchange operations with various Chinese university libraries, to view the conditions of Chinese libraries, and to purchase Chinese books. The report gives their impressions of the Peking University Library, the National Peking Library, the Tsinghua University Library, the Shanghai Municipal Library, and the Chianghsi University Library, which they describe as representative of libraries in China.

286. Perushek, Diane E. "Eleven Librarians Visit China." Committee on East Asian Libraries Bulletin No. 61: 55-64 (February 1980); No. 62: 45-53 (June 1980).

This two-part article is a report based on notes contributed by members of the group who visited China in 1979. The first part describes in detail visits to ten libraries. The second part discusses publishing, bookstores, the postal system, preservation of rare books, automation, the Pinyin system, and problems confronting major libraries.

287. Poarch, Margaret E. "A Librarian Visits Mainland China." Top of the News 36 (3): 293-295 (Spring 1980).

A study tour to China taken by twenty-two librarians and teachers from the U.S. in 1979 is described. It relates their impressions of the Shanghai Municipal

Public Library and the Peking Library as well as their general observations on China.

288. Roberts, Stephen. "The Chinese Are Eager to Learn Western Professional Ways." Library Association Record 86 (3): 117-118 (March 1984).

This is a record of the author's visit to China as a member of the Library Association of Australia's second China library study tour in 1983. It gives a glimpse into the current state of library and information development in China. It also describes the various libraries visited and discusses the following topics: public library services, free access to libraries, book supplies, closed stacks, standardization of cataloging, automation, buildings, and library administration and management.

289. Rogers, Sharon. "Academics Abroad: U.S. Librarians Visit the People's Republic of China." College and Research Libraries News 46 (8): 399-403 (September 1985).

Rogers describes the impressions of U.S. librarians who visited China in April 1985. Depending on whether they were interested in public or academic libraries, the sixty-five member delegation was divided into two groups and visited libraries in the following cities: Peking, Chengtu, Canton, Nanking, Shanghai, Wuhan, and Sian.

290. Shore, Elliot. "Chinese Libraries: Some Recent Impressions." Wilson Library Bulletin 57 (8): 652-656 (April 1983).

This presents the impressions of a librarian who visited China in 1982 on an individual visa. He recounts his visit to Chinese libraries without official arrangement and criticizes library operations and services at the National Library in Peking, a branch library of a large library system, and the Shanghai Municipal Library.

291. Stueart, Robert D. "A Leap Forward: China's Libraries in Transition; A Report on a Two Month Stay in China." Leads 24 (4): 1, 6-7 (Winter 1982).

Based on the author's observations during a visit, the article discusses library developments in China. It specifically comments on cataloging and classification schemes, standardization practices, plans for new library buildings, library and information science education, and an automated library and information services network.

292. "Touring Librarians Meet Eager Colleagues in China." American Libraries 10 (10): 572+ (November 1979).

The American Library Association representatives' visit to China at the invitation of National Library of Peking Director Liu Jiping is noted. It particularly mentions their arranged meetings with Chinese librarians, publishers, book dealers, museum officials, educators, and scholars in Peking, Sian, Nanking, Shanghai, and Canton.

293. Tsien, Tsuen-hsuin. "Some Remarks on Libraries in the People's Republic of China." Committee on East Asian Libraries Bulletin No. 61: 53-54 (February 1980).

This article presents personal observations on the recent development of Chinese libraries and their need to cooperate with American libraries. It comments on library collections, physical quarters, librarian training, and standardization of cataloging and classification systems.

294. Tsuneishi, Warren M. "American Library Delegation to China." Library of Congress Information Bulletin 39 (34): 318-319 (August 22, 1980).

A news item on a report presented at a session cosponsored by the International Relations Round Table and the Asian and African Section of the Association of College and Research Libraries. The report described a 1979 trip to China taken by three high officers of the American Library Association who were a part of a delegation of American librarians.

295. Tsuneishi, Warren M. "LC Delegation Visits Chinese Libraries." Library of Congress Information Bulletin 43 (39): 312-314 (September 24, 1984).

This is a detailed report on the two-week professional visit to China by an official delegation of the Library of Congress in 1984. The group visited Peking, Wuhan, Shanghai, Hangchou, and Kweilin. Their lectures and discussions with the Chinese included such topics as: managing change in libraries and planning for the future, the national and international role of the Library of Congress in automation and networking, collections and services for reference and research, contemporary American librarianship, the current exchange of publications program, training of staff, and library automation.

296. Tsuneishi, Warren M. "U.S. Librarians Visit the People's Republic of China." Library of Congress

Information Bulletin 38 (48): 487-488 (November 30, 1979).

This is a report on the American delegation of librarians who visited sixteen libraries in five Chinese cities in 1979. It briefly sketches their observations on each of the libraries visited.

297. Wan, Weiying. "Libraries in the People's Republic of China: A First Hand Report." University of Michigan Librarian 7 (22): 1-9 (May 6, 1976).

As head of the University of Michigan's Asia Library, the author made a three-week tour of the People's Republic of China in 1976. He reports on Chinese libraries and educational facilities. The report is divided into four parts: Part I is on China in general; Part II, on libraries and bookstores in China; Part III, on Hong Kong; and Part IV, on Japan. In Part II, Wan describes the current situation of the National Library of Peking, the Shanghai Library, the library of the Tsing-hua University, the Nanking University Library, the Hsin-hua (New China) Book Store, and several speciality stores in Peking.

298. Wang, Sing-wu. "National Library of Australia Delegation's Visit to China." East Asian Librarians' Group of Australia Newsletter No. 4: 2-3 (June 1980).

This is an account of an Australian delegation's visit to China in 1980 at the invitation of the National Library of Peking. It provides their observations on reading rooms, international exchange, and library associations.

299. Welsh, William. "Report on China Trip." In The Future of Scholarly Communication, pp. 51-55. Minutes of the 95th Meeting of the Association of Research Libraries, Washington, D.C., October 17-18, 1979. Washington, D.C.: Association of Research Libraries, 1980. (ED 187 327).

Invited by the National Library of Peking, a group of librarians from the Library of Congress, the Association of Research Libraries, and the Association for Asian Studies formed a delegation to visit China. Welsh, Deputy Librarian of Congress, talked about the Chinese concerns with library automation, preservation, training, standardization, collection, and exchanges. As consultants, the group advised the Chinese on standardization before automation, on-job training, and problems of preservation. It also established an exchange agreement between the National Library of Peking and the Library of Congress.

300. Yu, Priscilla C. "A Librarian's Visit to China." College and Research Libraries News 43 (4): 117-120 (April 1982).

A personal account of the author's visit to libraries in China in 1981 is recorded. The author visited the University of Peking Library, the National Library of China, Wuhan University Library, the Provincial Library of Hubei in Wuhan, and Chungshan University Library in Canton. She makes general remarks about each library, emphasizing individual exchange programs.

IV. REPUBLIC OF CHINA, 1945-PRESENT

301. Bao, You-yu. "Bibliographical Services Throughout the World: China." Bibliography, Documentation, Terminology 11 (4): 150-152 (July 1971).

Bao, the acting director of the National Central Library in Taiwan, reports on the development of bibliographical services in the Republic of China in 1969. He provides information on national institutions, professional associations, national bibliography, bibliographical desiderata, periodicals, interlibrary cooperation, and legal deposit.

302. Chandler, George. Libraries in the East: An International and Comparative Study. London and New York: Seminar Press, 1971. 214 pp.

This book provides scattered information on the national and public libraries in Taiwan. It includes a selected bibliography of 1950-70 publications.

303. "China (Taiwan)." In Bibliographical Services Throughout the World, 1965-69, compiled by Paul Avicenne, pp. 90-93. Paris: UNESCO, 1972.

This lists bibliographical activities in Taiwan. The list includes information on a national commission for bibliography, library cooperation, national bibliography, types of material, current bibliographies of special subjects, periodical indexes, training in bibliography, legal deposit, and archives.

304. FitzGerald, William A. "Library Mission in Taiwan." American Library Association Bulletin 53 (6): 490-493 (June 1959).

The author reports his two-year library mission in Taiwan as a consultant in the International Cooperation Administration Overseas Chinese Section. His special interests were to advise in the planning and construction of library buildings for universities and secondary schools, to advise in the selection of Western books, to assist in education for librarianship, to advise in the selection of Western textbooks for translation into Chinese, and to establish a close affinity and working relations with the Library Association of China.

305. Huang, Shih-hsion. "Library Career in the Republic of China: Looking Forward for the Next 30 Years." Journal of Educational Media and Library Sciences 20 (2): 169-172 (Winter 1983).

This article explores library automation, interlibrary cooperation, and library education and training of library staff from a personal point of view. It also proposes a way to cope with developments in the field of library science in Taiwan over the next thirty years. The text is in Chinese, with an abstract in English.

306. Ju, William C. "The Present Status of Library Services in Taiwan, Republic of China." In Proceedings of the First Conference on Asian Library Cooperation, edited by Tamkang College, pp. 99-112. Taipei: Tamkang College, 1974.

Based on a paper entitled "Library Services in Taiwan" by Chen-ku Wang, director of National Taiwan Normal University Library, this report discusses the current library situation in Taiwan. It includes information on the national library, college and university libraries, school libraries, and public libraries. It also explores library services, including bibliographical controls and index services.

307. Li, Tze-chung. "China, Republic of (Taiwan)." In ALA World Encyclopedia of Library and Information Services, edited by Robert Wedgeworth, pp. 139-140. Chicago: American Library Association, 1980.

Presenting an overview of the history of Chinese library development in Taiwan, this article provides general information and statistics for national libraries, academic libraries, public libraries, special libraries, and library associations.

308. Li, Tze-chung. "Some Aspects of the Recent Development of Librarianship in Taiwan." In International Librarianship, edited by George

Chandler, pp. 100-105. London: Library Association, 1972.

Outlining the development and building of libraries in Taiwan from the mid-1950's to the early 1970's, this article presents some aspects of recent developments in librarianship, with particular reference to the work of the National Central Library and the Library Association of China. Topics included in the discussion are bibliographical services, centralized process of cataloging, microproduction and reprints, reference services, and library education.

309. Li, Tze-chung. "Taiwan: Library Services and Development in the Republic of China." In Encyclopedia of Library and Information Science, vol. 30, edited by Allen Kent, Harold Lancour, and Jay E. Daily, pp. 48-56. New York: Marcel Dekker, 1980.

Based on surveys, observations, research results, and experience closely related to Chinese librarianship, the article is devoted to a general review and analysis of current library services, the profession, education, and the problems of libraries in Taiwan. It divides librarianship into three stages: (1) 1945-53 as a period of stagnation; (2) 1954-64 as a period of stability and growth; and (3) 1965-present as a period of progress. It describes national libraries, university and college libraries, school libraries, public libraries, special libraries, bibliographical services, library associations, library education, and future prospects. It includes a useful selected bibliography.

310. Pao, Ignatius T. P. "China, Libraries in the Republic of." In Encyclopedia of Library and Information Science, vol. 4, edited by Allen Kent and Harold Lancour, pp. 647-655. New York: Marcel Dekker, 1970.

This is an account of the libraries in Taiwan as of 1967, including one national library, two provincial libraries, eighteen city or county libraries, four private libraries, sixty-seven university and college libraries, and eighty-seven special libraries. It also discusses the library schools and in-service training as well as the future of Chinese libraries.

311. "Republic of China." In Library Development in Eight Asian Countries, by David Kaser, C. Walter Stone, and Cecil K. Byrd, pp. 72-88. Metuchen, NJ: Scarecrow Press, 1969. Also in NTU Library Science Circular No. 14: 1-14 (May 1966) under the title "Library Development in the Republic of China."

Chapter 3 of the book contains a detailed analysis of the current state of library activities in Taiwan. Topics under discussion include library planning; school, public, academic, foreign, and special libraries; the National Central Library; bibliographical control; professional associations; and library education.

312. Wang, Chen-ku. "China, Republic of (Taiwan)." In ALA World Encyclopedia of Library and Information Services, edited by Robert Wedgeworth, pp. 192-194. 2nd ed. Chicago: American Library Association, 1986.

Providing an outline of library history in Taiwan, this essay describes its national library, a branch of the national library, 245 public libraries, 139 university and college libraries, 2,456 school libraries, and 239 special libraries and information centers. It also discusses the library profession, the Library Association of China, an automation project, and library education in Taiwan.

313. Wang, Chen-ku. "The Development of Library Automation as a Foundation of the National Library Network in Taiwan." Journal of Educational Media and Library Sciences 20 (2): 101-108 (Winter 1983).

The article divides the development of librarianship in Taiwan into three stages: 1945-51, 1952-71, and 1972-present. It discusses the present status of national, public, university, school, and special libraries. It also describes library education, a library automation project, and plans for expanding the National Central Library.

314. Wang, Chen-ku. "Library and Information Services in Taiwan, ROC." In Proceedings of the First Asian-Pacific Conference in Library Science, March 1983, pp. 59-65. Seoul: The Centre, 1983. A revised and updated version of the article appeared in Papers of the Library Cooperation and Development Seminar, August 17-18, 1986, pp. 4.1-4.9. Taipei: National Central Library, [1987].

This paper gives a description of the recent development of library and information services in Taiwan, outlining the present status of library services and the education programs for librarianship. It also discusses library automation activities and the future of library and information services in Taiwan.

315. Wang, Chen-ku. "Library and Information Services in Taiwan, Republic of China." In Areas of Cooperation

in Library Development in Asian and Pacific Regions, edited by Sally C. Tseng, Hwa-wei Lee, and K. Mulliner, pp. 44-49. Athens, OH: Ohio University Libraries, 1985.

Presented at the 1983 Joint Annual Conference of the Asian/Pacific American Librarians Association and the Chinese-American Librarians Association, this paper traces the development of librarianship and discusses the current status of national, public, university, school, and special libraries in Taiwan. It also examines education for librarianship and library automation. It predicts a bright future for library services in Taiwan.

316. Wang, Chen-ku. "Library Services in Taiwan, Republic of China." In Proceedings of the Second Asian-Pacific Conference on Publications, January 9-15, 1978, Taipei, Taiwan, R.O.C., pp. 143-154 Taipei: Publishers Association of the ROC, 1978.

Concerned primarily with library development and service in Taiwan since 1945, this paper explores the current status of various types of libraries, bibliographical projects completed under the interlibrary cooperative system, and education for librarianship at the present time.

317. Wang, Chen-ku. "Thirty Years of Library Development in the Republic of China." Journal of Library and Information Science 1 (2): 41-69 (October 1975).

The article divides library development in Taiwan from 1945 to 1975 into three stages: 1945-52; 1953-61; and 1962-75. It examines the current situation of different types of libraries, such as national, public, school, college and university, and special libraries. It also discusses library education and training in Taiwan, the history and activities of the Library Association of China, and plans for future development. The text is in Chinese.

318. Wu, Pearl. "Taiwan: Continuation of New Patterns." Library Journal 87 (20): 4123-4132 (November 15, 1962).

This is one of six selected papers entitled "Libraries in the Far East: An Inquiry into the State of the Library Art in Burma, Taiwan, Communist China, Korea, Indonesia, and East Pakistan," edited by Paul Bixler. The paper reports on library development in Taiwan for the past fifteen years. It includes a description of libraries, general library practices adopted by most libraries, library training, and the activities and contributions of the Library Association of China.

4

Types of Libraries

I. NATIONAL LIBRARIES

319. Bottomley, Gesine. "The Peking Library." ALPA Bulletin 42 (4): 1+ (January 1979).

A brief sketch of the National Library of the People's Republic of China in Peking is presented, with particular interest in its large-scale development after 1949. The author notes the expanded collections, reading rooms, reference services, exchange programs, classification systems, and the library's 350,000 volumes of rare books.

320. Chang, Chuan-hsin. "The National Library of Peking." China Pictorial 1: 28-29 (January 1956).

Chang describes the history, working hours, lending service, exchange program, collection, and reader services of the National Library of Peking, the largest in China. He also outlines the Library's aim to serve the people, national economic construction, and scientific research.

321. Chang, Lucy Gi Dung. "History of National Central Library." Chinese Culture 5 (2): 87-91 (October 1963).

The author explores the history of the National Central Library according to four periods: (1) the preparatory stage; (2) the period during the Sino-Japanese War; (3) the post-war period and the removal to Taiwan; and (4) the period in Taiwan. He also mentions its rare book collections, publications, and special services.

322. Chen, Ping-jun. "Librarian Admits Staff Incompetence." China Daily 4: 3 (July 3, 1984).

This is a short note that the head of the business section of Peking's National Library has admitted that some young members of his staff are incompetent. He also indicates that improvement of the quality of staff is among the immediate goals of the library.

323. Chi, Yen-lang. "National Library of Peking: A Working Encyclopedia." New Zealand Libraries 24 (9): 205-206 (October 1961).

This presents the history of the National Library of Peking and its general collection, rare collections, gifts, circulation, international book exchange service, and reader services.

324. Chiang, Fu-tsung. "National Libraries in China." In Libraries in China, pp. 91-97. Peking: Library Association of China, 1935.

Tracing the history of the old Peking Library, this article discusses how it was combined with the Metropolitan Library to form the National Library of Peking, the leading library in China. It also reports on the establishment of the National Central Library in Nanking in 1933. The article recommends that more national libraries be established in China.

325. Chiang, Fu-tsung. "Rare Book Collection of the National Library of Peiping." China Today 9 (7): 24-29 (July 1966).

Chiang summarizes how the rare book collection of the National Library of Peking, which was comprised of more than 2,800 titles in about 21,000 volumes, was stored at the Library of Congress for safekeeping and microfilming before Peking was occupied by the Japanese in 1937, and was shipped back to Taiwan in 1965. He also gives an introduction to the origin, characteristics, and value of this book collection.

326. Chiang, Fu-tsung. "The Return of the Rare Book Collection of the National Library of Peiping Preserved in the United States." West and East 11 (3): 6-9 (March 1966).

The author introduces the characteristics of the collection, which consists of more than 2,800 titles in 21,000 volumes of rare books originally owned by the National Library of Peking. Because of the Japanese invasion, this collection was shipped to the Library of Congress for safekeeping and microfilming. In 1965, it was returned to the National Central Library in Taiwan.

327. Chiu, A. Kaiming. "National Libraries in China." The Library Quarterly 3 (2): 146-169 (April 1933).

Chiu describes the three national libraries in China: the Palace Museum Library, Peking; the National Library of Peking; and the National Sinological Library of Nanking. For each library, the following information is given: history, the nature and strength of its collection, and its organization for use, especially from the reader's point of view.

328. Chou, Pao-chen. "Peking Library--Treasure House of Culture." Peking Review No. 51: 21-23 (December 20, 1963).

This is a description of the Peking Library, China's largest collection of ordinary books and journals as well as the richest collection of works of antiquity in China, some of which date back to the thirteenth century. It also notes its library services.

329. "CLSI and National Library of China Working Together." Library Journal 112 (2): 24 (February 1, 1987).

This notes that the National Library of China in Peking will acquire a CLSI system, using SINOTERM III intelligent terminals and printers produced by Transtech International in Massachusetts, to automate the circulation of a 300,000 volume, all-Chinese collection. The installation of the system in Peking is set for October 1, 1987.

330. Ding, Zhigang. "Towards a Wider Library Resource Sharing." International Library Review 12 (1): 3-6 (January 1980).

Presented at the International Conference of Directors of National Libraries on Resource Sharing in Asia and Oceania, held in Canberra in 1979, this paper describes the views and methods of the National Library of Peking regarding the universal availability and interflow of library resources. The National Library of Peking has placed emphasis on the international exchange of publications and on international lending services as means to widen library resource-sharing.

331. Foramitti, Hans. "Die Chinesische Zentrabibliothek in Taipei, Taiwan [The Chinese Central Library in Taipei, Taiwan]" (in German). Biblos (Austria) 29 (4): 271-284 (1980).

332. "Friendship Through Books." Peking Review 3 (11): 22 (March 15, 1960).

This article describes the progress made during the first decade of the People's Republic of China in exchanging books, periodicals, and other publications through the International Exchange Section of the National Library of Peking. It reports that the Library is currently forming exchanges with libraries, academic institutions, people's organizations, museums, and publishing houses in more than one hundred countries in every part of the world.

333. Fung, Margaret C. "The Evolving Social Mission of the National Central Library in China, 1928-1966." Ph.D. dissertation, School of Library and Information Science, Indiana University, 1983.

This dissertation examines the National Central Library (NCL) from 1928 to 1966 to determine the degree to which its evolving social mission reflected the changes taking place in contemporary China. It first explores the mission of national libraries in general and then describes the historical background of the development of modern librarianship in China. It divides the development into five periods: (1) origin and conceptualization period, 1928-33; (2) the preparatory and formative years, 1933-37; (3) the war-stricken years, 1937-45; (4) the restoration period, 1945-53; and (5) the developing era, 1954-66. It maintains that both national consciousness and cultural tradition exerted a great influence on the life of the NCL. It concludes that the social mission of the NCL is the product of a number of environmental forces in modern China.

334. Fung, Margaret C. "Safekeeping of the National Peiping Library's Rare Chinese Books at the Library of Congress 1941-1965." Journal of Library History 19 (3): 359-372 (Summer 1984).

A detailed description of 102 boxes of selected rare Chinese books from the National Peking Library, which were sent to the Library of Congress for safekeeping and microfilming in 1941 because of the war, is provided. The collection remained in the Library of Congress until the Chinese government requested the return of the collection in 1965. The collection is now kept at the National Central Library (NCL) in Taipei, although the NCL does not claim ownership to the books.

335. Goette, John. "The New National Library of Peiping." China Weekly Review 55 (8): 284-285 (January 24, 1931).

This is a descriptive account of the new premises of the National Library of Peking made possible by grants from the returned American Boxer Indemnity Fund.

Included in the discussion are the Chinese palace-style building, the first domestically-produced large shelving unit, and the rare collection.

336. Hua, Shiping. "National Library of China Has One of the Largest Collections in the World." Library Times International 1 (4): 49-51 (January 1985).

Hua reports on the world's fifth largest library, the National Library of China. Topics include the library's old scripts collection, reader services, personnel, and vocational training to raise the educational level of its staff.

337. Huang, Junqui, and Zhao, Qikang. "Interlibrary Loan Service of the National Library of China." Interlending and Document Supply 11 (3): 109-111 (July 1983).

Based on a paper given at the International Federation of Library Associations (IFLA) General Conference in Montreal in 1982, the article traces the history of interlibrary lending in China since 1927, with emphasis on the services provided by the National Library of China. It calls for strengthening the compilation and management of bibliographies as important factors in developing resource-sharing among libraries.

338. Hunter, Edward. "China's Largest Library." China Weekly Review 59: 28+ (Reconstruction edition, December 19, 1931).

This article discusses the National Library of Peking, the largest library in China, which opened on June 25, 1931. It mainly describes its new building, finances, collections, and services to the community. It especially highlights the library's rare collections. It also points out that although the nominal director is Dr. Yuan-pei Tsai, the actual work is in the hands of the acting director, Tung-li Yuan.

339. Ju, William C. "A Brief Introduction to Chinese Rare Books Collected by the National Central Library, Republic of China." In Proceedings of the First Conference on Asian Library Cooperation, edited by Tamkang College, pp. 309-318. Taipei: Tamkang College, 1974.

The author, director of the National Central Library, describes the rich collections of rare Chinese books which are listed in the enlarged edition of the Catalog of Chinese Rare Books, printed in 1967. He points out that the collection is particularly rich in

(1) ancient imprints; (2) manuscripts by eminent scholars; (3) rare handwritten copies; and (4) Sung and Ming historical materials. He notes that the Author Index of Chinese Rare Books and Title Index of Chinese Rare Books are helpful guides for locating specific material in this collection.

340. Kwei, John Chih-ber. "A National Library for China." China Weekly Review 64 (11): 414 (May 13, 1933).

This article advocates establishing a national central library at the seat of Chinese government in Nanking to serve two functions: (1) as a storehouse of books and knowledge; and (2) as a laboratory for study and research.

341. "Library News from China." Libraries 35 (2): 74 (1930).

A news item on the merging of the Metropolitan Library of Peking and the Peking Library to form the National Library of Peking. It includes notes on new acquisitions and publications.

342. National Central Library. "The New Building Program of the National Central Library." Journal of Library and Information Science 4 (1): 25-39 (April 1978).

Faced with an explosion of publications in recent years, the National Central Library (NCL), located in Taipei since 1954, has serious space problems. The need for a new facility has become urgent. This paper describes the characteristics, missions, organization, and goals for the future development of the NCL. It also notes the design of the new facility. The text is in Chinese.

343. "The National Library of Peiping." China Institute Bulletin 6 (1): 3 (October 1941).

Summarizing the National Library of Peking's activities in free China, this report includes such topics as the war library, current journals, Chinese research materials, assistance to scholars, students, library clerks, and other libraries, and its publication, Quarterly Bulletin of Chinese Bibliography.

344. National Library of Peking. National Library of Peking and Its Activities. Peking: National Library, 1931. 16 pp.

This outlines the history of the National Library of Peking, including the library's origin and development, the new library building, collections, and services.

345. National Library of Peking. A Short Sketch of the National Library of Peiping. Peking: National Library of Peking, 1931. 9 pp.

This is an account of the origin and development of the National Library of Peking as well as a detailed description of its new library building.

346. "The National Library of Peking." Survey of China Mainland Press No. 2557: 19 (1961).

The activities of the National Library of Peking, the largest library in China with a collection of six million volumes, are described. It highlights the library's collection, rare ancient manuscripts and oracle tablets, international book exchange program, depository system for publications, and lending services.

347. "The NCL Library of the Future." National Central Library Newsletter 15 (3): 50-53 (November 1983).

This special report provides information on the construction of a new library building for the National Central Library (NCL) in Taiwan. There are charts providing a detailed design of the new building, scheduled for completion in 1985.

348. Parker, Katherine O. "National Library of Peking, People's Republic of China." In International Encyclopedia of Higher Education, vol. 6, pp. 2532-2535. San Francisco: Jessey-Bass, 1977.

Parker depicts the Peking Library, the largest and most important library in the People's Republic of China, which forms the apex of a system covering the entire country. She also gives information on its holdings, operation, union catalogs, classification system, library cards, and various activities, such as international exchange.

349. Phillips, Grace D. "Behind the Scenes in the Peiping National Library." Boone Library School Quarterly 7 3-4): 561-571 (December 1935).

The author describes her visit to the Peking National Library, where she was received by Tung-li Yuan, director of the library, and was allowed to see things not open to the public. She specifically comments on the fire-proof and all-steel building, stacks, arrangement of collections, special departments, staff, and reference services.

350. The Report of the Building Committee of the National Library of Peiping. Peking: The China Foundation for the Promotion of Education and Culture, 1933. 10, 13 pp.

On the completion of the National Library of Peking building in 1931, the Library Building Committee presented this report. It chronicles the development of the building since a national library was first proposed in 1925. It notes that the Committee, at the conclusion of the project, submitted the Library Construction Accounts and the Research Institute Construction Accounts for public information. The text is in both English and Chinese.

351. "Some Facts about the National Library of Peiping." Orient et Occident 1: 33-35 (1934).

This reports on the National Library of Peking which includes the library's history, objectives, organization and staff, location and buildings, collections, facilities, cataloging, publications, cooperation with other institutions, and needs.

352. "Special Collections in the National Central Library: The Republic of China." In Proceedings of the Second Asian-Pacific Conference on Publications, January 9-15, 1978, Taipei, Taiwan, ROC, pp. 155-162. Taipei: Publishers' Association of ROC, 1978.

This paper presents the background, special features, special collections, microfilm project, and comprehensive catalog of the National Central Library in Taiwan. The special features include holdings of ancient imprints, manuscripts by eminent scholars, rare handwritten copies, and Sung and Ming historical materials. Its special collections include oracle bones, Han wooden tablets, stone, and bronze rubbings.

353. Su, Ching. "From 'Exchange Bookstores' to 'The Bureau of International Exchange of Publications.'" Journal of Library and Information Science 4 (2): 180-183 (October 1978).

Covering the period from 1905 to 1934, this article traces the history of the international exchange of publications in China. It chronicles the origin, development, and activities of the Bureau of International Exchange of Publications at the National Central Library. The text is in Chinese, with an abstract in English.

354. Sun, Beixin. "Automation Development at the National Library of China." Library Resources and Technical Services 29 (4): 367-368 (October/December 1985).

Sun, the deputy director of the Automation Development Department of the National Library of China, chronicles the Library's automation planning, from the creation of a computer section in 1975 to the establishment of the Automation Development Department. Sun points out that the Library has enormous tasks to undertake as the national library of China.

355. Symons, Berry. "The National Library of Peking: An Australian Librarian's View." Australian Library Journal 27 (6): 88-90 (April 21, 1978).

Outlining the author's visit to the National Library of Peking in 1977, this article gives an overview of the Library, including its collection, rare items, building, staff, administration, and problems of dust.

356. Tan, Xiangjin. "Position and Role of the National Library of China in the Library Services of China." East Asian Librarians' Group of Australia Newsletter No. 7: 18-22 (December 1983).

Tan discusses the current status and role of the National Library of China (NLC) in the library services of China, covering the following functions: collection center, bibliographical center, library science research center, automation center, and international exchange center. He also describes the NCL's plans to erect a new building.

357. Tan, Xiangjin. "The Role and Functions of the National Library of China." Journal of Library and Information Science 9 (2): 146-153 (December 1984).

This article describes the main functions of the National Library of China (NCL) as: (1) the general repository of China's national collection; (2) the bibliographical center for Chinese books, journals, and other materials; (3) the center for modernizing, networking, and standardizing Chinese library sources; (4) the base of collecting, collating, storing, and disseminating information or knowledge; and (5) the center for the international interlibrary loan service, exchange of publications, and international cultural communication. It presents information on the NCL's acquisition policy; collection; bibliographies in preparation; automation program regarding acquisition, cataloging, and document retrieval; services; and new building under construction.

358. Walter, Carl E. "Facilities Offered for Research on Contemporary China by the National Library of Beijing." China Quarterly No. 85: 138-147 (March 1981).

This paper presents the author's personal experience in using the National Library of Peking, the largest library in China currently open to foreigners, for research in the field of economics during 1979 and 1980. The author comments on the general library regulations, the incompleteness of the catalog, the classification systems, the economics collection, the lack of consistency in dealing with internal materials, the large gap in the Library's periodical collection, copying services, and international exchange programs.

359. Wang, Chen-ku. "National Central Library of the Republic of China." Journal of Library and Information Science (India) 10 (1): 10-17 (June 1985).

Wang provides an historical account of the National Central Library of Taiwan and information concerning its functions, organization, collection, reader services, technical services, bibliographic services, major automation projects, promotion of librarianship and in-service training of librarians, international cooperation, and the Bureau of International Exchange of Publications. He concludes that the future will bring an expansion of many services and the latest technology at the new library facilities.

360. Wen, Ying. "China's House of Words Keeps Growing." East Asian Librarians' Group of Australia Newsletter No. 3: 6-8 (1979).

This article describes the history and current status of the National Library of Peking, with emphasis on the Library's rare collections. It points out that from the period of the imperial library to the present public library, both collections and readers have increased dramatically. It also notes that a new library is being planned, which will be at least three times the size of the present building.

361. Yang, Yu. "The National Peking Library." People's China No. 24: 33-34 (December 16, 1953).

This is a sketch of the largest library in China, the National Peking Library, with emphasis on the period after the founding of the People's Republic in 1949. The Library now has five departments: supply, antiquarian, cataloging, reading and reference, and the Soviet library department. The article also mentions the Library's primary tasks, book fund, and reader services.

362. Yu, Priscilla C. "National Library of China: The Acquisition of Foreign Language Materials." Library Acquisitions: Practice and Theory 8 (1): 1-9 (1984).

The study examines the growth of the acquisition of foreign language materials in the National Library of China. Divided into two periods (the pre-1949 period and developments since the 1950's), the article shows how historical and contemporary events affected the National Library's procurement of foreign materials. It presents seven tables which clearly indicate increasing acquisition of foreign science and technology materials to achieve China's goal of modernization.

363. Yu, Priscilla C. "Taiwan's International Exchange Program: A Study in Cultural Diplomacy." Asian Affairs 12 (2): 23-45 (Summer 1985).

Exploring the development and operations of the exchange programs of the Bureau of International Exchange of Publications of the National Central Library in Taiwan, this article traces and divides the history and activities of the Bureau into four periods: 1928 to 1936, the Sino-Japanese War and its aftermath (1937 to 1947), Taiwan from 1948 to the 1960's, and the 1970's. It also describes in detail the current activities of the Bureau. There are statistics and charts which indicate that the growth and utilization of international exchange serve Taiwan's specific national and scholarly interests.

364. Yuan, T'ung-li. "National Library of Peiping." Library Journal 57 (1): 55-59 (January 15, 1932).

Yuan, an associate director of the National Library of Peking, traces the development of the library since its inception in 1909, including its reorganization, new building, and collections.

365. Zeng, Jiguang. "Acquisition Work of the National Library of China: Organization and Functions." INSPEL 17 (3): 222-225 (1983).

Presented at the Annual Meeting of the International Federation of Library Associations (IFLA) in Montreal,

Canada in 1982, this paper discusses acquisitions at the National Library of China. At the National Library of China, the appropriation for acquisitions accounts for more than 60% of the total expenditure. The Library collects Chinese language titles as well as special collections, such as threadbound books, old and rare books, rubbings from stone tablets, oracle bones, maps, books in different national minority languages, Chinese revolutionary documents, newspapers and periodicals, and many foreign books, mainly through the international exchange programs.

366. Zeng, Jiguang. "Organization and Role of the Acquisition Department of the National Library of China." Paper presented at the International Federation of Library Associations Conference, Montreal, August 22-28, 1982.

This paper discusses the scope of responsibility and the organization of the Acquisitions Department, as well as its relationship with the acquisition committee of books and periodicals. It also covers the collection development of the National Library of China and the history and status of its international exchange programs.

367. Zhu, Nan and Zhu, Yan. "The National Library of China in Its Gradual Application of Modern Technology." Paper presented at the 49th Annual Conference of the International Federation of Library Associations, Munich, West Germany, August 21-27, 1983. 7 pp. (ED 239 635).

Sketching the history and development of the National Library of China, this paper summarizes what the Library has done and is doing in the preparation and experimental application of modern technology as follows: (1) setting the fundamental objective of the automation program for the library; (2) training personnel through utilization of foreign MARC; and (3) improving basic library skills to speed up Chinese bibliographic automation. The Library is currently strengthening the development and management of its collection by using modern technology and seeking library automation which would suit China's particular situation.

II. COLLEGE AND UNIVERSITY LIBRARIES

368. "Ask Books for Chinese Libraries." American Library Association Bulletin 32 (10): 710 (October 1, 1938).

This is an appeal by the American Library Association for books for Chinese colleges and universities whose libraries were destroyed by the Japanese invasion. Most needed are materials in the fields of science, technology, medicine, literature, and general reference.

369. "Baker and Taylor to Provide Books to Chinese Libraries." Wilson Library Bulletin 59 (1): 12 (September 1984).

This announces that as part of a five-year initiative to rebuild Chinese library collections, an agreement has been reached between Baker and Taylor Company and China for supplying U.S. scholarly books to over 100 university libraries throughout China.

370. Bishop, Enid. "University Libraries in China: Some Personal Observations." Australian Academic and Research Libraries 5 (1): 25-28 (March 1974).

Bishop reports on a three-week visit to China by the first Australian university group in 1973. He highlights the collections and staff of four libraries: the National Library of Peking, and the Peking, Liao-ning, and Chung-shan university libraries. He also comments on library buildings, rare book collection, reference service, professionally trained librarians, and the limited range of current publishing.

371. Boettcher, Cheryl. "Library Organization and Current Activities: A Letter from Peking University." Chinese-American Librarians' Association Midwest Chapter Newsletter, pp. 3-5 (April 1984).

Presenting the author's observations of the Peking University Library during her stay in 1983-84, this letter briefly traces the history of the Library from 1902 and describes the facilities, services, administration, and problems the Library faces today.

372. "Books for China." Wilson Bulletin for Librarians 13 (2): 132-133 (October 1938).

Authorized by the Executive Board of the American Library Association, this is a national appeal for books to be sent to China, especially to the college and university libraries which were destroyed by the Sino-Japanese war. It notes that the need for scientific and technical works as well as Western literature is particularly great.

373. "Books to China." College and Research Libraries News 43 (4): 118 (April 1982).

A news item on a program organized by the Foundation for Books to China, which welcomes donations of academic books and journals in the sciences, social sciences, and humanities for Chinese institutions.

374. Castagna, Edwin. "A Visit to Two Chinese Libraries." Wilson Library Bulletin 52 (10): 789-792 (June 1978).

Reporting on a visit to the Peking University Library and the Shanghai Municipal Library in September 1977, this article presents observations on the former's collection, acquisitions, reading room, and the new classification as well as general impressions of the latter, the largest city library in China. It also notes the impact of Mao Tse-tung and the Gang of Four upon these libraries.

375. Chen, Robert Pin-chuan. "Library Resources for American Studies in Taiwan: An Evaluation." International Library Review 9 (4): 441-454 (October 1977).

Chen reports on a survey conducted in 1975, which examines four libraries of academic institutions that offer American Studies programs and seven major libraries that provide support to these programs. The survey was designed to determine whether the library resources at academic institutions are adequate to support their existing American Studies programs and to assess the adequacy of the total library resources for American Studies in Taiwan. The study concludes that the growth of such resources has lagged behind the expansion of teaching and research, and that the total library resources are not adequate for graduate or faculty research in Taiwan.

376. Den, G. L. "A Wartime Library in Free China." Wilson Library Bulletin 20 (6): 40-41 (February 1946).

This article describes the West China Union University Library and its four branch libraries at Chengtu, the nerve center of education in Free China during the Japanese invasion. It also reports that the Library was a depository center for receiving selected periodicals and important theses in microfilm from the U.S.

377. Dennis, William H. "Science Via Microfilm." Library Journal 68: 414-416 (May 14, 1943).

Dennis presents an account of American efforts to supply scientific and technical information via microfilm to Chinese readers during the Japanese invasion. Chinese universities, libraries, and technical centers selected specially designed "vest pocket" projectors and more than 300 titles of journals for microfilming. These materials were sent to Chungking, where most of the universities are located, during the latter part of the war.

378. Fan, Zheng. "Consulting Service at the Library of Tianjin University." College and Research Libraries 42 (5): 483-485 (September 1981).

This is a research note on the consulting service provided by the Literature Searching and Consulting Group of the Tientsin University Library. It identifies categories of inquiry and gives examples. It concludes that the service is an important link in the library, saves researchers' time, and speeds up the development of research.

379. Ferguson, Anthony W. "Taiwan College and University Libraries: Problems and Prospects." International Library Review 10 (4): 397-405 (October 1978).

Based on the author's survey of college and university libraries in Taiwan from 1975 to 1976, the article identifies and discusses five major library problems which are related to inadequate funding: (1) lack of trained librarians; (2) lack of job openings for professionals; (3) inadequate book collections; (4) overabundance of departmental libraries; and (5) lack of trained leadership. The article recommends more adequate funding and wiser management for overcoming the problems and for future improvement.

380. Ferguson, Anthony W. "Taiwan College and University Library Collections: A Preliminary Statistical Profile." Committee on East Asian Libraries Bulletin No. 53: 34-52 (July 1977).

381. Fiske, Edward B. "Peking Tries to Fill a 10-Year Gap in the Shelves of Its University Libraries." New York Times (July 1, 1984).

This article is on the rebuilding of a generation of scholarship and scientific discovery lost during the ten year period of the Cultural Revolution, 1966-76. It reports that the Chinese signed an agreement with Baker and Taylor, the largest wholesale distributor of books to libraries in the U.S., to import $4 million worth of scientific books over the next two years in order to minimize the gap.

382. Gupta, R. K. "Academic Library Scene in the People's Republic of China and India." Annals of Library Science and Documentation 18 (4): 167-172 (December 1971).

Comparing the academic library in China and India, this article points out that although both countries began developing academic libraries in the late 1940's, China is clearly ahead of India in this field. The article discusses the political, economic, and educational factors affecting library development. It also reviews the users, international exchange programs, Western publications, expenditures on libraries, centralization of control and operations of the Chinese library system, and school libraries.

383. "Have the Libraries in Institutions of Higher Education Well Run." Survey of China Mainland Press No. 1448: 10-12 (January 11, 1957).

This article reports on a conference on library work in institutions of higher education. It points out that libraries should play an important role in planning for improving the quality of teaching, developing academic research work, and engaging in scientific research. It also examines the activities of the libraries of these institutions in revising the regulations governing how books may be read in the libraries, relaxing the restrictions placed on the number of books that may be borrowed, simplifying the book-borrowing procedure, and introducing more facilities for the readers.

384. Ho, James. "Is the Larger the Better? A Quantitative Analysis of Sixteen University Libraries in the Republic of China." Journal of Educational Media and Library Sciences 22 (4): 295-328 (Summer 1985).

Based on data collected during visits to twenty-six college and university libraries in Taiwan between late 1982 and early 1983 by the Library Evaluation Team, commissioned by the Ministry of Education of the Republic of China, this study provides a statistical analysis of the size and condition of library services among the sixteen largest academic libraries. It concludes that (1) there is no direct correlation between the condition of library services and the library size; (2) government-funded university libraries are better off financially and, thus, provide better library services; (3) private university libraries are generally larger in size but poorer in services; and (4) libraries ranked lower according to size or services are not necessarily inferior in their overall reader services.

385. Hu, Shu-chao. "Evaluating Chinese Academic Libraries from the Standpoints of American 'Standards for College Libraries.'" Journal of Library and Information Science 8 (2): 213-220 (October 1982).

Based on a 1981 survey of sixteen college and university libraries in Taiwan, the article evaluates these libraries by using the "Standards for College Libraries" adopted in the U.S. It compares the average collections of these libraries, the average collections of national university libraries, and the average collections of private university libraries in terms of U.S. standards. It concludes that except for the second category, they are well below the average of U.S. standards for college libraries. The text is in Chinese.

386. Huang, Hong-chu. "A Study on the Computerization of Foreign Publications Ordering Procedures in the ROC." Journal of Library and Information Science 5 (1): 104-110 (April 1979).

This study examines the ordering procedures for foreign publications in private college and university libraries in Taiwan and discusses in detail the possibilities and problems of computerizing these procedures.

387. Keenan, Barry. "Library Resources for Qing Studies in Nanjing." China Exchange News 12 (3): 10-12 (September 1984).

Working on the social history of education in Kiangsu from 1885 to 1927, the author spent from 1982 to 1983 at Nanking University as a researcher with the National Program for Advanced Study and Research in China. He describes the research facilitates at the Nanking Library and Nanking University, with special comments on twentieth-century books, Ch'ing materials, the reference room, and the History Department Library.

388. Kuo, Frank F. "An Inside Look at an Academic Library in the People's Republic of China." PNLA Quarterly 45 (4): 2-4 (Summer 1981).

This presents the personal observations of an audiovisual consultant to the Hua Chung Teachers College, including comments on bookstacks, staff, budget, and circulation.

389. Kwei, John Chih-ber. "National Central University Library." China Weekly Review 62 (4): 160-161 (September 24, 1932).

This is an historical account of the National Central University in Nanking and its library.

390. Kwei, John Chih-ber. "The Shantung University Library." China Weekly Review 37 (3): 58 (June 19, 1926).

Presenting a brief historical sketch of the Shantung University Library, this item comments on the library's catalogs, building arrangement, and lively collection of books.

391. "LAC Standards for University Libraries." NTU Library Science Circular No. 2: 1-10 (February 1966).

Prepared by Yung-hsiang Lai of the National Taiwan University, this presents the final draft of the "Standards for University Libraries." The draft was discussed article by article by the Committee for Improvements of Library Services in Taiwan Province and was approved by the Library Association of China (LAC) in 1963. It contains forty-eight articles divided into five groups: basic principles, library materials, planning and facilities, staff and budget, and services, as well as an addendum governing university libraries in Taiwan.

392. Lai, Yung-hsiang. "National Taiwan University Graduate Library: A Brief Introduction." NTU Library Science Circular No. 10: 1-5 (December 1968).

This article gives an introduction to the building and equipment, services and organization, and the collection of the Graduate Library of the National Taiwan University, which was formally opened in October 1968.

393. Lee, Linda Tzeng. "A Survey of the Western Social Sciences Literature among Seven Taipei Major Libraries and a Discussion of the Importance of Establishing a National Social Sciences Information Center." Journal of Educational Media Science 18 (3): 87-102 (Spring 1981).

Based on a survey conducted in 1980, the article provides statistical data on Western social science collections in seven major libraries in Taipei. It explains how some libraries handle social science literature and how they provide services to users. It concludes that the collection of Western social science literature in Taiwan is extremely inadequate. It suggests establishing a national social science information center to provide better services. The text is in Chinese, with an abstract in English.

394. Li, Siao-yuen. "The Reserved Book Situation in College Libraries in China: A Report." University of Nanking Magazine 16: 31-39 (November 1927).

Read at the Library Section of the Biennial Conference of the Higher Christian Association in 1926, this paper reports on a questionnaire survey of the reserved book situation in thirty-three college libraries in China. It discusses their services, their administration of the reserved books, the cost involved, and the problems connected with the college reserved books.

395. Li, Tze-chung. "A Survey of Library Resources for the Teaching of American Studies in Taiwan." International Library Review 2 (4): 437-444 (October 1970).

This is a revised version of a survey report presented at the Third Conference of the Joint Council on Sino-American Co-operation in Humanities and Social Sciences in 1969. The survey was designed to investigate present library resources on American Studies in Taiwan and to discover if they are adequate to support the teaching of American Studies. The survey indicated that the library resources are inadequate and the report therefore recommends building a Center for American Studies.

396. Lin, Sharon Chien. "Tsing Hua University Library." International Library Review 15 (1): 115-127 (January 1983).

This article describes the present status and possible future developments of the Tsing Hua University Library. It covers a review of its history, organization and staff, collections, acquisitions, cataloging and classification, periodical and reference services, and reader services (including monographs, periodicals, circulation and copying service, circulation stations, interlibrary loan, and an exchange program).

397. Lo, Henrietta. "The Obstacles to Reform: China Modernizes Its University Libraries." College and Research Libraries 48 (6): 504-512 (November 1987).

Based on the author's research on university libraries in China during 1983 and 1985, this paper examines the development of librarianship in modern China, outlines the problems facing both university libraries and their users, and points to China's political and social structures and economic conditions as obstacles in reforming Chinese libraries. It also discusses user services, a new development mandated for university libraries by the Chinese government.

398. Ma, Shiyi. "A Brief Introduction to College and University Librarianship in China." Chinese-American Librarians Association Newsletter No. 31: 12 (December 1984).

This reports on the National Working Conference of College and University Libraries held in Peking in 1981. It outlines the functions and activities of the National Working Committee of College and University Libraries, including the issuance of the "Rules of College and University Libraries."

399. Miller, John N. "The Chinese Disconnection: An American in China Finds His Students Severed from the Library Books They Need." American Libraries 15 (1): 22-24 (January 1984).

Speaking from the perspective of an English teacher at the Central China Teachers College in Wuhan from 1981 to 1982, the author expresses dismay over library service in China. He cites the limited admission, confused card catalog, unfriendly staff, and closed stacks as walls blocking access to information in a library.

400. "A Note on Chinese Libraries and the Chinese Library Association." Library World 32: 5-7 (1929).

This is a short article on the development of the Boone University Library, the establishment of the Chinese Library Association, and the Association's first conference.

401. Pastine, Maureen. "An International Library Exchange in China: Academic and Research Libraries in the PRC." College and Research Library News 47 (6): 392-399 (June 1986).

This is a report contributed by several members of a delegation of U.S. librarians who visited China in 1984. They visited several major university libraries, schools or departments of library and information science, and large provincial libraries. The report includes comments on salaries, automation, classification schemes, library associations, stacks, mobile libraries, cooperative acquisition exchange, and personnel training.

402. "Possible Changes in Chinese Library Administration." Leads 24 (2): 8 (Summer 1982).

Based on a review of Chinese library literature, this article presents the demographic makeup of the university library leadership in China and Taiwan. It discusses the massive retirement program for personnel over sixty in China. It also comments on personnel in library administration and describes the systems and methods of managing libraries in Taiwan.

403. Repp, Joan M. "Kwangtung Teachers' College Library, People's Republic of China." International Library Review 10 (4): 407-410 (October 1978).

Repp describes the building, reading rooms, collections, and cataloging system of the Kwangtung Teachers' College Library. He outlines the Chinese system which uses twenty-two letters of the English alphabet to identify the subdivisions.

404. Schwintzer, Ernst. "Foreign Student Use of Libraries in Shanghai." China Exchange News 12 (3): 15-18 (September 1982).

The author discusses the library at Futan University and the Shanghai Municipal Library from the viewpoint of an advanced graduate student at Futan University during 1982-84. He also mentions other archives and libraries in the Shanghai area.

405. Seng, Samuel T. Y. "The Recent Progress of Boone University Library, and Its Future Development." Library Journal 38 (5): 284-286 (May 1913).

An abridged version of an article which appeared in the December 1912 issue of Boone Review, this piece pertains to the growth and progress of the Boone University Library in Wuchang, China. It also appeals for building up the library.

406. Shaw, Charles B. "China's Christian Libraries." Library Journal 75 (4): 243-245 (February 15, 1950).

This paper recounts the difficulties of the libraries in thirteen Christian or missionary colleges and universities which are partially supported by American funds. It points out that despite the problems, the United Board for Christian Colleges in China decided the libraries would continue to receive grants and be supplied with new books.

407. Shaw, Charles B. The Libraries of the Christian Colleges in China. New York: United Board for Christian Colleges in China, 1948. 87 leaves.

Surveying conditions of the libraries of the Christian colleges in China in 1947, the author closely examines thirteen libraries. He reports on their situation, notes their pressing needs, and suggests some of the steps and procedures which would aid in the development of these libraries. He concludes with recommendations on the techniques of library work, education in librarianship, the reference service, gifts, the physical plant, and cooperative activities.

408. Shyu, Jin-fen. "A Study on Job Satisfaction of the University Library Staffs in the Republic of China." Journal of Library and Information Science 11 (2): 207-234 (October 1985).

This study is based on a 1985 survey of 312 employees at sixteen university libraries in Taiwan. The data are analyzed by the t-test, ANOVA, and Scheffe method. The study indicates that (1) at present, the university library staff have not achieved satisfaction on their job; (2) education, departmental affiliation, marital status, and types of university do not produce differences among the respondents; and (3) scores on job satisfaction differ significantly by sex, age, professional education, supervisory level, tenure, and career orientation. The article outlines suggestions for future improvements. The text is in Chinese, with an abstract in English.

409. "Steady Flow." Library Journal 70: 31 (January 1, 1945).

This is a note on the wartime transmission of scientific, technological, and medical materials on microfilm to Chinese universities and research centers.

410. Wang, Chen-ku. "A Survey of College and University Libraries in Taiwan." Journal of Library and Information Science 2 (1): 74-101 (April 1976).

This paper analyzes a 1975 survey of 100 college and university libraries in Taiwan in terms of the library administration, collections, personnel, budget, buildings and facilities, technical services, and reader services. The survey was designed to access the standing of college and university libraries in Taiwan, with the final goal of drafting a new "Standards for College and University Libraries." Valuable suggestions are made as the result of the survey. The text is in Chinese, with an abstract in English.

411. Wang, Chung-fu. "The Suggestions of Current Period in University Libraries Development." Journal of Educational Media and Library Sciences 20 (4): 374-384 (Summer 1983).

Exploring the important factors which influenced the development of contemporary university libraries in Taiwan, this paper also provides suggestions to improve conditions in the university libraries. The text is in Chinese, with an abstract in English.

412. Wong, Sanford Ch'ang P'ing. "The Problem of Selecting Occidental Reference Books for Chinese College Libraries." M.S. thesis, School of Library Services, Columbia University, 1934. 68 pp.

This thesis surveys the libraries of seventeen liberal arts colleges in China to discover the problems which affect the selection of Occidental reference books in English, French, and German.

413. Wong, Vi-lien. The Low Library--A History. Shanghai: St. John's University, 1924. 12 pp.

Covering the period from 1894 to 1923, this booklet presents an historical sketch of the expansion of the St. John's University Library, the Low Library, in Shanghai. It traces the growth and development of the library in four periods: the Main Building period, 1894-1904; the Yen Hall period, 1904-11; the Administration Building period, 1911-15; and the Anniversary Hall period, 1915. It includes comparative statistics on circulation and accession.

414. Wong, Vi-lien. "Reflections on the Profession of College Librarianship in China." College and Research Libraries 10 (4): 401-405 (October 1949).

The author traces the development of the modern library movement in China in three stages, with the first stage credited to the visit of Arthur E. Bostwick in 1925, the second stage credited to the Rockefeller Foundation, and the third credited to the United Board for Christian Colleges in China. He also explores problems and difficulties facing the profession of college librarianship in China.

415. Wong, Vi-lien. "A Study of Chinese College Library Personnel." The Library Quarterly 7 (3): 401-432 (July 1937).

This study analyzes the present status of personnel in Chinese college libraries. Its purpose is twofold: to discover the present status of library personnel in institutions of higher learning and to discover the immediate needs of these librarians. The study includes the areas of personnel appointments and promotions, qualifications, duties, academic status, salaries, working conditions, and staff privileges and welfare. Conclusions and recommendations are drawn from the analysis.

416. Wood, Frances. "Peking University Library." Focus on International and Comparative Librarianship 7 (3): 27-28 (1976).

This article provides a general description of the Peking University Library, founded in 1899. It is devoted to the arts collection, which serves approximately 7,000 students and 4,000 staff. The article focuses on two main features of the Library: (1) a rigid separation into subject divisions; and (2) closed access and an unreliable catalog. The author observes that because of censorship, many books are unlisted; however, these books are obtainable upon request.

417. Wood, Mary Elizabeth. "Boone College Library, Wuchang, China." Library Journal 34 (2): 54-55 (February 1909). Reprinted from the Boone Review (August 1908).

Wood describes the plan to build a library in Boone College and discusses the current state of the library collection and its fund-raising status.

418. Wood, Mary Elizabeth. The Boone Library and Its Outlook for the Future. Wuchang: Boone University Library, [1918]. 17 pp.

This outlines the library work carried out by the Boone University Library in Wuchang and its recent activities. "Statistics of the Boone University Library" and "Programs of the Boone University Library Extension Lectures for Students of Government Schools and Government Institutions in Wuchang" are appended.

419. Wood, Mary Elizabeth. "Library Work in a Chinese City." American Library Association Bulletin 1 (3): 84-87 (May 1907).

Wood describes Wuchang, one of the greatest literary centers in China, and library work at the Boone University Library. She also advocates establishing a large public library in the city.

420. "Year of Progress at Low Library, China." Library Journal 60: 117 (February 1, 1935).

This is a note on the growth of the book collection at the Low Library, St. John's University, Shanghai, during 1933-34.

421. Yeh, Thomas Y. "A Profile of Academic Libraries in China." College and Research Libraries 46 (6): 499-503 (November 1985).

Describing common characteristics and problems facing academic libraries in China, this article points out that although the use of academic libraries is very high, most of these libraries trail behind the U.S. libraries in budget, personnel management, building design, and public services. It also notes that since China has placed a high priority on academic library services, its library systems should be greatly improved in the near future.

422. Zhu, Chenggong. "Some Problems in Designing the University Library Buildings in China: A Developing Country University Librarian's View Based on His Own Experience." Paper presented at the 48th Annual Meeting of the International Federation of Library Associations, Montreal, Canada, August 22-28, 1982. 9 pp. (ED 227 876).

The author presents the history of the Tsing Hua University Library in Peking and discusses the library facilities there. He stresses the importance of the comparison between Chinese library building designs and those of other countries, the flexibility in library space design, and the cooperation between librarians and architects in designing libraries. He recommends that the Chinese learn from other countries' experience, pay attention to future changes, enhance the flexibility of library function, and have a proper cooperation between the librarians and architects for new building design.

III. PUBLIC LIBRARIES

423. Bostwick, Arthur E. "Public Library in China." China Weekly Review 34 (12): 273-275 (November 21, 1925).

Bostwick stresses free access of the public library and home use of library books in this address which he delivered before the Chinese Social and Political Science Association in Peking. He discusses the plan to establish experimental public libraries by requesting money from the Indemnity Fund Commission.

424. Chen, Feng. "Communist China's Cultural Work in 1965." In Communist China 1965, vol. 2, pp. 123-141. Hong Kong: Union Research Institute, 1967.

This is an account of the mobile bookstalls operated by the Hsinhua Book Company to supply reading materials for the general readers in the village libraries. It also mentions other cultural activities serviced by the bookstalls.

425. Chin, Kung. "A Village Library Station." Survey of China Mainland Press No. 2989: 7-9 (May 29, 1963).

Chin describes library services established in a suburb of Peking to meet the needs of young readers working in the countryside. The establishment of a village library station, with simple regulations governing the borrowing of books and basic systems of cataloging books, has greatly encouraged young readers in suburban Peking to read more.

426. "China's Libraries Assist Scientific Research." Survey of China Mainland Press No. 2536: 23-24 (1961).

This article describes how China's public libraries are providing special facilities for research work by engineers, scientists, technicians, and workers. It particularly depicts the roles played by the two national library committees in Peking and in Shanghai. It also notes that the networking among libraries facilitates interlibrary exchange, cataloging, and staff training.

427. Chinese Communist Party. Liling Hsien Committee. "How Do We Run Libraries?" Selections from Chinese Mainland Magazines No. 758-759: 36-39 (August 20-28, 1973). Originally published in Chinese in Red Flag No. 8 (August 1973).

This is an account of the establishment of small libraries in the communes of the Liling Hsien area. It explores their space, book supply, and library management problems. It also discusses the mode of activity in most libraries in Liling Hsien.

428. "Delivering Books to Rural Readers and Occupying the Cultural Position in the Countryside." Survey of China Mainland Press No. 3588: 10-12 (December 1, 1965).

This is a report on the Ching Hsien Cultural Center, Anhwei Province, which helped fifty-seven production brigades from twenty-four communes set up more than

100 libraries or reading rooms and made more than 200 circulating book shelves or boxes during the past few years. By the end of 1964, more than 16,000 volumes were kept in the centers or stations in Ching Hsien, of which 13,000 copies (roughly 80% of the total collection) were circulated among rural readers.

429. Doo, Ding U. "Public Libraries and Adult Education in China." In Libraries in China, pp. 129-132. Peking: Library Association of China, 1935.

The author describes the promotion of library work in China during the 1930's through adult education. He outlines the library services rendered to adult readers by the Popular Library in Wuhsi. He also articulates the hope for greater achievements in the future.

430. Eliot, Charles W. "An American Free Public Library in Peking." Library Journal 39 (9): 688-689 (September 1914).

Based on personal observations made in China in 1912, this report to the trustees of the Carnegie Endowment for International Peace recommends the establishment of a public library along American lines in the city of Peking.

431. Gray, Karen. "Looking into Public Libraries of the People's Republic of China." Illinois Libraries 62 (8): 686-689 (October 1980).

These are impressions gained during the author's visit to five public libraries in China in 1980: a commune library, a city library, two provincial libraries, and the Peking Library. The author observes that library services are limited to circulation and reference and that collections are stagnant and in poor condition in most libraries she visited.

432. "Greater Library Service Provided for Rural Areas in Shansi." Survey of China Mainland Press No. 2870: 15 (November 30, 1962).

Reporting on the mobile booklending points set up by workers at the library of Yangkao Hsien, Shansi, this short note describes library service in the rural area.

433. Hayford, Charles W., and Nathan, Andrew J. "Sixty Good Books on China: A Basic Collection for the General Reader." Library Journal 97 (13): 2341-2347 (July 1972).

This list of sixty books, plus a short list of current periodicals, emphasizes reportage, eye-witness accounts, biography, politics, and society in modern China. The entries are arranged by subject and are briefly annotated. The selection is suited to the needs of branch libraries.

434. "Increase in Rural Mobile Libraries Around Peking." Survey of China Mainland Press No. 2877: 20 (December 11, 1962).

This reports on the establishment of thirty mobile libraries in various counties around Peking under the people's communes in 1962. The libraries are run by production teams, with the assistance of the cultural centers.

435. Lee, Michelle Shaio-lan. "Private Public Libraries of Taiwan, Republic of China: Two Additional Examples." Public Library Quarterly 4 (4): 57-60 (Winter 1983).

Lee describes two private public libraries in Taipei, which are oriented towards special needs of the public: the Hong Chian-chuan Audio-Visual Library and the Taipei Hsing Tien Temple Library. The former is devoted primarily to audio-visual material, and the latter holds a large collection in religious studies. The article provides information on the collections and services of each library.

436. Li, Augustine Fong-fu. "Financing of Chinese Public Libraries." M.A. thesis, Faculty of Library Services, Columbia University, 1936. 93 leaves.

The thesis analyzes the present financial status of Chinese public libraries. It also presents an historical survey of the development of public libraries in China, discusses the present library status and support, points out the weaknesses in the present system of library support and administration, and offers suggestions for its reconstruction.

437. "The Library Comes to the Mountain." Peking Review No. 24: 32 (June 14, 1960).

This is an account of how the library services were extended to the northwestern region of Kansu Province by a team from the Kansu Provincial Library.

438. "Library Expansion in China Begun." Library Journal 43 (10): 764-765 (October 1918).

This short article notes on the beginning of public library development in China. It also presents sample pages of a modified Dewey system of classifying Chinese books, adapted by Samuel T. Y. Seng.

439. Liu, I-cheng. "The Provincial Libraries in China." In Libraries in China, pp. 99-115. Peking: Library Association of China, 1935.

This is a summary of the history, organization, collection, public service, publications, and budget of sixteen provincial libraries in China: Kiangsu, Chekiang, Anhui, Kiangsi, Hupeh, Hunan, Szechuan, Hopei, Honan, Shantung, Shensi, Kansu, Fukien, Kwangsi, Yunnan, and the Northeastern Provincial Libraries. Some libraries were not included in the survey due to the lack of sufficient information.

440. "Mobile Book Centers Set Up in Chiehyang Hsien." Survey of China Mainland Press No. 3570: 8 (November 2, 1965).

The establishment of mobile book centers in the rural villages of Kwangtung Province since March 1965 is reported. It notes that about 2,600 books were sent to the P'ao-t'ai Commune alone. It criticizes the former practice of merely waiting for readers to borrow books and suggests the library take initiative in reaching readers in the rural areas.

441. "More Books Supplied to Rural Readers in Suburban Areas of Peking." Survey of China Mainland Press No. 2870: 15 (November 30, 1962).

This is a note on the cultural clubs, Hsinhua Bookstores, and other relevant departments in the suburban areas of Peking that take part in supplying more books to rural readers. It mentions that more than thirty mobile libraries have been established.

442. "Neighborhood Libraries in Central China City." Survey of China Mainland Press No. 5410: 22 (July 9, 1973).

The establishment of libraries in the city of Changsha in Central China is described. It particularly notes their services, facilities, and collections.

443. "Northeast China City Library Brings Books to Peasant Readers." Survey of China Mainland Press No. 3594: 17 (December 5, 1965).

This article reports on the mobile library service of the Shenyang Municipal Library, which brings books to 30,000 peasant readers on the outskirts of the Northeast China industrial center. There are thirty-five mobile libraries staffed by eight volunteers who are guided by the library's staff members.

444. Nutting, N. "Libraries in Shanghai." New Zealand Libraries 15 (4): 89-90 (May 1952).

This is a letter which notes the great library developments in modern China. During her two-year stay in Shanghai, Nutting especially observed changes in the Shanghai Municipal Library including its expansion, increased acquisition funds, a new librarian, and full-time library workers.

445. Otness, Harold M. "The Private Public Libraries of Taiwan." Public Library Quarterly 4 (4): 51-56 (Winter 1983).

This article describes the Lee Family Library in Taipei, Taiwan, which is funded through charitable foundations to serve neighborhood needs. It points out that although the library does not have card catalogs or cataloging procedures, a reference collection or service, interlibrary loans or non-print materials, a large budget, or a professionally trained librarian, the library is extremely popular and efficient in servicing student and adult needs.

446. "'People's Libraries' Set Up in Shanghai Streets and Lanes." Union Research Service 43 (16): 233-248 (May 24, 1966).

Six reports dealing with the activities of the "people's libraries" in Shanghai since 1958 are included. These reports describe the collections, circulation, and ideological, political, and propaganda activities of the people's libraries.

447. "Promotion of Public Libraries." Quarterly Bulletin of Chinese Bibliography, New Series 2 (1/2): 56 (June 1941).

A news item on the Ministry of Education's promulgation of a set of sixteen articles governing the promotion of public libraries as an important educational institution. It lists five articles for the provincial and city authorities to observe.

448. Public Libraries for Asia: The Delhi Seminar, pp. 157-158. Paris: UNESCO, 1956.

While this is a general book on public libraries in Asia, it does cover public library development in Taiwan (p. 157) and the People's Republic of China (pp. 157-158).

449. "The Provincial Library of Chekiang." Orient et Occident 2: 117-119 (1935/36).

The history, organization, collections, and recent development of the Provincial Library of Chekiang and its two branch libraries are traced. The article also mentions the Imperial Library, the Ssu K'u Ch'uan Shu, and the library's book sales and printing shop.

450. "Success of Dr. Bostwick's Mission to China." Libraries 31 (1): 78 (January 1926).

Reporting on the success of using returned Boxer indemnity funds for library extension and improvement in China, this also notes the China Foundation's decision to establish six other libraries in various parts of the country as a result of Dr. Bostwick's visit and his presentation of the educational value of the public library.

451. Wang, Jane. "The Information Service Practice of the Public Library in Taiwan." Journal of Educational Media and Library Sciences 21 (1): 92-98 (Autumn 1983).

The author defines the information service as the most direct, effective, and efficient method of social education. She points out that with government support in Taiwan, the public libraries are rapidly developing. She discusses the work flow of the information services and the establishment of a network to serve the public libraries in Taiwan. The text is in Chinese, with an abstract in English.

452. Wang, Julie. A Study of the Criteria for Book Selection in Communist China's Public Libraries, 1949-1964. Hong Kong: Union Research Institute, 1968. 160 pp.

This is an outgrowth of the author's M.A. thesis presented to the faculty of the Department of Librarianship at San Jose State College in 1966. The study describes the size and scope of book collections in Communist China's public libraries and examines the criteria for book selection in these libraries. It covers the historical background of Chinese Communist public libraries, library organization and interlibrary organizational structure, characteristics of book collections, and the criteria for book selection.

453. Wood, Mary Elizabeth. "A Library as a Phase of Mission Work." Outlook 86 (2): 618 (July 20, 1907).

This is an appeal by the Episcopal Mission in China for U.S. support in establishing a public library in Wuchang, one of the foremost educational centers in China.

454. Wu, K. T. "Public Library Service in China." China Critic 3: 509-511 (1930).

A survey of public library conditions in China is presented. Wu suggests two types of public libraries that are most urgently needed: (1) technical and scientific libraries; and (2) libraries for the average student and the general public. Wu maintains that although the libraries are beset with many difficulties, they are becoming more favorably regarded.

455. Yoh, Peter Liang-mu. "American Methods of Public Library Extension and Their Possible Application in China." M.A. thesis, Faculty of Library Service, Columbia University, 1936. 119 leaves.

The study surveys the development of the public library extension movement and types of extension agencies in America with the hope of finding a formula which might be adaptable to conditions in China. It also discusses the development of the public library movement in China and compares the present status of public libraries and other agencies in China with those in the U.S.

456. Yu, Chin-fang. "Some Considerations for the Planning of Public Library Building." Journal of Educational Media and Library Sciences 21 (4): 430-440 (Summer 1984).

In order to meet library needs, services, technologies, and systems which are rapidly changing, the author urges libraries in Taiwan to consider greater flexibility in the design, construction, and utilization of library space when planning a public library building. The author also suggests taking into account publication and population explosions when designing a public library building. The text is in Chinese, with an abstract in English.

457. Yu, Po-cheng. "A Street Library in Shanghai." China Reconstructs 14 (10): 44-46 (October 1965).

This article deals with the Plum Fragrance Street Library in Shanghai, which was established by the residents. It shows the library service as an educational center for socialism and describes the services and reading materials provided by the Library.

IV. SPECIAL LIBRARIES

458. Campbell, Marguerite E. "Peking Union Medical College Libraries." In Methods and Problems of Medical Education (Sixth Series), pp. 1-8. New York: Rockefeller Foundation, 1927.

Campbell describes two libraries of the Peking Union Medical College: the medical library in the chemistry building and the general library in Lockhart Hall, where the Premedical School is located. She remarks on the current journal reading room, the main reading rooms, the periodical reading room, and others. She also discusses the library's administration, interlibrary loans, book selection, classification, duplicates, bindery, and budget.

459. Ch'en, C. D. Henry, "The Chinese Social and Political Science Library." Chinese Social and Political Science Review 7: 117-124 (July 1923).

The article details the progress of the Chinese Social and Political Science Association and traces the origin as well as the development of its library since 1915. It includes a description of the "Decimal Classification" of books with a detailed outline of the class "Sociology," the library's reference use, and its collection of Chinese books. It welcomes suggestions as well as criticisms on the growth and development of the library and the institution.

460. "China Information Library Is a Bimonthly Current Awareness Service." Information News and Services 7 (8): 225+ (October 1975).

This is an information item on the China Information Library, which provides easy access to up-to-date information on China, including news stories, commerce and trade reports, features, book reviews, and reference guides from China and all over the world.

461. "China's Oldest Library Helps Scientific Research." Survey of China Mainland Press No. 2577: 19 (1961).

This short article describes China's oldest library, founded in Ningpo, Chekiang Province between 1561 and 1566 by the book collector, Fan Chin. The library is currently under special state protection to repair damaged volumes, photocopy more than 180 rare books, and make facsimile editions in order to aid scientific research.

462. Chiu, A. Kaiming. "The Destruction of the Commercial Press Library." Library Journal 57 (14): 649-651 (August 1932).

The article traces the history of the Oriental Library, one of the subsidiary institutions of the Commerical Press in Shanghai and known to Chinese scholars as Han Fen Lou. It was destroyed by the Japanese invasion in 1932.

463. Cummins, J. S. "Present Location of the Pei-t'ang Library." Monumenta Nipponica 22 (3/4): 482-487 (1967).

Cummins presents an historical description of one of the mission libraries, the library of the North Church or Pei-t'ang Library in Peking. Established in the seventeenth century by Jesuit priests, the library has survived numerous wars and is currently being absorbed into the Rare Books Section of the Peking Municipal Library. Rare items collected by the Pei-t'ang can still be found at its new location.

464. Erickson, Linda J., and Ford, Barbara J. "Cooperation with the People's Republic of China." Special Libraries 77 (3): 129-132 (Summer 1986).

The authors report on their visit to China as a part of a delegation of American librarians. The authors, who visited the library of Chengtu Institute of Radio Engineering (CIRE), describe the library's collection, staff, services, and computer center. They also outline opportunities for exchanging materials and personnel and engaging in other cooperative efforts. They append a set of proposals made by CIRE to promote international exchange and cooperation.

465. Fu, Ssu-nien. "Note on Chinese Libraries." Journal of the American Oriental Society 67 (4): 327-328 (October/December 1947).

Fu examines the conditions of the library which was attached to the Institute for the Study of Humanities in China in Peking and subsequently turned over to the Academia Sinica after World War II. He also outlines steps to be taken to make this valuable collection readily available.

466. Fukudome, Takao. "The China Medical Board and Medical Libraries in the Far East." Medical Library Association Bulletin 56 (2): 150-156 (April 1968).

The article describes the situation of medical libraries in the Far East in relation to the China Medical Board's grants. Among the recipients are the Peking Union Medical College of China and the National Defense Medical Center of Taiwan, where libraries and collections are built, and librarians are trained.

467. He, Daxun; Cai, Fenlan; and Wu, Zijun. "The Status and Development of Biomedical Libraries in China." INSPEL 21 (1): 5-8 (1987).

Tracing the history of medical libraries from the Western Chou Dynasty (1,066-771 B.C.) to the present, this paper describes the current status of medical libraries in China, with an emphasis on medical college libraries and the information services and the user education function they provide. The paper also points out that the establishment of the Chinese Medical College Library Association not only contributed to the development of medical college libraries but also made a great impact on the development of medical librarianship as a whole.

468. Huang, C. K. "A Leap Forward in Medical Librarianship: A Glimpse of the Biomedical Information Centre and Network, People's Republic of China." Bulletin of the Medical Library Association 71 (3): 299-303 (July 1983).

This article describes the Biomedical Information Centre and Network Project (BNIC), a cooperative agreement signed by the World Health Organization and the Chinese Ministry of Public Health in 1978 to develop a national health information system and modernize China's medical libraries. It presents details on the resources, personnel, facilities, network, and automation of the project. It points out that the final goal is to develop a MEDLARS-like data base in the network, which will have a significant impact upon future medical librarianship in China.

469. Liu, Ellen Fan. "Medical Monographs: A Comparison of Core Lists and Their Potential Uses in Taiwan." Journal of Library and Information Science 8 (2): 174-194 (October 1982).

Focusing on medical monographs, this article compares four core lists in terms of the authority of the core lists, purpose, intended users, size of the core collection, subjects covered, and characteristics.

The purpose of the study is to find out if these lists can be adopted or modified for use in hospital libraries and academic medical libraries in Taiwan. It concludes that direct adoption would include materials not applicable in Taiwan and suggests that this be taken into consideration before modifying them for local users.

470. Liu, Ellen Fan. "A Selected List of Core Books for the Medical Libraries in the R.O.C." Journal of Educational Media and Library Sciences 20 (3): 253-276 (Spring 1983).

The author explains the importance of acquiring and maintaining a core medical collection to aid scholars and physicians in their continuing education and daily work in the biomedical institutions in Taiwan. She first studies and compares the core collections currently used in the U.S. and England. To accommodate local needs, she surveys the opinions of physicians and specialists in Taiwan. She then identifies and provides a selected list of 260 English titles and 22 Chinese titles as the core collection for medical libraries in Taiwan. The text is in Chinese, with an abstract and list in English.

471. Liu, Ellen Fan. "A Selected List of Core Journals for the Medical Libraries in the R.O.C." Journal of Educational Media and Library Sciences 21 (4): 441-465 (Summer 1984).

This is a second study of the acquisition and maintenance of a core medical collection for the medical libraries in Taiwan. The author studies and compares twelve core lists from the U.S., Canada, and England. She then surveys the Chinese medical journals and solicits opinions on these journals from physicians and specialists in Taiwan. As a result, she identifies and provides a selected list of 156 English titles and 17 Chinese titles as the basic information needed by the small and medium-size medical libraries in Taiwan. The text is in Chinese, with an abstract and list in English.

472. Liu, Helen. "A Description and Brief History of the History and Philology Library, Academia Sinica." M.L.S. research paper, School of Library Science, Kent State University, 1970. 37 leaves.

Based on information provided by the librarian of the History and Philology Library, this paper discusses the history, building and equipment, and collection of this research library. The main part of the study is in Chapter 3 which is a detailed description of the

Library's collection, divided into the following areas: Chinese rare books, archives of the Ming and Ch'ing Dynasties, "Veritable Records" of the Ming Dynasty, Chinese local gazetteers, rubbings, the Chinese folk song collection, periodicals, special catalogs and indexes, microfilms, the reference collection, and the special collection. The paper also discusses some plans for the Library's future.

473. Otness, Harold M. "Map Librarianship in the Republic of China." Western Association of Map Libraries Information Bulletin 13 (2): 124-128 (March 1982).

This article describes the state of map librarianship in Taiwan. The author points out that map collections open to the public are virtually nonexistent in the public and university libraries of Taiwan. He comments on various map collections at the major university and national libraries. He also shares his experience as a visiting associate professor teaching a first-ever course on "Geography and Map Librarianship" to library science students at the National Taiwan University.

474. Otness, Harold M. "The Morrison Libraries: A Tale of Two Private Chinese Collections." Journal of Library and Information Science 8 (2): 159-164 (October 1982).

Otness depicts two Morrison libraries which were formed almost a century apart, one in Canton and the other in Peking, by unrelated individuals. The first Morrison Library was built by a missionary, Dr. Robert Morrison, in the early nineteenth century in Canton and has a collection of 10,000 volumes, including many rare and valuable editions of the Chinese classics. Today, the collection is in the School of Oriental and African Studies in London. The other Morrison Library was formed by George Ernest Morrison in the early twentieth century in Peking and has 20,000 volumes of Western language materials concerning China. The library was sold to the Japanese in 1924 and remains in the Oriental Institute in Tokyo today.

475. Peng, Guiyuan. "Research and Development Challenge Better Services in Scientific and Technical Libraries." Paper presented at the 49th Annual Conference of the International Federation of Library Associations, Munich, West Germany, August 21-27, 1983. 9 pp. (ED 239 653).

This paper traces the development of the reader services at the Central Library of the Chinese Academy of Sciences in Peking since 1949, dividing it into two periods: (1) from the 1950's to the eve of the Cultural Revolution in 1966; and (2) the new stage of development since 1966. The Library has now become a national comprehensive scientific research system, consisting of 140 research institutes. The paper outlines the functions and accomplishments of the system. The author believes that the development of modern science and technology will challenge library and information work and will provide the library with new means and technology. He encourages librarians to do their best to make use of the achievements in science and technology in promoting library work and better library services.

476. Powell, John. "Special Report: My Father's Library." Wilson Library Bulletin 60 (7): 35-37 (March 1986).

This is a description of a special library, the China Weekly Review Library of Shanghai, which is one of the best newspaper libraries in the Far East.

477. "Private Library Donated to Chinese Academy of Sciences by Local Inventor." Survey of China Mainland Press No. 16/57: 4 (January 23, 1957).

A news item on the donation of 20,000 books, chiefly on agriculture, to the Chinese Academy of Sciences South China Botanic Research Office in Canton. They were donated by Ng Sau-yin, inventor of DDT in vapor form and chairman of the Hong Kong Association of Inventors.

478. "The Research Library of the College of Agriculture and Forestry, University of Nanking." Agricultural Library Notes 3: 289-291 (1928).

Based on the annual report of the College for 1926-27, this article describes one of the most important Chinese agricultural libraries--the Research Library of the College of Agriculture and Forestry of the University of Nanking. It reports on the library's collection, cooperation with the Library of Congress, activities in indexing current periodicals, and the compilation of Agricultural Encyclopedia Sinica. It also notes the completion of a bibliography of Chinese literature in agriculture.

479. Shari'at, M. J. "The Library of the Tung-hsi Mosque at Peking." Asian Affairs 67 (1): 68-70 (February 1980).

Translated from Persian, the article describes a special library in Peking, the library of the Tung-hsi Mosque. The author was surprised to find Persian manuscripts in the library. He provides a list of these titles.

480. Shen, Jialian. "How About the 'Ugly Duckling' in China? Some Investigations on the Use of Patent Literature in This Country." World Patent Information 4 (3): 102-104 (1982).

Providing a profile of users at the Patent Library of the Institute of Scientific and Technical Information of China, this article investigates the characteristics, language capabilities, and needs of users.

481. Shen, Jishian. "The Patent Library in the Institute of Scientific and Technical Information of China." World Patent Information 3 (4): 175-176 (October 1981).

This paper is presented as a follow-up of A. Wittmann's "A Patent System for the People's Republic of China--Impressions from an Official Visit" (see #720). It describes the Patent Library in the Institute of Scientific and Technical Information of China, which houses China's largest patent literature collection. The library functions as a patent documentation and information center and offers other information facilities.

482. Sung, Yu. "Cooperation and Computerization of Science and Technology Orientated Libraries in R.O.C." In Proceedings of the First Conference on Asian Library Cooperation, edited by Tamkang College, pp. 558-574. Taipei: Tamkang College, 1974.

The problems facing the science and technology-orientated libraries in Taiwan and their efforts to solve them are closely examined. The author identifies problems in the areas of acquisition budget and acquisition process, competent staff, space, facilities, speed and quality of service, and duplication and omissions. The author points out that in order to solve some of the problems, libraries formed a cooperative organization to handle interlibrary loan and cooperative acquisition of serial titles and instituted experimental automation projects. The author proposes four recommendations to push for more cooperation and computerization in Taiwan.

483. Tai, Julie Rummelhoff. "Medical Libraries in China: A Survey." In Libraries in China, pp. 117-127. Peking: Library Association of China, 1935.

This article summarizes the development of Western medicine and medical training in China since the nineteenth century. It also reports on a questionnaire survey of libraries in medical schools and hospitals which examined their collection size, number of periodicals subscribed to, annual budget, and seating capacity. It cites the lack of money, equipment, and trained library staff as problems facing medical libraries in China.

484. Wang, John K. C. "Industrial Research Libraries: How Can They Put Information to Work in the 1980's?" Journal of Library and Information Science 7 (2): 194-203 (October 1981).

Wang reviews the work, organization, and services of industrial research libraries, which are a dynamic unit for the acquisition, organization, dissemination, retrieval, and transfer of scientific and technical information. He also presents models to support the development of such libraries in Taiwan.

485. Wang, John K. C. "Special Libraries in Taiwan." Journal of Educational Media Science 18 (3): 31-36 (Spring 1981).

This article gives an overview of 101 special libraries in Taiwan, which are divided into three groups: libraries of research institutes, industrial and business libraries, and government libraries. It also notes such problems as charges made to librarians for missing or damaged materials, and delays in receiving publications due to foreign currency regulations. It suggests recommendations for the improvement of service and management of special libraries in Taiwan.

486. Wu, Grace. "A Survey of Special Libraries in Taiwan." M.L.S. research paper, School of Library Science, Kent State University, 1970. 39 leaves.

This paper is based on a questionnaire survey of thirty special libraries in Taiwan, twelve of which are included in this study. The first chapter outlines the purposes, need, methodology, and limitations of the study, and the second discusses the general characteristics of special libraries, such as size, location, and major function. The third and final chapter presents a general discussion and statistical analysis of the survey data.

487. Yan, Lizhong. "A Brief Introduction to the Library of Academia Sinica." Chinese-American Librarians Association Newsletter No. 30: 8 (June 1984).

Introducing the Library of the Chinese Academy of Sciences, established in 1951, this short note focuses on the library's collections, organization, publications, and exchange programs. It points out that in addition to its own professional work, the library, as the center for a network of library and information services, also has the responsibility of providing assistance to the libraries of its affiliated institutions.

V. SCHOOL/CHILDREN'S LIBRARIES

488. Chen, Paul T. H. "China's Tricycle Libraries." Library Journal 67 (4): 138 (February 15, 1942).

In an attempt to provide more useful books for the children of Shanghai, the author, a librarian at Nanking Theological Seminary, plans to select a collection of the best children's literature and make it accessible through traveling libraries, to be put on four tricycles and carried around in the residential districts.

489. "A Children's Library." China Reconstructs 23 (8): 39 (August 1974).

This short paper describes the Wuhan Children's Library in central China. Established in 1958, the Library now has about 200,000 volumes of children's books, serves 1,000 readers a day, and offers a variety of activities to entertain and educate children after school.

490. Chou, Nancy Ou-lan. "A Survey of School Libraries in Taiwan." Journal of Library and Information Science 7 (1): 72-98 (April 1981).

Chou reports a 1980 survey of libraries in 188 senior high schools, 183 senior vocational schools, 626 junior high schools, and 2,380 elementary schools in Taiwan. She investigates the buildings, facilities, administration, budgets, collections, technical services, public services, and community services of these libraries. She also analyzes the survey results in light of library standards in foreign countries. Using statistical data, she points out problems and offers suggestions for future improvements. The text is in Chinese.

491. Fung, Margaret C. "Library Services for Children in the Republic of China." In On Library and Information Science, pp. 123-130. Taipei: Student Book Company, 1982.

The author presents an historical sketch of Chinese library development in five periods and discusses these periods of advances and setbacks as an introduction to the present state of children's librarianship in Taiwan. She comments on reader services and technical services for school and children's libraries. She also proposes measures for improving children's library services, including compiling a simplified decimal classification system for Chinese children's collections, revising and updating library standards, increasing publication of high quality children's literature and bibliographies, and increasing emphasis on the training of children's librarians.

492. Giblin, James Cross. "Green Heart: Notes on Children's Cultural Activities in China." The Horn Book 51 (6): 564-570 (December 1975).

Giblin, who toured China as a member of the American Friendship Delegation, relates his personal impressions of the children's program. In addition to discussing children's cultural activities, the author comments on the library of the Nankai Middle School in Tientsin, the book publishing industry before and after the Cultural Revolution, the impact of the Cultural Revolution on Chinese libraries and reading rooms, and children's literature in China.

493. Heng, Siew Ngoh. "List of Recommended Chinese Periodicals for Primary School Libraries." Singapore Libraries 4: 30-31 (1974).

This is an annotated list of sixteen periodicals for primary school libraries. Each entry includes the title in both English and Chinese, frequency of publication, price, and where to order the title.

494. Khoo, Sait Poh. "Recommended Chinese Periodicals for Secondary School Libraries." Singapore Libraries 3: 55-56 (1973).

This article lists twenty-three titles of Chinese periodicals recommended for secondary school libraries. The entries include the title in both Chinese and English, subscription information, and annotations.

495. Lai, Chao-yen. "The Use of School Libraries of Junior High School Students in Yunlin County: A Study." Journal of Educational Media and Library Sciences 21 (2): 190-198 (Winter 1984).

Based on a questionnaire survey of 510 junior high school students in Yunlin County, the study explores the degree of understanding of the functions of school libraries, the state of the use of these libraries and information, and the cultural backgrounds of the students. The results indicate that teachers as well as school and government authorities should pay more attention to teaching library use and that teachers should have a better understanding of the functions of school libraries. The text is in Chinese, with an abstract in English.

496. Lin, Tana Man-chen. "The School Library in Taipei, Taiwan, R.O.C. Survey." Journal of Library and Information Science 10 (2): 184-215 (October 1984).

A 1973 survey of school libraries in Taipei revealed problems in such areas as the role and function of the school library, the scope of library materials, the training of professional librarians and assistants, and technical services. The purpose of this article is to discuss the essential requirements for setting up school libraries and to emphasize the establishment of standards for school library development in Taiwan. It also describes the fundamental principles of management in the "information age" and points out the concept and types of management to be emphasized.

497. "Question of Placing School Libraries in the Services of Teaching and Scientific Research Discussed." Survey of China Mainland Press No. 1448: 9-10 (January 11, 1957).

This is a report on a discussion that took place at the National Conference on Library Work in Institutions of Higher Education in Peking in 1956. It relates that there was a consensus that the library has the task of serving teaching and scientific research in the school. The library must supply the essential reference books and publications, and it should procure different kinds of books and publications according to the scientific research plan of the school. The report identifies staff training, acquisition and classification of books, and capital construction work as the major problems facing the library and suggests ways to solve them.

498. Shaw, Ernest T. "A School Administrator's Experiences in Developing a Library for Primary and Junior Middle School Students in China." Educational Review (Shanghai) 22 (2): 166-176 (April 1930).

From a school administrator's point of view, this article describes the development of the library for students at the Yü Ying Boys' School in Peking during the late 1920's. It discusses the plan for the school library, the involvement of the library on the basis of the school curriculum, the library as a center of school life, the library's collection, and the administration of the library. It also explores such problems as talking in the library, the loss of books, little use of the catalog, and purchasing suitable books.

VI. ARCHIVES

499. Bartlett, Beatrice S. "An Archival Revival: The Qing Central Government Archives in Peking Today." Ching-shih Wen-t'i [Topic in Ching History] 4 (6): 81-110 (December 1981).

Bartlett, a research fellow at the Fairbank Center for East Asian Research, Harvard University, spent ten months in Peking at the First Historical Archives. She presents a detailed report on the Ming and Ch'ing archives of China, the world's oldest national archives. Although the Ming-Ch'ing Archive is largely limited to official central government document traffic, the nine million items collected represent more than fifty government agencies. She also outlines in detail how the catalogs of the archives are organized and provides valuable suggestions for researchers to follow.

500. "Bureau of State Archives Calls Conference to Exchange Experiences of Work Concerning Scientific and Technological Archives." Survey of China Mainland Press No. 2739: 1-3 (May 16, 1962).

This is a report of a conference called by the Bureau of State Archives in Peking to exchange experiences of work on scientific and technological archives of research institutes on natural sciences. Attended by over 1,100 people, including personnel in charge of technological archives and scientific and technological researchers, the research institutes discussed measures to improve and organize scientific and technological archives.

501. Cheng, Pei-kai. "A Visit to the Ming-Ch'ing Archive in Peking." Ch'ing-shih Wen-t'i [Topic in Ch'ing History] 4 (1): 94-100 (June 1979).

Based on the author's interview with two members of the Ming-Ch'ing Archive's staff, this presents a summary of an article that appeared in the Hong Kong magazine Tou Sou (No. 29, September 1978, p. 11-19).

It discusses the history of the Archive and its collection, cataloging of materials, publishing of archival documents for scholarly use, preservation, facilities, and the exchange of materials among the various archives.

502. Ghausi, Marilyn. "An American Archivist's First View of the Chinese Archives." The American Archivist 43 (4): 505-508 (Fall 1980).

The author, a museum archivist, visited Peking's Palace Museum (Ming-Ch'ing) Archives in 1979. In this article, she traces the history of the Archives and describes its current activities, including preservation, arrangement, publication, research, and Manchurian translation. She also reports her discussions with her hosts about the possibility of organizing a study tour for the members of the Society of American Archivists.

503. Goodman, Bryna. "The Shanghai Municipal Archives." China Exchange News 12 (3): 18-20 (September 1984).

This is a report on the use of the collection at the Shanghai Municipal Archives during 1983 and 1984 by an advanced graduate student at Futan University. Goodman found that the Archives house an extensive collection of books, periodicals, and archival documents on the history of Shanghai and the history of the Chinese Communist Party, which is underutilized for research in both fields.

504. Lary, Diana. "The Second Historical Archives, Nanjing." Modern China 7 (4): 498-501 (October 1981).

The author's personal experience at the Second Historical Archives, Nanking, in 1981 is related. It describes the physical plant, staff, and documents of the Republican Period. The author cites research methods and the lack of a catalog or index for documents as the most difficult problems facing foreign scholars in using the facilities at the Archives.

505. Lo, Hui-min. "Some Notes on Archives on Modern China." In Essays on the Sources for Chinese History, edited by Donald D. Leslie, Colin Mackerras, and Gungwu Wang, pp. 203-220. Canberra: Australian National University Press, 1973.

Lo presents general information on the establishment of archives; the state of Chinese archives; foreign archives on China; and foreign missionary, business, and personal archives. It also discusses archives as an historical source.

506. Moseley, Eva. "Visiting Archives in China." The American Archivist 50 (1): 137-141 (Winter 1987).

Based on information gathered during a 1986 visit to Chinese archives, this article describes the history, organization, staff, special features, education, training, and problems of the following archives in China: Shanghai Municipal Archives, Chekiang Provincial Archives in Hangchou, Second Historical Archives in Nanking, First Historical Archives in Peking, Chengtu Municipal Archives, and Wenchiang County Archives in the suburbs of Chengtu. The author notes that there are 3,006 archives and 28 archival education programs in China.

507. Moss, William W. "Archives in the People's Republic of China." The American Archivist 45 (4): 385-409 (Fall 1982).

This article is an account of the Society of American Archivists' study tour of seven archives in China in 1982. It reviews archives and administration in China and presents the state of the art of archival work. It also describes the holdings, buildings, stock areas, and research provision of each of the seven archives visited. It comments on conservation, records management, and acquisition policy. It concludes that the U.S. can help China with equipment and modern technology in order for China to advance in the future.

508. Moss, William W. "Archives in the People's Republic of China Revisited." The American Archivist 49 (4): 481-490 (Fall 1986).

This is an update and supplement to an earlier article on the same subject (#507). Based on readings of Chinese archival literature and on information gained during a 1986 study tour of Chinese archives, this article focuses on the organization and structure of the Chinese archival system, documentation and archives management, and dissemination and use of archives in China. It concentrates on the post-1949 records and its revolutionary antecedents, beginning with the May Fourth Movement of 1919. It briefly notes the earlier archives of imperial dynasties and of various governments between 1911 and 1949.

509. Murata, S. "The Administration of Documents in the People's Republic of China." Joho Kanri [Journal of

Information Processing and Management] 25 (5): 409-417 (August 1982).

Dealing with various aspects of document administration in the Chinese People's Republic, this article includes such topics as archives administration, the staff involved in the document administration, foreign documents, scientific and technical documents, and the distribution and technical aspects of document administration. The text is in Japanese.

510. Pong, David. A Critical Guide to the Kwangtung Provincial Archives Deposited at the Public Record Offices of London. Cambridge, MA: East Asian Research Center, Harvard University, 1975. 203 pp.

This guide book deals with documents belonging to the Kwangtung and Liang-Kwang archives at Canton, which were captured by the British forces in 1858. The book traces the history of the Kwangtung Provincial Archives, which contain around 20,000 documents, and provides a critical evaluation of these archives. The documents are arranged chronologically under six topics: (1) opium trade and the Opium War; (2) central and local administration, 1765-1857; (3) foreign relations and foreign trade, 1810s-57; (4) rebellions, secret societies, military organization and operation, and rebellion suppression, 1811-57; (5) the first phase of the Second Anglo-Chinese War, 1856-57; and (6) maps and illustrations.

511. Wang, Yeh-chien. "Working at the First Historical Archives in Beijing." China Exchange News 12 (3): 8-10 (September 1984).

This article is based on the author's personal experience in conducting research at the First Historical Archives (FHA) in Peking, which houses the central government archives of the Ming and Ch'ing periods and has more than nine million documents. Wang discusses the publications of the FHA, important regulations in using the facility, and personal frustrations and gives advice to future researchers.

512. Zhang, Tien-ming. "Report on the State of Chinese Archives." The American Archivist 45 (2): 224-226 (Spring 1982).

Based on a translation of Zhang's speech on the Chinese archives system prepared by William Moss of the John F. Kennedy Library, this report centers on the organization of Chinese archives, which are under the supervision and direction of the State Archives

Bureau, founded in 1954. Two central archives are introduced: the First Historical Archives in Peking and the Second Historical Archives in Nanking. It also briefly notes other types of archives in China, on-job training, the publication of two archival journals, and the establishment of the Society of Chinese Archivists.

513. Zhang, Zhong. "Aperçu sur les Archives d'État de la République Populaire de Chine" [Overview of the National Archives of the People's Republic of China]. Gazette des Archives No. 116: 30-35 (1st Quarter, 1982).

This paper provides an overview of the Chinese national archives system which consists of: (1) the Central Archives, which maintain the archives of the Party and the organs of state since 1949; (2) the Primary Historic Archives, which maintain the archives of the dynasties; (3) the Secondary Historic Archives, which maintain the Nanking government, Kuomintang, and War Lord archives; and (4) specialized ministerial archives. It also considers the local archives, which collect materials of all periods. It notes that the archives have been used increasingly since 1980 when some materials were opened to the public. The text is in French.

5

Technical Services Activities

I. CATALOGING AND CLASSIFICATION

514. Anderson, Dorothy. "IFLA's Visit to the People's Republic of China: Notes on Bibliographic and Cataloguing Activities." IFLA Journal 8 (2): 184-187 (1982).

This is a report of discussions and observations during a visit to China in 1981 by International Federation of Library Associations (IFLA) representatives, who were invited by the China Society of Library Science. It gives a brief summary of the visit, with emphasis on the standardization of Chinese cataloging, the problems of automation, and the need to ensure that Chinese libraries become part of the developing Machine Readable Catalog (MARC) network. It also outlines the important points that should be considered in cataloging standards.

515. Anderson, James D. "The Arrangement of Chinese-Language Author-Title Catalogs." The Library Quarterly 44 (1): 42-59 (January 1974).

Presenting a summary of the author's doctoral dissertation at Columbia University, 1972, this article compares four different methods of arranging Chinese-language author-title catalogs in terms of the information needed to locate entries. It also surveys catalog users to determine the extent to which they obtain bibliographic information about Chinese language materials only in romanized form. It concludes that although arranging methods differ enormously, the amount of information required does not differ much. It also indicates the trend toward strictly alphabetical arrangement of Chinese-language library catalogs on the basis of romanized entries.

516. Anderson, James D. "Cataloging and Classification of Chinese Language Library Materials." In Cataloging and Classification of Non-Western Material: Concerns,

Issues, and Practices, edited by Mohammed M. Aman, pp. 93-129. Phoenix, AZ: Oryx, 1980.

Anderson provides an excellent survey on the growing standardization of library operations relating to Chinese language materials, the increasing efforts to establish cooperative and centralized systems for cataloging and classifying these materials, and the need for integrating East Asian librarianship into the mainstream of Western librarianship. He raises and discusses problems concerning descriptive cataloging, subject access, cooperative cataloging, the arrangement of Chinese language catalogs, and the application of computers to the bibliographic control of Chinese language materials.

517. Anderson, James D. "A Comparative Study of Methods of Arranging Chinese Language Author-Title Catalogs in Large American Chinese Language Collections." D.L.S. thesis, Columbia University, 1972. 147 pp.

518. Anderson, James D. "Standardization in Chinese Language Library Catalog Arrangement Methods." Committee on East Asian Libraries Bulletin No. 45: 42, 49-53 (November 1974).

This article argues that the arrangement of Chinese language author-title catalogs should be alphabetical according to romanized entries. It investigates whether standardization based on the adoption of the alphabetical arrangement could be defended. It also recommends replacing the Wade-Giles system with the Pinyin romanization system in libraries.

519. Beal, Edwin G. "The Library of Congress Expediting Production of Cards for Chinese Books." Committee on East Asian Libraries Bulletin No. 42: 6 (December 1973).

520. Cambridge University. Library. Classification of Chinese Books: FB, FC. Cambridge: Cambridge University Library, 1961. 24 leaves.

This outlines the classification scheme of Chinese books adopted by the Cambridge University Library.

521. "[CEAL Subcommittee on Technical Processing Held a Special Meeting on March 31, during the Annual Conference of the Committee on East Asian Libraries of the Association for Asian Studies]." Library of Congress Information Bulletin 38 (26): 244 (June 29, 1979).

This is a report on CEAL Subcommittee's meeting to discuss automation, AACR II, and the Pinyin romanization of Chinese language materials. The Chinese-English Translation Assistance Group (CETA) reported on the development of a computer-based Chinese text, dictionary, and bibliographic files. The Library of Congress reported on the plan to train its staff in the implementation of AACR II and reviewed the advantages and disadvantages of abandoning the Wade-Giles romanization scheme in favor of Pinyin romanization.

522. Chen, Lawrence Hsing-hsia. "A Comparative Study of Six Representative Chinese Classification Schedules." M.S.L.S. thesis, University of North Carolina, 1968. 160 pp.

Chen compares a selected number of Chinese classifications to better understand the factors involved in constructing and adopting a classification scheme for Chinese materials. From among the nineteen better known Chinese schemes published between 1911 and 1958, he chooses six representative ones for intensive analysis and comparison. He categorizes the six schemes into adaptations of the Dewey Decimal System, imitations of it, or independent structures. He also proposes suggestions for future development.

523. Chiang, Fu-tsung. "The Beginning of Library Cataloguing in China." Chinese Culture 8 (4): 144-158 (1967).

Tracing in detail the origin of cataloging in China, this scholarly work divides Chinese catalogs into two kinds: those with commentaries and those without. On the basis of historical evidence, it concludes that Liu Hsiang's Ch'i-lüeh-pieh-mu (Han Dynasty) was the forerunner of the Chinese catalog.

524. Chinese Catalogue Cards and How to Order and Use Them. Peking: National Library, 1936. 12 pp.

This is a pamphlet in English for foreign subscribers on methods initiated by the National Library of Peking in 1936 for ordering and using the catalog cards for Chinese books. It also provides information on the scope and characteristics of the cards.

525. Chiu, A. Kaiming, with the assistance of Feng, H. Y., and Yue, Zunvair. A Classification Scheme for Chinese and Japanese Books. Washington, D.C.: Committee on Far Eastern Studies, American Council of Learned Societies, 1943. 359 pp.

Presenting an historical account of a classification scheme for Chinese and Japanese books, this article introduces the genesis of the Harvard-Yenching system and its application. It is followed by a detailed table of the main classes, a summary table of classes, and the nine classification schemes. It also includes appended tables, the arrangement of shelflist, and the classed catalog. The text is in both English and Chinese.

526. Chiu, A. Kaiming. "Classification in China." Library Journal 52 (8): 409-414 (April 15, 1927).

The author outlines the existing Chinese classification systems, which include the Chinese fourfold classification scheme and systems of classification in current use in libraries. He also proposes a system of classification for Chinese and Japanese books in American libraries.

527. Chiu, A. Kaiming. "How to File Books in Chinese." Library Journal 52 (19): 1007-1011 (November 1, 1927).

Chiu reviews different methods which have been used to file Chinese characters: meaning, form, pronunciation, and Wong's system of Chinese lexicography. He also discusses a system of book and work numbers, author numbers, title or work numbers, and edition numbers.

528. Chiu, A. Kaiming. "Printed Cards for Chinese Books." Library Journal 64 (5): 178-180 (March 1, 1939).

This article introduces the "Unit Cards" system for Chinese books used by the Yenching University Library, Peking, and the Harvard-Yenching Institute Library at Harvard University. It provides the characteristics of the cards, instructions on how to use and order them, and samples of the cards.

529. Chou, Nelson. "A New Alphameric Code for Chinese Ideographs: Its Evaluation and Applications." Ph.D. dissertation, University of Chicago, 1972. 142 pp.

The study surveys current research on coding Chinese ideographs, explains the alphameric coding systems, explores error detection and corrections, designs a statistical experiment for comparative evaluation, and applies it to descriptive cataloging. It concludes that with proper training, a coder with little knowledge of the Chinese language should be able to do some descriptive cataloging on certain kinds of Chinese materials by using this coding system.

530. Chu, T. F. "My System of Word Cataloging." China Critic 3 (3): 53-57 (January 16, 1930).

A review of three existing word cataloging systems for filing Chinese characters is presented in this article. These systems are: (1) dividing the vocabulary into as many groups as there are numbers of strokes; (2) grouping the words under as many radical headings as there are; and (3) a combination of the above. It also describes the author's own system of arranging words by kinds of strokes. The author believes that his method would increase efficiency and usefulness in most kinds of index services.

531. Cohen, Monique, and Lucas, Alain. "The Romanization of Chinese: Towards the Adoption of Pinyin as an International System." UNESCO Journal of Information Science, Librarianship and Archives Administration 1 (3): 180-183 (July/September 1979).

Offering an historical background of romanized schemes of Chinese drawn up by non-Chinese, the authors point out the advantages of the Pinyin scheme which was developed in China as a potential international standard to facilitate exchanges of all kinds between China and the rest of the world.

532. Cressaty, Margaret. "Integration of Chinese Publications." College and Research Libraries 13 (1): 38-40 (January 1952).

This is a discussion on a simpler method of cataloging and classifying 500 titles of Chinese language materials in the von KleinSmid Library of World Affairs at the University of Southern California.

533. Doo, Ding U. Book Classification. Shanghai: The Shanghai Library Association, 1925. 63 pp.

Doo furnishes a general introduction to book classifications and includes a chapter on the Chinese book classification system. He also incorporates a detailed topography and geography of China (districts and provinces) for easy classification purposes.

534. Feng-Chen, T. Y. "The Development of Chinese Catalogue." Orient et Occident 2: 39 (1935/1936).

This is a brief account of Chinese catalog development and three initiatives for establishing the catalog: the emperor's, private person's, and public body's. It outlines Chinese cataloging and presents classifications of the catalogs.

535. Holmes, Olive. "The Pinyin Syndrome." Scholarly Publishing 11 (3): 221-227 (April 1980).

Although about twenty systems of romanization have been developed for the Chinese language, only the Wade-Giles system and the Pinyin system are used in scholarly works and in libraries today. The article compares the two systems and explores the effect on editors and librarians in switching from Wade-Giles to Pinyin. It discusses the problems they will meet and the ways they can deal with them. It singles out librarians' special problem of cataloging as the driving force behind the protest over the switch and the failure of the Library of Congress to adopt Pinyin in U.S. libraries.

536. Howard, Richard C. "Chinese Cooperative Cataloging." Committee on East Asian Libraries Newsletter No. 44: 17-28 (July 1974).

This contains a synopsis of the proceedings of the first three conferences on Chinese Cooperative Cataloging from 1972 to 1974 and related documents. It also presents background information and proposals for such a cooperative program.

537. Hsu, Marjorie Y. "The Chinese Subject Catalog: A Study of Its Arrangement in Classified Form Versus Alphabetical Subject Headings." M.A. thesis, University of Chicago, 1968. 70 pp.

538. Hu, David Y. "Problems of Cataloging Chinese Books." Journal of Library and Information Science 3 (1): 42-54 (April 1977).

The author identifies four distinct problems of cataloging Chinese books to be main entry, issue date, establishing geographical names as subjects, and subjects divided by period. He suggests that the Library of Congress publish its authority file in book form as a reference aid, establish a national union catalog for Chinese books, publish a Chinese cooperative catalog, and use the Online Computer Library Center (OCLC) data base for cataloging and resource-sharing as some of the possible solutions for the practical problems of cataloging Chinese books.

539. Kishibe, K. "Cataloging Books in Chinese." International Cataloguing 3 (1): 4 (January/March 1974).

The author's experience in cataloging a sizable collection of books in Chinese at a branch library of the Toronto Public Libraries is summarized. The author decided to put the author, title, imprint, and collation in Chinese script and to identify a particular title by a special title code. The author notes that producing these special catalogs is expensive and time-consuming.

540. Kwei, John Chih-ber. Bibliographical and Administrative Problems Arising from the Incorporation of Chinese Books in American Libraries. Peking: Lender Press, 1931. 138 pp.

A Ph.D. dissertation at the Graduate Library School at the University of Chicago, this study examines the extent and variety of collections of Chinese books in America, deals with the physical characteristics of Chinese books, and determines how Chinese books may be handled in American libraries. Although the study focuses on Chinese collections in the U.S., it provides valuable information in administering libraries in China.

541. Lai, Yung-hsiang. "Notes on Chinese Descriptive Cataloguing Rules." In International Co-operation in Oriental Librarianship, edited by Enid Bishop and Jean M. Waller, pp. 43-48. Canberra: National Library of Australia, 1972.

The National Central Library's Cataloguing Rules for Chinese Books is discussed. The book is divided into two parts: the first part deals with ordinary books; the second part supplements the first and deals with Chinese rare books and other non-book materials. The article also discusses personal authorship, romanization of Chinese characters, and standardization.

542. Lan, Chien-chang. "Guidelines for Technical Services in the Libraries of the Republic of China." Journal of Library and Information Science 10 (1): 63-82 (April 1984).

Based on recent surveys carried out by the National Central Library, this paper examines the overall cataloging practices used in national, public, academic, school, and special libraries in Taiwan. It formulates a revised policy toward a more satisfactory classification scheme for Chinese materials. It then presents two major topics on subject cataloging: the revision of the Chung-kuo t'u shu fen lei fa and the newly completed List of Subject Headings for Chinese Materials. The former is still in progress and the latter is based on Sears Subject Headings and the Library of Congress Subject Headings. However, these are presented as experimental information since the codes need to be modified as the work proceeds. The text in Chinese, with an abstract in English.

543. Lan, Chien-chang, and Wu, Ming-ter. "The New Chinese Cataloging Rules as the Foundation of the Chinese MARC." In Information Interaction: Proceedings of the 45th ASIS Annual Meeting, Columbus, Ohio, 17-21, October 1982, edited by Anthony E. Petrarca, Celinna I. Taylor, and Robert S. Kohn, pp. 155-157. White Plains, New York: Knowledge Industry Publications (for the American Society for Information Science), 1982.

Prepared by the Cataloging Rules Working Group of the Library Automation Planning Committee, Library Association of China, Taipei, this paper reports on the preparatory work on a new code for the bibliographic description of library materials since 1980. The new rule serves as a foundation of bibliographic control by means of the Chinese MARC. It not only retains the essence of traditional Chinese bibliographic descriptions, but also complies with international codes in both format and description. The paper summarizes the guidelines and features of the new code.

544. Lee, C. F. "The ISBDs and Chinese Cataloguing, and Their Application in Hong Kong Libraries." International Cataloguing 10 (1): 10-12 (January/March 1981).

This is an updated version of a paper presented at the International Federation of Library Associations Conference in Manila in 1980. It reports on a survey sent to institutions with Chinese collections in Peking, Taipei, Singapore, Australia, the United Kingdom, and the U.S., which was designed to examine the problems in applying the ISBDs to non-roman script publications. The article includes specific reference to the numbered ISBD section, with suggestions for amended or expanded wording. It notes its application in Hong Kong libraries.

545. Lee, Thomas H. "Chinese Cooperative Cataloging." U. W. Library News 18 (4): 6-9 (April 1973).

Lee reports on the main activities of the 1973 annual meetings of the Committee on East Asian Libraries of the Association for Asian Studies in Chicago. To avoid cataloging duplication among East Asian libraries, an Ad Hoc Committee was formed to investigate and identify the problems of Chinese cataloging. The Committee urged the Library of Congress (LC) to set up a National Program for

Acquisitions and Cataloging for Chinese materials or to designate a "coordinating agency" to carry out cooperative cataloging activities. The paper also reports on a survey of the percentage of LC printed catalog cards used in major research libraries. It reports that the Library of Congress discussed what it can and cannot do, given its resources.

546. Lee, Thomas H. "More about Chinese Cooperative Cataloging." U. W. Library News 18 (7/8): 7-8 (September/October 1973).

This is a follow-up report to update and to revise the previous one on "Chinese Cooperative Cataloging" (see #545).

547. Lee, Thomas H. "Results of a Survey on Pinyin vs. Wade-Giles as the Standard Romanization System for Chinese in North American Libraries." Committee on East Asian Libraries Bulletin No. 59: 40-49 (June 1979).

548. Lee, Thomas H. "Romanized Titles on East Asian Catalog Cards." U. W. Library News 16 (3): 15-19 (March 1971).

The paper describes the improvement the Library of Congress made on the East Asian catalog cards during the past years. The Library of Congress moved the romanized titles at the bottom of the card to a more prominent position so that it is much easier for library users and staff to identify a title.

549. Lee, Thomas H. "A Study of the New Chinese Uniform Cataloging Code: A Possibility for Shared Cataloging." Committee on East Asian Libraries Bulletin No. 66: 15-25 (October 1981).

Comparing the new Uniform Cataloging Rules for Ordinary Books in the Chinese Language (compiled by the Peking Library) and the new edition of the Anglo-American Cataloguing Rules, this article attempts to find out if the catalog cards produced in China could be used by American libraries. It concludes that with the addition of the romanized access points and the Library of Congress classification and subject headings, shared cataloging by Chinese and American libraries is possible.

550. Lee, Thomas H. "A Survey on Pinyin vs. Wade-Giles as the Standard Romanization System for Chinese in North American Libraries." Committee on East Asian Libraries Bulletin No. 59: 34-39 (June 1979).

551. Leide, John E. "Classification Development Effected from Graphical Hierarchies." Ph.D. dissertation, Library School, Rutgers University, 1975.

The study analyzes the graphical structure of the Chinese Lesser Seal characters to develop a classification that will generate a numerical surrogation for each character and produce a partial ordering. It concludes that the technique of such a classification can provide a means of accessing information that is recorded in non-alphanumeric notations, and it can assist the library in arranging and retrieving a significant category of materials.

552. Li, Ying-chiang. "Proposal of Classification Scheme for Books on Chinese Medical Science." _Journal of Educational Media and Library Sciences_ 20 (2): 173-184 (Winter 1983).

Because of the insufficient classification system for Chinese medical literature, the author proposes adopting the Western languages classification theory to classify medical books into seventeen classes. Each class is coded by a roman alphabet, followed by three numerical digits to indicate the subdivisions. The article includes the complete schedule, area table, and chronological table which are applicable for books on Chinese medicine published anywhere in the world. The text is in Chinese, with an abstract in English.

553. Library Automation Planning Committee. Chinese Cataloging Rules Working Group. "The Shaping of 'Chinese Cataloging Rules.'" _Journal of Library and Information Science_ 7 (1): 44-71 (April 1981).

Presented at the International Workshop on Chinese Library Automation in Taipei on February 14-19, 1981, this paper traces the development and drafting of the new Chinese cataloging rules, designed to accommodate the increased number and variety of publication formats. The Working Group sets down the following principles as guidelines: the rules should be applicable to all types of publications, the description should be based on ISBD, the feasible part of the National Central Library rules should be retained, merits of AACR II and Nippon Cataloging Rules should be adopted, and UNIMARC should be consulted. The paper identifies special features of the first two chapters of the new rules, followed by the draft of these two chapters. The text is in Chinese, with an abstract in English.

554. "Library Considering Pinyin Romanization." Library of Congress Information Bulletin 38 (26): 239-240 (June 29, 1979).

The article outlines the reasons why the Library of Congress (LC) is considering Pinyin romanization: (1) many sources of current information about China for American library users romanize Chinese by the Pinyin system; (2) documents issued by the Chinese government use Pinyin; (3) the Journal of Asian Studies intends to use Pinyin; (4) Pinyin is used more frequently in teaching; (5) the British Library uses Pinyin; and (6) the United States Board on Geographic Names uses Pinyin for PRC names. The LC is to make a final decision by January 1980.

555. "Library to Continue Wade-Giles Romanization." Library of Congress Information Bulletin 39 (18): 149 (May 2, 1980).

The Library of Congress announces in this note that it will continue using the Wade-Giles system of romanization in cataloging Chinese language materials rather than the Pinyin system. The decision was based on the preference expressed by the American library community in recent surveys.

556. Liu, Ching. "An Explanation of the 'Five Laws of Library Science' and Some Notes on 'Problems in Librarianship.'" Journal of the Hong Kong Library Association 4: 55-59 (November 1977).

This article is a critical study of Ranganathan's five laws of library science supplemented by an explanation of the laws by Min Ku of the National Central Library in his book Problems in Librarianship. It discusses the third and fourth laws and applies the two to the cataloging of Chinese materials. The author suggests standardizing all Chinese subject headings, using Chinese for the headings, and compiling a comprehensive list of subject headings for libraries holding valuable collections of Chinese books. The text is in Chinese, with an English summary.

557. Liu-Lengyel, Hong-ying. "The Development and Use of the Chinese Classification System." International Library Review 19 (1): 47-60 (January 1987).

The study traces the development of the Chinese classification system, explores problems encountered in using the system, and discusses benefits gained in using the system. It pays special attention to the Chinese Library Book Classification, published in 1975 and revised in 1979, which is expected to be used as the National Standardized Classification System in the near future.

558. Lu, Ho-sheng. "An Essay on the Revision of 'Chinese Chronological Subdivision Table.'" Journal of Educational Media and Library Sciences 22 (4): 361-366 (Summer 1985).

The author comments on the "Chinese Chronological Subdivision Table" of the New Classification Scheme for Chinese Libraries, a cataloging tool widely adopted by libraries in Taiwan. He points out errors and outlines suggestions for revision. The text is in Chinese, with an abstract in English.

559. Matsumi, Hiromichi. "The Assimilation of Occidental Cataloging Rules among Oriental Librarians: The Opinion of Ch'iao Yen-kuan and Lau Chien-chang in Taiwan" (in Japanese). Annals of Japan Society of Library Science 20 (2): 57-65 (October 1974).

560. Matsumi, Hiromichi. "Construction and Annotation of Wong's System for the Uniform Classification of Chinese and Foreign Books." Toshokan-kai [The Library World] 21 (1): 8-16 (May 1969).

Describing the classification system outlined in Wong's book published in 1967, this article identifies the main features of the Wong's system as follows: (1) the application of Dewey's classification system to Chinese books by adding codes to Dewey's numbers to denote books of Chinese origin, text, and subject; (2) the representation of authors' and place names as a combination of figures by translating both Chinese characters and letters of European language alphabets into ten digits, so that there is no need to transliterate into English. The text is in Japanese.

561. "Memorandum: Method of Recording Volumes of Chinese and Japanese Books." American Library Association Bulletin 10: 410-411 (1916).

Providing a summary of a survey of several American libraries regarding their method of counting Chinese and Japanese books, this article concludes that the unchangeable unit is the fascicule and notes that Harvard recommends that this method be adopted.

562. Öhman, Einar. "Alphabetic Indexes to Chinese Classification Systems." In General Classification Systems in a Changing World, pp. 36-42. The Hague: Fédération Internationale de Documentation (FID), 1978.

The article describes in some detail the Academia Sinica Library Classification System, Index published in Peking in 1959, gives some information on another system, and discusses some general problems pertaining to Chinese indexes. A brief discussion on questions regarding the Chinese language and its recent development precedes the main topic.

563. Ohta, Beatrice Chang. "The Impact of AACR 2 on Chinese and Korean Headings." Committee on East Asian Libraries Bulletin No. 62: 55-59 (June 1980).

The major impact of the implementation of the second edition of the Anglo-American Cataloguing Rules on Chinese and Korean name headings is discussed. It particularly notes headings for persons, geographical areas, and corporate bodies. Samples are given to demonstrate the changes.

564. Ohta, Beatrice Chang. "The Library of Congress and Chinese Romanization." Journal of Library and Information Science 6 (2): 151-153 (October 1980).

The author discusses the pros and cons of the Wade-Giles system and the Pinyin system of Chinese romanization. Ohta states that based on the preference of the American library community and on consultation with the Committee on East Asian Libraries of the Association for Asian Studies, the Library of Congress will continue to use Wade-Giles romanization for processing Chinese materials.

565. Ohta, Beatrice Chang, and Tucker, Ben. "Pinyin vs. Wade-Giles for Library Purposes." Committee on East Asian Libraries Bulletin No. 61: 36-41 (February 1980).

Pinyin and Wade-Giles--the two most widely used romanization schemes for the Chinese language--are discussed. The authors argue that although the library community has been using the Wade-Giles system, catalogers should consider replacing it with Pinyin to better serve users.

566. Ohta, Beatrice Chang. "Post Wade-Giles and the Implementation of Pinyin Cross References for Chinese Headings at the Library of Congress." Committee on East Asian Libraries Bulletin No. 63: 56-61 (October 1980).

567. "People's Republic of China: Notes on Cataloguing Activities." International Cataloguing 10 (3): 28 (July/September 1981).

This notes the various cataloging activities in the People's Republic of China such as the publication of New Books Catalogue of PRC. It also mentions centralized card service, the Pinyin romanization, the classification scheme, and problems of automation facing the libraries.

568. "People's Republic of China: Standardization of Descriptive Cataloguing." International Cataloguing 11 (2): 16 (April/June 1982).

This short note summarizes two articles by Huang Jungui which appeared in Chinese library journals during 1980: "The Standardization of Descriptive Cataloguing" (in Library and Information Science 3: 17-22, 1980) and "Notes on Drafting the 'General Principles for a Chinese Standard Catalogue Entry'" (in Information Science [Harbin], 4: 67-75, 1980). Huang argues the pressing need for standardization and outlines the complete Chinese standard for descriptive cataloging in preparation for future mechanization programs.

569. "Preliminary Rules and Manual for Cataloging Chinese, Japanese, and Korean Materials." Cataloging Service Bulletin 42: 1-22 (July 1957).

This is a revision of the A.L.A. Cataloging Rules for Author and Title Entries, the Rules for Descriptive Cataloging by the Library of Congress, and a Manual of Romanization, Capitalization, Punctuation, and Word Division by the American Library Association and the Library of Congress to develop standardized rules necessary for the cataloging of Chinese, Japanese, and Korean materials in U.S. libraries.

570. "Recommendations for Expanding Classification Schedules for Chinese Materials." Committee on East Asian Libraries Newsletter No. 45: 38-41 (November 1974).

Submitted to the Library of Congress in 1974, this paper reports on the recommendations in two groups: (1) recommendations in chart form, covering a wide range of topics; and (2) recommendations dealing mainly with classification numbers for Chinese philosophy, local history, institutions, and individuals.

571. Rydings, H. Anthony. "Subject Headings for a Local Catalog." Library Resources and Technical Services 19 (1): 24-30 (Winter 1975).

This article describes the methods adopted to modify the Library of Congress headings in the process of compiling a union catalog of materials relating to Hong Kong that were available in the local libraries. It provides examples of special form, subject, geographical headings, and the problem of Chinese names.

572. Shu, Austin. "Chinese and Western Cataloguing Methods: A Comparative Study." Majallah Parpustakaan Singapura [Singapore Library Journal] 1 (1): 9-12 (April 1961).

Comparing old Chinese catalogs and modern Western library catalogs, this article points out that the old Chinese catalogs are either based on the seven-epitome classification or the four-fold classification. They are compiled to annotate and most often are in book form, while the Western catalogs are for a particular collection and in card-catalog format. However, the guiding principles of classification, cross references, and analytical entries for both cataloging methods are similar.

573. Shu, Austin. "Historical Development in Chinese Cataloguing Methods." The Repository No. 1: 33-38 (Autumn 1962).

Tracing the history of Chinese cataloging from the Former Han Dynasty to the present, this paper outlines some of the most important cataloging schemes and compares modern cataloging rules with the old Chinese catalogs.

574. Su, Meng-fen. "On Cataloging and Classifying Chinese History." Cataloging and Classification Quarterly 4 (2): 51-71 (Winter 1983).

By studying the cataloging and classification of Chinese history, the author reveals the inadequate period divisions presented in the Library of Congress Subject Headings (LCSH) and the Library of Congress Classification (LCC) Schedule D. She investigates LCSH, 9th edition and supplements through June 1981, and LCC "D" schedule 2nd edition and additions and changes through #202. Comparing LCSH and LCC, she concludes that the two do not correspond well and foresees problems in expansion and revision.

575. "Taiwan Library Starts Cataloging in Source Plan." Library of Congress Information Bulletin 31 (7): 74 (February 17, 1972).

This is a note on the inauguration of a Cataloging in Source project on September 1, 1971. It aims to standardize cataloging, better bibliographical control, and save other libraries time and work.

576. Tan, Chek-neng. "Chinese Personal Names." Library Association Record 88 (11): 551 (November 1986).

Tan discusses the problems of using correct forms of Chinese names, even in librarianship circles. He suggests that for purposes of library cataloging, a standardized form be adopted to conform to the AACR II and to avoid confusion among non-Chinese.

577. Ting, Lee-hsia Hsu. "Problems of Cataloging Chinese Author and Title Entries in American Libraries." The Library Quarterly 36 (1): 1-13 (January 1966).

Based on the author's M.L.S. thesis at the University of Texas, the article discusses the problems facing American libraries in entering books by Chinese authors and considers whether it is desirable to use as much romanization as is required by the revised rules. Personal authors, corporate bodies as authors, and title entry are given special attention.

578. Ting, Lee-hsia Hsu. "Problems of Entry of Chinese Names and Titles in American Libraries." M.L.S. thesis, Graduate School of the University of Texas, 1964. 67 leaves.

This thesis attempts to discuss various problems in entering books by Chinese authors, to determine whether the current Library of Congress rules and practice have helped in achieving the objectives implicit in the rules of entry, and to make recommendations to facilitate the cataloging of works by Chinese authors. The thesis is divided into five chapters: Chapter 1 describes the Chinese language and its romanization; Chapters 2, 3, and 4 deal with personal authors, corporate bodies as authors, and title entry; Chapter 5 presents her conclusions and recommendations.

579. Tsen, Mark H. S. "Chinese Cataloging Principles and Practices in the Ch'ing Dynasty, 1644-1900." M.S. thesis, School of Library Service, Columbia University, 1937. 53 pp. Abstract of the thesis appeared in Catalogers' and Classifiers' Yearbook, compiled by the Catalog Section of the American Library Association, No. 7: 80-82. Chicago: American Library Association, 1938.

Based on catalogs available in the U.S., this thesis examines Chinese cataloging principles and practices of the Ch'ing period and compares them with China's modern cataloging systems. The study concludes that the cataloging trend in the Ch'ing Dynasty was not only to list titles but also to annotate, criticize, and describe works in a systematic way; the ultimate aim of modern cataloging is to help patrons in locating books and thus make library materials more accessible to the public.

580. Tsien, Tsuen-hsuin. "A History of Bibliographic Classification in China." The Library Quarterly 22 (4): 307-324 (October 1952).

This is a comprehensive study of the development of Chinese classification systems and their contribution to scholarship. It discusses the sevenfold classification, the fourfold classification, and other classical systems. It also identifies the characteristics and problems of Chinese classification and recommends solutions to eliminate confusion and duplication in the control of Chinese materials.

581. Wang, Joseph En-po. "Chinese Cataloging in the United States." Journal of Library and Information Science 5 (1): 51-55 (April 1979).

The lack of cataloging standards for Chinese language materials has been considered the major problem in cataloging in the Far Eastern libraries in the U.S. The author notes the tremendous changes and developments since the Library of Congress Far Eastern Cataloging Section was established in 1957. One of the most helpful methods is the Cooperative Cataloging Project for Far Eastern materials, which follows the traditional rules set by the American Library Association, and later the Anglo-American Cataloguing Rules.

582. Wang, Sze-tseng. "Books for Establishing Chinese Personal Names." Library Resources and Technical Services 16 (4): 445-452 (Fall 1972).

Wang lists twenty-one selected books in Chinese and other languages which are useful in establishing Chinese personal names for cataloging purposes. The books are divided into three categories: (1) works covering several periods; (2) works limited to a specific period; and (3) works dealing with a specific profession. Each book is described and evaluated from a cataloger's viewpoint.

583. Wang, Sze-tseng. "Cataloging Pirated Chinese Books." Library Resources and Technical Services 15 (3): 385-392 (Summer 1971).

The problems in cataloging pirated editions of Chinese materials produced in Hong Kong and Taiwan are discussed. The article illustrates various types of pirated Chinese books and describes the basic steps for proper identification of these books. It also makes suggestions in case the original is discovered after the book has already been cataloged according to the information provided in the pirated book.

584. Wang, Sze-tseng. "An Explanation of Author Notations and Tables Used in Library of Congress Schedule for Chinese Literature." Library Resources and Technical Services 18 (1): 51-60 (Winter 1974).

Because the Library of Congress (LC) schedule fails to explain both terminology and procedures in classifying, the author discusses the author notations and the table provided in the LC schedule for Chinese literature. Special examples are provided to clarify ambiguity.

585. Wang, Sze-tseng. "The Structure of Library of Congress Subject Headings for Belles-Lettres in Chinese Literature." Library Resources and Technical Services 17 (2): 231-237 (Spring 1973).

The author discusses the literary genres and the chronological subdivisions of Library of Congress (LC) subject headings for belles-lettres in Chinese literature, with examples taken from LC cards. He recommends that more romanized Chinese terms be adopted and more period subdivisions be introduced to the headings for literary history.

586. Wei, Karen T. "AACRII in Chinese Cataloging: The Illinois Experience." Committee on East Asian Libraries Bulletin No. 64: 65-71 (1981).

This article describes the University of Illinois experience in first applying the new Anglo-American Cataloguing Rules (AACRII) to process Chinese materials. It emphasizes the three chapters which affect most of the rule changes: "Headings for Persons" (Chapter 22); "Geographic Names" (Chapter 23); and "Headings for Corporate Bodies" (Chapter 24). Examples are provided to demonstrate the differences between the first and the second edition of the rule.

587. Wu, K. T. "Ten Years of Classification and Cataloging in China." In Libraries in China, pp. 19-58. Peking: Library Association of China, 1935.

This paper reviews the historical development of classification systems in China, introduces general methods of classifying books in modern Chinese libraries, and outlines the schemes devised or in use in Chinese libraries and special collections. It also discusses Chinese works on cataloging, subject headings, book catalogs and card catalogs, and cooperative cataloging. It briefly reports on the resolutions regarding cataloging and classification of Chinese books formulated during the Library Association of China's plenary meetings in 1929 and 1933.

588. Wu, Louis To. "Dewey Decimal Classification and Chinese Books." Majallah Perpustakaan Singapura [Singapore Library Journal] 2 (1): 18-24 (April 1962).

Wu discusses the importance of having a single systematic and standardized classification scheme for all Chinese books. He recommends the use of the Dewey Decimal Classification with modifications, based on an analysis of the special features of Chinese books. The article is in Chinese, with an English summary.

589. Wu, Louis To. "Dewey Decimal Classification for Chinese Books." Majallah Perpustakaan Singapura [Singapore Library Journal] 3 (2): 58-65 (April 1964).

The author modified Dewey classification schedules for Chinese literature and Chinese Ching and forwarded to the Forest Press, copyright holder of the Dewey Decimal Classification, for publication. The outline of the modified schedules for Chinese literature is listed, with explanatory notes.

590. Xu, Yi-ping, and Terragno, P. James. "The U.S. Patent Classification or the International Patent Classification: Which System Should the People's Republic of China Adopt?" World Patent Information 2 (3): 125-131 (1980).

This is an extract from a report which studies the history, philosophy, principle, and structure of the U.S. Patent Classification System (USPCS) and the International Patent Classification System (IPC). It compares their structures, principles of classification, reference tools, and international aspects. It concludes that China should adopt the IPC as its primary basis of patent classification for reasons of economy and its international scope.

591. Yae, Kwoon-choh. "Computer Conversion from Wade-Giles Romanization to Pinyin or from Pinyin to Wade-Giles." Journal of the Hong Kong Library Association 5: 67-72 (1980).

592. Yan, Lizhong; Bai, Guoyin; and Li, Bing. "Profile on Chinese Cataloguing and Subject Cataloguing." International Cataloguing 16 (1): 6-8 (January/March 1987).

Presented at the Fifty-second IFLA General Conference in Tokyo in 1986, this paper summarizes current cataloging and subject cataloging practices in libraries in China. It reports that eight titles of national standards in the area of library and information services have been developed. The article sums up the special features of Chinese cataloging and outlines three most popular and well-known classification systems in China: China People's University Library Classification, Classification of the Library of Academia Sinica, and Classification of Chinese Libraries.

593. Zeng, Lei. "An Introduction to Thesauri and Classification Systems in the People's Republic of China." International Classification 13 (1): 24-28 (1986).

Providing an overview of thesauri and classification systems currently in use in China, this article discusses the history, purposes, and characteristics of the Chinese Thesaurus, with emphasis on its vocabulary and treatment of relationships. It briefly mentions other specialized thesauri. It also explains the principles and structure of three classification systems: the library classification of the People's University of China, the library classification of the Chinese Academy of Sciences, and the Chinese library classification.

594. Zhou, You-guang. "The Romanization of Chinese: Development and Outline of Pinyin." UNESCO Journal of Information Science, Librarianship and Archives Administration 1 (3): 175-179 (July/September 1979).

This paper considers the Pinyin romanization of Chinese, which was developed in the twentieth-century. It outlines the historical background of the Chinese written language and its romanization. It also notes the special features and application of Pinyin romanization since its adoption for publication by the

National People's Congress in 1958. A table of Chinese syllabary is appended.

II. CHINESE COLLECTIONS AND ACQUISITIONS

595. Beal, Edwin G. "Chinese Collection in LC Subject of New Reference Works." Library of Congress Information Bulletin 34 (11): 95-97 (March 14, 1975).

This article describes two publications by the Association of Research Libraries' Center for Chinese Research Materials: Chinese Collections in the Library of Congress: Excerpts from the Annual Report(s) of the Librarian of Congress, 1898-1971, compiled by P. K. Yu; and Chinese Materials on Microfilm Available from the Library of Congress, compiled by James C. Y. Soong. The former is a three-volume reference pertaining to China and the development of the Library of Congress's Chinese collections. The latter is a comprehensive listing of items available on film.

596. Bishop, Enid; Chan, Yim-sang; and Miller, W. George. "Recent Australian Experience with China and Southeast Asia." Library Acquisitions: Practice and Theory 6 (2): 149-160 (1982).

As one of the papers in an issue devoted to library acquisitions from the Third World, this article describes in detail the experiences of the Australian National University (ANU) in acquiring materials from China and Southeast Asia between 1977 and 1982. An increase in published materials from China and a decrease in republishing production from Taiwan have changed acquisition activities considerably. In addition, limited budgets are contributing to cooperation among Australian libraries, especially ANU and the National Library of Australia.

597. Chen, Robert Pin-chuan. "The Acquisition, Organization, and Utilization of Chinese Government Publications in Libraries in Taiwan." Government Publications Review 14 (2): 169-186 (1987).

Based on surveys, interviews, and site visits, this study examines how Chinese government documents are acquired, organized, and used by libraries in Taiwan. It also identifies major problems libraries in Taiwan face in the acquisition, organization, and utilization of these publications. The findings indicate that Chinese documents have not received adequate attention either from the government publishing agencies distributing them or from the libraries acquiring and organizing them. The lack of bibliographic control of such publications poses the biggest problem to users. Based on survey results and the latest document-related developments, the study lists eight recommendations to correct the current situation.

598. "Chinese Cooperative Catalog Is Reviewed." Library of Congress Information Bulletin 34 (34): 334-335 (August 22, 1975).

This is a review of the Chinese Cooperative Catalog, a monthly bibliography of Chinese materials cataloged by the Library of Congress (LC) and libraries holding major Chinese collections in the U.S. The Library of Congress produces the title as a vehicle for disseminating bibliographic information among libraries with Chinese collections as well as for studying the extent of the LC's role in the acquisition and cataloging of current Chinese-language materials.

599. Chinese Periodicals in the Library of Congress, compiled by Han Chu Huang. Washington, D.C.: Library of Congress, 1978. 521 pp.

This volume includes Chinese language serials in the Chinese collection of the Library of Congress (LC), which were issued between 1868 and 1975. It consists of more than 6,400 titles on all except legal subjects. Entries are arranged in alphabetical order with titles romanized according to the Wade-Giles system, followed by Chinese titles in characters, English title or other title information, place of publication, publisher, date, and LC holdings.

600. Chung, E. W. H. "Chinese Collections in the United States." M.L.S. thesis, University of Mississippi, 1969. 68 pp.

601. "Discussions Held at Library on Chinese Acquisitions." Library of Congress Information Bulletin 34 (34): 336 (August 22, 1975).

This is a news item on the Task Force on (Chinese) Libraries and Research Materials' meeting with members of the Library of Congress to discuss problems on the acquisition and bibliographic control of Chinese publications by American libraries, with special attention to the role of the Library of Congress in the overall process.

602. Fouts, Judi. "Observations on the Acquisition of Library Materials in the People's Republic of China."

Library Acquisitions: Practice and Theory 10 (1): 71-78 (1986).

Fouts reports on the first "People to People" Library and Information Science Delegation to China in 1986. She states that the visit of thirteen libraries in five cities was slow-paced and somewhat frustrating because of the language barrier and limited time. She also presents information about the selection and acquisition of materials in various libraries.

603. Hu, Shu-chao. The Development of the Chinese Collection in the Library of Congress. Boulder, CO: Westview Press, 1979. 259 pp.

This book is an historical study of the Chinese collection in the Library of Congress, the largest collection of its kind in the Western world. The author examines the social, cultural, and political forces that led to the growth of the collection from 950 books in 1869 to more than 430,000 volumes in 1977. He also discusses acquisition policies, sources of personal and financial support, and methods by which the library has built up its collection.

604. Li, S. K. "Developing a Collection for Chinese Studies." College and Research Libraries 24 (2): 131-136 (March 1963).

Aimed at assisting acquisition librarians in developing a collection for Chinese Studies, the article reviews publications from the Chinese Mainland, Taiwan, and the U.S. It discusses major sources, including directories, journals, reference tools, and series.

605. Lo, Karl. "Acquisitions for Chinese Studies: A Response to the Lindbeck Report." In An Evaluation of Chinese Studies in American Universities and Colleges, 1958-1975, edited with an introduction and preface by Paul K. T. Sih, pp. 75-81. New York: Center for Asian Studies, St. John's University, 1978.

Presented at the Seventh Annual Conference of the American Association for Chinese Studies in New York in 1975, this paper identifies six steps, out of the eleven essential steps to develop Chinese Studies suggested by Lindbeck, which have a direct impact on library collections. It highlights the four most important factors--motivation, language ability, bibliographic knowledge, and access--that have a direct impact on library acquisitions. It includes proposals to achieve a more economical and effective service through acquisitions to make library materials available to users in Chinese Studies.

606. Ma, John T. "Some Remarks on Chinese Materials." In Library Resources on East Asia, pp. 43-46. Zug, Switzerland: Inter Documentation Company, 1967.

Because of a tremendous increase in the demand for all kinds of Chinese materials in recent years, there are problems in the current supplies of these materials from Mainland China, Taiwan, Hong Kong, and Japan. This paper concentrates on the problem of developing resources on Chinese materials and offers a few remarks concerning the acquisition, development, and coordination of older and new reproduction projects.

607. Massachusetts Institute of Technology. Libraries. Current Holdings of Communist Chinese Journals in the M.I.T. Libraries. Prepared under the sponsorship of the National Science Foundation. Rev. ed. Cambridge, MA: The Institute, 1961. 14 pp.

This bibliography contains 138 entries of Communist Chinese serials and journals currently in the M.I.T. libraries. The entries are arranged alphabetically by Wade-Giles romanization within broad subject fields. It lists bibliographic, general scientific, and university publications at the end. It provides indexes for the romanized and translated or Latin titles.

608. "New Asian Acquisitions: News from Berkeley." Library Journal 99 (1): 11-12 (January 1974).

This is a news item reporting UC Berkeley's acquisition of the largest collection of books to be brought out of China in twenty-five years. A total of 4,500 volumes, or nearly 3,000 titles, representing various subjects, were purchased for its East Asian collection.

609. Ng, Tung-king. "The Chinese Collections in Canada: A Review of Their Development and Status in Academic Libraries." In Essays in Commemoration of the Golden Jubilee of the Fung Ping Shan Library (1932-1982): Studies in Chinese Librarianship, Literature, Language, History and Arts, edited by Chan Ping-leung and others, pp. 39-57. Hong Kong: Fung Ping Shan Library, University of Hong Kong, 1982.

The historical development of Chinese collections in Canadian institutions of higher learning in the past half century is reviewed. It provides a fuller report on the two largest collections at the universities of

Toronto and British Columbia. Largely based on a questionnaire, this paper attempts to identify the strengths and weaknesses of the Chinese collections and to plan for the future development of Chinese libraries in Canada. It points out that cooperation seems to be the key to success in planning for the future development of Chinese collections.

610. Ng, Tung-king. "The University of British Columbia Chinese Library Collection: A Report." Pacific Affairs 50 (3): 473-485 (Fall 1977).

Ng traces the history of the development of the Chinese collection since 1960 when the Asian Studies Division of the University of British Columbia Library was established. He records an impressive growth of the Chinese collections, from the initial 45,000 stitch-bound volumes almost entirely in the humanities to the approximately 141,000 volumes covering various subjects today.

611. Perushek, Diane E. "Features in Managing East Asian Studies Collections." Collection Management 5 (3/4): 89-101 (Fall/Winter 1983).

This is a survey of collection activities relating to China, Japan, and Korea, with emphasis on the People's Republic of China. The author points out that during the Cultural Revolution (1965-69), the publishing industry in China was drastically curtailed and few titles were available outside China. The situation changed in the late 1970's when many more titles became available and exchanges with learned institutions became a reality. Statistics are provided for both China and Taiwan publications.

612. Schiltman, Maria J. "Acquisition of Publications from Asiatic Countries: Dutch Problems." Paper presented at the Annual Conference of the International Federation of Library Associations, Manila, Philippines, August 18-12, 1980. 9 pp. (ED 208 809).

The Dutch experience with the international exchange of publications, especially publications from China and Indonesia, is presented. The problems different institutions are facing in acquiring their library materials are summarized as follows: lack of depository systems, restrictive export policies, inadequate national bibliographies, excessive commercial prices, and time-consuming delivery systems. The author calls for cooperation among libraries to achieve universal availability of publications in the most efficient and economical way.

613. Swingle, Walter T. "The Chinese Collection in the Library of Congress." Library Journal 42 (2): 104-105 (February 1917).

Presented to the District of Columbia Library Association in 1916, Swingle reports on the Library of Congress's recent acquisition of Chinese materials and notes that this is the first time a library in the Western world has acquired such materials. He also discusses the classification of these materials and introduces some of the other rare collections the Library possesses.

614. Swingle, Walter T. "The Chinese Collection of the Library of Congress." Public Libraries 22: 101 (1917).

Same talk as above (#613), reported by T. W. Koch.

615. Tsuneishi, Warren M. "Acquisition of Library Materials from China, Japan and Korea." Library Resources and Technical Services 7 (1): 28-33 (Winter 1963).

Addressed to general acquisition librarians, this article comments on acquiring library material from East Asia. It discusses the problems facing each of the three East Asian countries--China, Japan, and Korea. It provides valuable opinion, and contact information.

616. Tung, Shih-kang. "Library Collections and Research Materials on Chinese Studies: Where to Now?" In An Evaluation of Chinese Studies in American Universities and Colleges, 1958-1975, edited with an introduction and preface by Paul K. T. Sih, pp. 70-74. New York: Center of Asian Studies, St. John's University, 1978.

This is a summary of the author's remarks presented to a panel entitled "Library Collections and Research Materials on Chinese Studies," at the Seventh Annual Conference of the American Association for Chinese Studies in New York in 1975. It consists of two parts: the first part concerns the general condition of East Asian collections in American libraries; the second part briefly comments on Chester Wang's paper, "Growth of Research Resources for Chinese Studies, 1958-1975" (#619), and Karl Lo's paper, "Acquisitions for Chinese Studies: A Response to the Lindbeck Report" (#605). It also includes the author's reflections on some library problems on the subject.

617. "University of California Librarian Brings Back to Berkeley the Biggest Collection of Books to Come out

of China in a Quarter-Century." College and Research Library News 34 (5): 225 (October 1973).

This is a news item on the purchase of 4,500 volumes on various subjects, some art folios, woodblock watercolor prints, illustrated children's books, and folktales, many of which were not available outside China. The purchase was made by Raymond N. Tang, head of the UC Berkeley East Asiatic Library and the first university librarian to visit the People's Republic of China.

618. Wang, Chester C. "East Asian Acquisitions: A Bibliographer's Practical View." Madison: University of Wisconsin, [n.d.] 11 leaves.

Although this paper deals with East Asian acquisitions in general, it has a separate section on the acquisition of Chinese materials from both Taiwan and Mainland China. The paper indicates that both bibliographic control and the supply of Chinese materials are poor.

619. Wang, Chester C. "Growth of Research Resources for Chinese Studies, 1958-1975." In An Evaluation of Chinese Studies in American Universities and Colleges, 1958-1975, edited with an introduction and preface by Paul K. T. Sih, pp. 82-93. New York: Center for Asian Studies, St. John's University, 1978.

Wang presents a statistical summary of Chinese collections in U.S. universities and colleges and highlights the development of the following library-related institutions: the Center for Chinese Studies (UC Berkeley), the Chinese Materials Center (San Francisco), the Center for Chinese Research Materials (Washington, D.C.), and the Center for Research Libraries (Chicago). He also discusses problems in the growth of research collections for Chinese Studies. The "Growth of Reprint and Microform Projects" and the "Growth of Bibliographies" are appended.

620. Wang, Sing-wu. "The Chinese Collection in the National Library of Australia." East Asian Librarians' Group of Australia Newsletter No. 7: 1-9 (December 1983).

621. Wong, William Sheh. "Acquiring Library Materials from the People's Republic of China." Library Acquisitions: Practice and Theory 7 (1): 47-57 (1983).

Focusing on collection development in academic libraries in the U.S., this paper explores the Chinese book publishing industry since 1971 when normal publishing activities resumed, outlines its characteristics, and discusses problems and strategies for the acquisition of Chinese materials. It includes valuable notes and a good bibliography.

622. Wu, Eugene. "Bibliographical Controls for Chinese Studies: Present Status and Future Developments." Harvard Library Bulletin 20 (1): 38-48 (January 1972).

Prepared for the library panel, "Bibliographical Controls for Asian Studies," at the annual meeting of the Association for Asian Studies held in 1970, this paper attempts to determine why the Chinese collections, which comprise 61% of all East Asian language materials held by libraries in the U.S., lack effective bibliographical control. It also reviews the corrective measures that have been taken and considers what remains to be done.

623. Wu, K. T. "Library of Congress Chinese Collection Helps Scholars East and West." China and America 1 (1): 7-15 (March 1948).

Tracing the steady development of the Chinese collections in the Library of Congress which are the largest outside of the Far East, this article notes that from an initial gift made by the Manchu Emperor in the mid-nineteenth century, the Library of Congress's collections have grown to be a bridge of true understanding between the East and the West. The author remarks on the categories which merit special attention: rare books and manuscripts; local histories; collectanea and encyclopedias; books on agriculture and husbandry, herbs and materia medica, medicine and prescriptions; the Yung-lo Ta-tien; books on music and manuals for playing the lute; multicolor printing; Manchu, Mongol, and Tibetan books; and biographies and literary collections.

624. Yang, Richard H. "Statement [on Library Collections and Research Materials on Chinese Studies]." In An Evaluation of Chinese Studies in American Universities and Colleges, 1958-1975, edited with an introduction and preface by Paul K. T. Sih, pp. 94-98. New York: Center for Asian Studies, St. John's University, 1978.

This statement presents the author's observations and comments on the subject. He points out the need to reassess Chinese Studies programs, to implement deelitization and decentralization through national or regional institutional cooperation, to provide a qualitative diversification approach to Chinese Studies, to preserve indispensable probity, and to support library collections in the field of Chinese Studies.

6

Automation and Information Services

625. Agenbroad, James E. "Chinese Library Automation Workshop Held." Library of Congress Information Bulletin 40 (14): 108 (April 3, 1981).

This is a news item on the International Workshop on Chinese Library Automation held in Taiwan on February 14-19, 1981, where thirty papers were presented in sessions devoted to the Chinese character code for information interchange, Chinese language and the computer, Chinese cataloging rules and the Chinese MARC, case studies, and international cooperation.

626. Agenbroad, James E. "Personal Names and the Chinese Character Code for Information Interchange, Vol. 1: (CCCII/1) -- Adequacy and Implications." Journal of Library and Information Science 7 (2): 152-160 (October 1981).

Presented at the International Workshop on Chinese Library Automation, February 14-19, 1981, this paper reports the results of an experiment to test if the first volume of the Chinese Character Code for Information Interchange contains enough characters to represent a small sample of Chinese personal names. It also considers two alternative responses when the needed characters are absent: do without them or add them.

627. "Automated Chinese Character Processing for CETA Tested." Library of Congress Information Bulletin 37 (28): 402-404 (July 14, 1978).

This is a report on the test run of a 3M Beta COM 800 device, which is capable of producing microfiche that can include Chinese characters as well as alphabetic script, by the Library of Congress for the Chinese-English Translation Assistance Group (CETA). In addition to several projects cited in the report, CETA also pursues information about new computer processing techniques.

628. Baark, Erik. Information Infrastructures in India and China. Lund: Research Policy Institute, 1983. 62 pp.

The study compares the structure of information dissemination in China and India, focusing on scientific and technical periodicals. It also reviews the organizational structure of information services, compares the formation and implementation of information policies, and analyzes the effectiveness of information utilization in the Indian and Chinese context.

629. Baark, Erik. "Information Policy in India and China." Information Development 1 (1): 19-30 (January 1985).

Providing a comparative survey of the development of national information infrastructures and the formulation of national information policy in India and China, this article discusses the influence of foreign models, traditions of library and information work, indigenous development, and language and the patterns of information use. It also compares the existing organizational structures for scientific and technological information and considers the policy implications of introducing modern information technology.

630. Baark, Erik. "The Institute of Scientific and Technical Information of China: A Short Presentation." China Exchange News 8 (2): 35-36 (April 1980).

Reprinted from the RPI China Acquisition List No. 3, November 1979, this article summarizes the three tasks of the Institute of Scientific and Technical Information of China (ISTIC): (1) to collect and arrange scientific and technical information from China and abroad; (2) to translate and report on science and technology; and (3) to provide documentation services. It also describes ISTIC's organization, library activities, and computerized searching and machine translation.

631. Bhatia, Mohan. "Science, Technology and Development in China--Secondary Sources of Information." Annals of Library Science and Documentation 28 (1/4): 54-63 (1981).

Covering Chinese and Western literature on science and technology, this study investigates eighty-eight bibliographies in order to provide a better understanding of the availability of such literature in China. It concludes that little is known about information activities in China, although the Institute of Scientific and Technical Information of China has been in existence for some time. The study stresses the need to compile detailed, annotated, and up-to-date bibliographies on specific aspects of development in China.

632. Bishop, Enid. "Conference on International Cooperation in Chinese Bibliographical Automation." Australian Academic and Research Libraries 13 (4): 265-266 (December 1982).

This is a report on the Conference held in 1982 at the Australian National University, where sixteen papers were presented on four themes: (1) "On an International Chinese Character Code for Information Interchange"; (2) "Developments in Technology for Chinese Bibliographical Data Processing"; (3) "Developments in Chinese MARC"; and (4) "Future Development of Chinese Bibliographical Automation."

633. Black, Donald V., and Fung, Margaret C. "Information Systems and Services in China and Japan." In Annual Review of Information Science and Technology, vol. 18, edited by Martha E. Williams, pp. 307-354. New York: Knowledge Industry Publications for American Society for Information Science, 1983.

Divided into five sections, this lengthy chapter reviews the literature on information systems and services in China, Japan, and Taiwan published in the period 1920 to 1983. It provides information on cultural background, recent and current trends, current information systems and services, computer technology for information services, and future trends in Taiwan. It also discusses recent trends in the People's Republic of China. For Japan, the information includes standards, recent trends, the information industry, videotext, educational systems, and specialized information services. It includes an extensive bibliography.

634. Brawne, Michael, and Schwarz, Stephan. "Development of the Institute of Scientific and Technical Information of China (ISTIC)." Report prepared for the government of the People's Republic of China by the United Nations Educational, Scientific, and Cultural Organization (UNESCO), March 31, 1981. 93 pp. (ED 213 411).

Prepared by two UNESCO consultants following a one-month visit to China and based largely on verbal data, this report provides observations and advice for the development of ISTIC. It includes recommendations to

ISTIC, background information on existing facilities, ISTIC's plans for computer application, computer and software options for bibliographic information services, an architectural brief of the ISTIC building, and building problems and proposals. It also includes a thirteen-item bibliography of documents produced by ISTIC.

635. Broadbent, Kieran P. Dissemination of Scientific Information in the People's Republic of China. Ottawa: International Development Research Centre, 1980. 60 pp.

Based on the author's visit to China in 1979, this is a report of findings concerning library and information services and their problems, as well as the applications of computer technology in China. Other topics include conversion of Chinese script to machine-readable format, professional training, awareness of literature, and current trends and developments in science and technology information.

636. Broadbent, Kieran P. "The Modernization of Information Services in the People's Republic of China." Journal of Information Science 3 (5): 227-233 (November 1981).

This paper reviews the history, recent lines, and present situation of information services in China. It also outlines ways in which China is currently attempting to meet such problems as technical and political constraints and written language. It discusses machine translation, optical character recognition, facsimile transmission, and organizational matters. It notes that China hopes to provide modern information services by the end of the decade.

637. Campbell, Harry. "Information and Library Automation in the People's Republic of China: Notes from a Visit, March-July 1984." Focus on International and Comparative Librarianship 15 (3): 26-27 (1984).

Concentrating on the topics of information science and library modernization, this briefly discusses activities in retrospective catalog conversion, staff training in computer information methods, and modernization of library and information science instruction.

638. Chang, Chung-tao; Huang, Jack Kai-tung; Yang, Chen-chau; and Hsieh, Ching-chun. "The Design of a Cross-Reference Data Base for Chinese Character Indexing."

Journal of Library and Information Science 7 (2): 144-151 (October 1981).

Presented at the International Workshop on Chinese Library Automation in Taipei on February 14-19, 1981, this paper describes an experimental design of a cross-reference data base for identifying and indexing Chinese characters stored in computer. It discusses the characteristics of Chinese character indexing, the content and structure of the cross-reference data base, and the data structure of files. The authors hope that the data base will provide service of code conversions and cross-referencing as well as a base for further studies on Chinese characters.

639. Chang, Chung-tao; Hsieh, Ching-chun; Yang, Chen-chau; Huang, Jack Kai-tung; and Mei, K. "The Development of Software Tools for Sinology." Journal of Educational Media and Library Sciences 21 (2): 129-159 (Winter 1984).

This reports on the scope of a project undertaken by the Chinese Character Analysis Group for the use of computers in the study of the Chinese language and its developmental progress. It presents some preliminary results to demonstrate the power of the computer for literature searches, subject retrieval, and keyword searches.

640. Chartrand, Robert Lee. "Our China Adventure." Bulletin of the American Society for Information Science 6 (4): 10-14 (April 1980).

Chartrand reports on his trip to China in 1979 to deliver a series of lectures to educate and orient key government and academic personnel in aspects of information science and technology. It outlines basic steps in information handling in eight sessions. It also provides his impressions of the Peking Municipal Computing Center and the Peking University Computing Center.

641. Chen, Binggang. "A Tentative Survey of Information Demands of Scientific and Technical Personnel in China." In The Use of Information in a Changing World: Proceedings of the 42nd FID Congress Held in The Hague, The Netherlands, 24-27 September 1984, edited by A. Van der Laan and A. A. Winters, pp. 111-119. North-Holland, The Netherlands: Elsevier Science Publishers B.V., 1984.

This is an analysis of a comprehensive questionnaire survey of the conditions of document utilization by a portion of the scientific and technical personnel in

China. It evaluates various modes of present information services and summarizes the opinions and suggestions of the scientific and technical personnel. It also makes recommendations for improving scientific and technical information services.

642. Cheng, Heng-hsiung. "Chinese Indexes." Journal of Library and Information Science 8 (1): 77-95 (April 1982).

Various definitions, types, and functions of Chinese indexes are discussed. It is followed by a selected and annotated bibliography of Chinese indexes. The text is in Chinese, with an abstract in English.

643. "China Specialists Study LC's Automation Practices." Library of Congress Information Bulletin 41 (38): 289-290 (September 7, 1982).

This reports on the activities of two librarians from the National Library of China who studied the development and status of automated operations at the Library of Congress and other U.S. libraries.

644. "Chinese Automation Gains Charted." Library Journal 108 (2): 80 (January 15, 1983).

This is a news item on a report by Enid Bishop, chairperson of the Conference on International Cooperation in Chinese Bibliographical Automation, which focuses on progress in Chinese bibliographical data processing, the Chinese MARC, and new frontiers on Chinese bibliographic automation.

645. "Chinese Library Automation Workshop." College and Research Libraries News 42 (5): 152 (May 1981).

The International Workshop on Chinese Library Automation, held in Taipei in 1981 is briefly noted. Thirty papers on the automation of Chinese characters and languages were read and fourteen computer manufacturers demonstrated several Chinese library automated systems. The note highlights the formation and preparation of Chinese Character Code for Information Interchange and the Chinese MARC Format for Books.

646. Chinese MARC Format for Books, compiled by the Chinese MARC Working Group, Library Automation Planning Committee. 2nd ed. Taipei: Library Association of China, 1981. 204 pp.

This book details the task of designing the Chinese MARC format, which facilitates data processing for

Chinese materials and promotes international resource-sharing and exchange. It is divided into two major parts: (1) the first part explicates the scope, application, definition of terms used, and structure of the communication format of the Chinese MARC; and (2) the second part includes such appendixes as catalog card format, special character set, changes from the first edition, fields and subfields, Wade-Giles system of romanization, geographical area codes, chronological coverage code, codes for the representation of names of countries, and a revised list of languages and language codes.

647. "Chinese Record Entered into RLIN Database." Wilson Library Bulletin 58 (3): 171 (November 1983).

This reports that on September 12, 1983 the Library of Congress created the first online cataloging record in the RLIN database to contain Chinese vernacular.

648. Chou, Nancy Ou-lan; Fung, Margaret C.; Lee, Lucy Te-chu; and Wu, L. L. "Chinese MARC Format and Bibliographic Databases." In Proceedings of the ASIS Annual Meeting, Columbus, Ohio 17-21, Oct. 1982, vol. 19, edited by A. E. Petrarca, C. I. Taylor, and R. S. Kohn, pp. 58-91. White Plains, NY: Knowledge Industry Publications for American Society for Information Science (ASIS), 1982.

Presented at the Forty-fifth ASIS Annual Meeting, this paper reports on the development of the Chinese MARC format for books and non-book materials in Taiwan, discusses the structure of the Chinese MARC format for Chinese library materials and library practices, and presents the current status of Chinese bibliographic data bases.

649. Chou, Nancy Ou-lan. "A Chinese MARC-Oriented Study on the Establishment Feasibility of the East Asian MARC System." Journal of Library and Information Science 11 (1): 1-23 (April 1985).

Using the design and implementation experience of the Chinese MARC format, the author does a pilot study on its adaptability to Korean and Japanese materials and the feasibility of establishing an East Asian MARC system. She introduces the Chinese MARC system, compares the Chinese MARC and UNIMARC, and explores the adaptability of the Chinese MARC. She recommends that China, Japan, and Korea adopt UNIMARC as their standards for data structures and communication format in order to increase compatibility and information interchange among East Asian nations.

650. Chou, Nancy Ou-lan, and Chiang, Hsiu-ying. "The Computerized Bibliography of Chinese Rare Books." Journal of Educational Media and Library Sciences 21 (2): 160-168 (Winter 1984).

As one of the contributions to an issue devoted in part to "Computer Technology and Applications in Chinese Information Systems," this article describes the methods, purpose, and scope of the Machine-readable Catalog (MARC) File for Chinese rare books in Taiwan. It also explores the function and use of the File in hopes of helping Sinologists find an easy and scientific access to data on Chinese rare books.

651. Chou, Nancy Ou-lan. "The Development of Library Automation and Chinese Computer Technology in Taiwan, R.O.C." Paper presented at the Asian African Section, Conference of the American Library Association, Dallas, Texas, June 25, 1984. 5 pp.

Reporting on the development of library automation in Taiwan during the past few years, this paper hails the establishment of a Chinese MARC Data Base and the introduction of DIALOG and ORBIT systems since 1981. It also discusses the new progress and roles played by the National Central Library as well as information-sharing and service in the development of library automation in Taiwan.

652. Chou, Nelson. "Design a Chinese Input/Output System and Its Evaluation." Journal of Library and Information Science 1 (1): 49-59 (April 1975).

The author reviews and evaluates three existing Chinese experimental methods of the input/output system: (1) based on Chinese pronunciation; (2) based on the shape and structure of the Chinese characters; and (3) based on a coding system. It also outlines important points to be considered when designing a complete Chinese input/output system for library use. The text is in Chinese.

653. Chou, Nelson. "Information Retrieval and the Chinese Language." In Essays in Commemoration of the Golden Jubilee of the Fung Ping Shan Library (1932-1982): Studies in Chinese Librarianship, Literature, Language, History and Arts, edited by Chan Ping-leung and others, pp. 80-91. Hong Kong: Fung Ping Shan Library, University of Hong Kong, 1982.

Chou discusses the process of information retrieval which involves four elements: (1) the data base; (2) the retrieval mechanism; (3) relevance judgment; and (4) feedback procedures. The second half of the paper examines the Chinese language in terms of its capacity to be retrieved by a computerized information retrieval system. The author points out that future research should be conducted in three different phases in the following order: modern writings and spoken language, classic writings, and religious writings. He also suggests that the actual research may take place as follows: verification, observation, establishment of machine algorithm, and experiments.

654. "Circuit Exhibition of Scientific and Technological Information Service Warmly Welcomed by Scientists and Technicians." Survey of China Mainland Press No. 3147: 10-11 (January 27, 1964).

By describing the circuit exhibition, this article tries to introduce the general condition of scientific and technological literature in the world. It also announces the methods of information service work and kinds of service offered by the China Scientific and Technological Information Research Institute.

655. Computer Information Systems in the People's Republic of China: Current Advances and Prospects to 1995, compiled and edited by Harry Campbell. Toronto: China Business Consulting, 1986.

This is a special report on the First International Chinese Symposium on Computerized Information Retrieval, held in Peking in October 1985 and sponsored by the China Society for Scientific and Technical Information. Divided into seven chapters, this report deals with online retrieval systems design, Chinese data base online retrieval, information and communication networks, English/Chinese data base compatibility, Chinese language automated indexing and key word searching, library and information science education, and business opportunities in computer information systems to 1995. It includes a list of sixty-four recent papers on information retrieval in China.

656. "Computer Technology and Applications in Chinese Information Systems." Journal of Educational Media and Library Sciences 21 (2): 119-168 (Winter 1984).

This is a collection of three papers, which are edited versions of papers presented at the Forty-sixth Annual Meeting of the American Society for Information Science in Washington, D.C. in 1983. The papers are: (1) "Productive Use of Information Through New Technologies and Information Systems in Taiwan R.O.C." by Margaret C. Fung (#663); (2) "The Development of Software Tools for Sinology" by C. T. Chang, et al.

(#639); and (3) "The Computerized Bibliography of Chinese Rare Books" by Nancy Ou-lan Chou and Hsiu-ying Chiang (#650).

657. Date, Munetsugu. "Science Technology Information Activities in China." Joho Kanri [Journal of Information Processing and Management] 14 (9): 555-558 (December 1971).

Date presents general information on the development and activities of Chinese information centers since 1958. He also includes a discussion on bibliographic information and the processing of Chinese characters.

658. Fang, Zheng; Zhou, Zengwen; and Weng, Huiyu. "Information and Communication Networks." In Computer Information Systems in the People's Republic of China, compiled and edited by Harry Campbell, pp. 3.1-3.9. Toronto: China Business Consulting, 1986.

This paper describes the Information Retrieval Network System (IRNS) with Distributed Database using the Honeywell DPS-6, a project undertaken by the Shanghai Interuniversity Computer Network and one of the first of such systems to appear in China. It introduces the "Common Search Command Set (CSCS)," which is similar to the DIALOG system. It also discusses the interface problem between application and network software, system and data structures, as well as the function of IRNS.

659. Fayen, Emily Gallup, and Slamecka, Vladimir. "China Modernizes Scientific Communication System." Information Processing and Management 22 (1): 71-77 (1986).

Observations on the progress in building a modern network of scientific and technical information services in China since 1974 are presented. The article examines major accomplishments, including a Chinese science thesaurus, the installation of computers for searching over seventy Western and Japanese data bases, and the near-operational capability of computer processing Chinese text. It also describes overall structural and functional characteristics of the planned national scientific and technical information network.

660. Fu, Lansheng; Sun, Boqing; and Yu, Hong. "Chinese Language Automated Indexing and Key Word Searching." In Computer Information Systems in the People's Republic of China, compiled and edited by Harry Campbell, pp. 5.1-5.6. Toronto: China Business Consulting, 1986.

This paper reports on the development of a nationwide abstracting and indexing system in China since the 1950s. It describes the extent of indexing and discusses what type of subject index is better. It also mentions free terms indexing and comments on the conceptual coordination method versus the literal coordination method in using the data bases.

661. Fung, Margaret C. "The Development of Chinese MARC in Taipei." Journal of Educational Media Science 19 (4): 357-368 (Summer 1982). Also in On Library and Information Science, pp. 149-159. Taipei: Student Book Company, 1982.

Presented at the 1981 Annual Conference of the American Library Association, Resources and Technical Services Division, Committee on Cataloging, Session on Cataloging of Asian and African Materials, this paper reviews the development of the Chinese Machine-readable Format (MARC) and the Chinese Character Code for Information Interchange (CCCII), which facilitate computer processing of Chinese materials. It discusses the structure of the Chinese MARC format, its publication, the character set, and the facilities available. It reports that both the Chinese MARC format and the CCCII have been tested, published, and found authoritative since 1981.

662. Fung, Margaret C. "Library Automation in the Republic of China." Journal of Library and Information Science 6 (1): 1-16 (April 1980).

Presented at the CEAL Plenary Session of the Association for Asian Studies held in Washington, D.C. in 1980, this paper describes the history, development, and current status of library automation in Taiwan. It provides information on the early experiments on computer applications for libraries and current projects. It also outlines four basic preparatory tasks for the future overall, unified, and centralized implementation of library automation in Taiwan.

663. Fung, Margaret C. "Productive Use of Information Through New Technologies and Information Systems in Taiwan R.O.C." Journal of Educational Media and Library Sciences 21 (2): 121-128 (Winter 1984).

An edited version of a paper presented at the Forty-sixth Annual Meeting of the American Society for Information Science in 1983, this article describes the state of art in information systems and networking activities in Taiwan. It examines data processing facilities for Chinese materials, structures of data bases and information systems, standards for processing non-roman Chinese materials, automated library systems, and online information services. It also addresses important issues in developing effective information services in Taiwan.

664. Fung, Margaret C. "State of the Art: Library Automation in Taipei, R.O.C." In On Library and Information Science, pp. 131-147. Taipei: Student Book Company, 1982.

Presented at the Chinese-American Association for Science and Technology Second Annual Meeting in Seattle in 1981, this paper reports on automation activities carried out in Taipei since 1973. It focuses on the essentials of Chinese data processing, requirements for Chinese library automation, computer processing of Chinese vernacular materials, computer processing of Roman alphabet library materials, and recent research in Chinese data processing.

665. Gong, Y. T. "The Library and Information System of the Chinese Academy of Sciences: A Brief Overview." Journal of Information Science 12 (1/2): 59-62 (1986).

Gong describes the objectives and structure of the Library and Information System of the Chinese Academy of Sciences (LISCAS). The author also explores major programs and recent activities carried out by LISCAS, including coordination projects, the integration of library and information science, standardization and library automation, information retrieval services, and staff training.

666. Herbert, P. A. "A Reader's View of East Asian Catalogue Automation." East Asian Librarians' Group of Australia Newsletter No. 5: 7-12 (June 1981). Also in Journal of Educational Media and Library Sciences 20 (4): 293-301 (Summer 1983).

This is a discussion paper on whether automated cataloging can and should be applied to East Asian materials and, if so, what are the problems involved and how is automation best achieved. The paper also provides some comments on the history of library classification and cataloging in China, the romanization of Chinese characters, the cost, and future projections of automated East Asian collections.

667. Hirohashi, T., and Hasegawa, N. "Scientific and Technological Information Policy and Information Activities in China" (in Japanese). Joho Kanri

[Journal of Information Processing and Management] 27 (1): 35-51 (April 1984).

668. Hsieh, Ching-chun; Huang, Jack Kai-tung; Chang, Chung-tao; and Yang, Chen-chau. "The Design and Application of the Chinese Character Code for Information Interchange (CCCII)." Journal of Library and Information Science 7 (2): 129-143 (October 1981).

Presented at the International Workshop on Chinese Library Automation in Taipei on February 14-19, 1981, this paper introduces volume two of the Chinese Character Code for Information Interchange (CCCII), which intends to cover all existing Chinese characters of more than 80,000 for general data processing. This character set includes all characters being used in data processing centers in Taiwan, the characters used in Chinese libraries, the standard characters announced by the Ministry of Education, and many others. It provides detailed technical surveys of Chinese characters, the placement of characters, the organization of CCCII, and its applications.

669. Hsieh, Ching-chun. "Full Text Processing of Chinese Language: An Experimental System for Studying Chinese History Literature." Journal of Library and Information Science 11 (2): 125-142 (October 1985).

This paper was presented at the CEAL Sub-Committee on Library Technology, at the Thirty-eighth AAS Annual Conference held in Chicago in 1986. The author argues the importance of full-text data bases and associated processing technology for library automation and online information service systems. He presents an experimental Chinese text processor for studying history literatures in order to find out the feasibility of using computers as a tool for history studies. The system provides both free-text and controlled vocabulary search for the text, which the author proves to be highly feasible by applying existing technology. He introduces details of the system, text representation, the access method, an auto-indexing method for Chinese text, and its application.

670. Hu, David Y. "Computer Processing of Chinese Library Materials in Taiwan." Information Processing and Management 19 (5): 285-293 (1983).

Based on the ASIS-82 Special Symposium on Computer Processing of Chinese Library Materials and Computer Assisted Chinese Language Instruction held in Columbus, Ohio, the paper describes the progress made in library automation and information systems in

Taiwan during the past two years. It summarizes the papers presented at the symposium with emphasis on standards, technological breakthroughs, current developments of Chinese library automation systems, the solution of Chinese linguistic problems, and the computer-assisted Chinese language instruction system.

671. Huang, Hong-chu. "From the Utilization of UDAS to Outlook the Development of Bibliographic Information Retrieval System in the R.O.C." Journal of Educational Media Science 18 (2): 84-98 (Winter 1980).

This article introduces the Universal Database Access Service (UDAS), an international online, real-time bibliographic information retrieval system inaugurated in 1979. It examines the elements and procedures of establishing the data base and investigates the current status of its utilization in the field. It also provides suggestions for developing bibliographic information retrieval services in Taiwan. The text is in Chinese, with an abstract in English.

672. Huang, Hong-chu. "MARC: Basic Concepts of Its Structure and Application." Journal of Educational Media and Library Sciences 20 (3): 235-252 (Spring 1983).

Huang describes the general characteristics of the Machine-readable Catalog Format (MARC) and outlines the desired preparation when it is used in automation. She places special emphasis on the problems of applying the Chinese MARC to Chinese library automation. The text is in Chinese, with an abstract in English.

673. Huang, Jack Kai-tung. "The Diagonal Symbol Encoding System (DSES): A Simplified 3-Corner Coding Method and Its Feasibility for CJK Adoption." Journal of Library and Information Science 11 (1): 33-50 (April 1985).

The design of the Diagonal Symbol Encoding System (DSES), a simplified input system of the Three Corner Coding Method for casual users of Chinese, Japanese, and Korean (CJK) materials in library management and office automation, is introduced. The system employs four digits representing an entire CJK vernacular character, encoding the two symbols which occupy the diagonal corner or diagonal position of a given CJK script. The author claims that anyone can learn to input within thirty minutes, and after sixty hours of on-job-training, the user may reach an input speed of twenty-seven characters per minute, the average speed of Chinese handwriting.

674. Huang, Shih-hsion. "The Feasibility of East-Asian Library Cooperation: From the Point of View of C.J.K. Materials Cataloging." Journal of Educational Media and Library Sciences 22 (3): 213-223 (Spring 1985).

This article traces the historical background of cataloging practices in Japanese libraries, cataloging rules in Korean libraries, and problems in Chinese processing in CJK. It then explores Chinese character processing techniques related to the establishment of a cooperative information network and examines the feasibility of cooperation among the three nations. It also outlines steps to build a comprehensive Chinese Bibliographic Data Base in the Taiwan area, which would turn into an authority data base and would be widely accepted internationally.

675. Huang, Shih-hsion. "Microcomputer and Libraries." Journal of Educational Media and Library Sciences 21 (3): 300-307 (Spring 1984).

The author analyzes features of microcomputers, explores how they are selected for library use, and introduces some successful systems for library and information science usage. He hopes that the library profession will pay more attention to the growth of the microcomputer market in Taiwan and its application in library operations. The text is in Chinese, with an abstract in English.

676. Huang, Shih-hsion. "Micrographic Productions and National Standards in the Republic of China." Journal of Educational Media and Library Sciences 20 (1): 55-63 (Autumn 1982).

Because of the increased usage of microforms and the establishment of the microform system in public and private institutions in Taiwan, the need to set up an agreement on the standards for microform specification becomes imperative. This paper discusses the basis for the establishment of national standards for the production and processing of microform, quality, and long-term preservation.

677. Huang, Shih-hsion. "Progress in Telecommunications Technology and Library Network Endeavors in the Taiwan Area." Journal of Educational Media and Library Sciences 21 (4): 329-340 (Summer 1984).

Surveying the present situation of telecommunications technology in Taiwan, this paper reports on the current stage of progress in library cooperation systems, and discusses the prospects for applying telecommunications technology to such systems. The author hopes that by combining elements from the telecommunications industry and computer technology, a library and information center can fully develop its function of maintaining the free flow of information.

678. Hung, William. "Indexing Chinese Books." Chinese Social and Political Science Review 15 (1): 48-61 (April 1931).

The author announces a grant to help publish the Harvard-Yenching Institute Sinological Index Series for purposes of improving methods of research and increasing access to books in Sinology. He summarizes the operations involved in publishing an index: choosing a book and the particular edition to be indexed, marking the text for copyists, copying each entry on a card and carefully checking the card, arranging the cards, copying the properly numbered and arranged entry cards, printing, proofreading, and preparing and printing the prefatory matter.

679. "Information Science in China." Bulletin of the American Society for Information Science 6 (4): 5, 10-18 (April 1980).

This is a collection of four papers representing visits and observations of American Society of Information Science members to China. The four papers are: "Recent Development in Library and Information Science in China," by Ching-chih Chen (#249); "Our China Adventure," by Robert Lee Chartrand (#640); "A Beijing Journal," by Charles Benton (#264); and "Education and Training in Information Science in the People's Republic of China," by Ching-chih Chen (#738).

680. International Workshop on Chinese Library Automation, February 14-19, 1981, Taipei, Republic of China. Taipei: Science and Technology Information Center, National Science Council, 1981.

Divided into five sections, this is a collection of papers presented at the Workshop held in Taipei in 1981. They are: Section A deals with Chinese character code for information interchange; Section B explores the Chinese language and computer; Section C discusses the Chinese cataloging rules and MARC; Section D concentrates on case studies of applying Chinese information; and Section E is on international cooperation.

681. Jiang, Xiang-dong, and Liu, Xiao-quing. "The Computer Applications in Some Libraries and Information Institutes in China." Electronic Library 1 (4): 279-285 (October 1983).

This paper deals with computer applications in information retrieval, library management, and Chinese character processing in several information organizations and institutions in China. It outlines the current state of information retrieval in terms of personnel, equipment, bibliographic data bases, information retrieval programs and systems, and service status. It also notes the progress of library automation experiments.

682. Ku, Karl Min. "The Development of Library Automation and Information Services in Taiwan Region, ROC, 1978-1984." In Proceedings of IMC's 1985 Asia-Pacific Regional Information and Micrographic Management Congress, July 11-13, 1985, pp. 625-643. Taipei: The Congress, 1985.

Examining the computer-based library information system currently being developed in Taiwan, this paper discusses the basic concept and background of library automation, the information organization, the characteristics of data bases, and the nationwide library automation project. It also includes a discussion of the problems and prospects for the future development of library automation in Taiwan.

683. Lee, Hwa-wei. "Coordination and Networking: The Chinese Case." In Management of Information Centres in China: Results of a Course Held in Kunming, Yunnan Province, People's Republic of China, 6-18 December 1982, edited by K. P. Broadbent, pp. 208-217. Ottawa, Ont.: International Development Research Centre, 1984.

This is a two-part lecture. The first part reviews the recent development of library and information networks in China. The second part is devoted to a discussion of the important considerations in the national planning for a coordinated and cohesive development of library and information networks. The paper examines the early stage of network development from 1957 to 1965, the revival of network development since 1976, the basic library tools compiled, the leadership role of the National Library of China, future plans, and major considerations.

684. Lee, Hwa-wei. "Recent Breakthroughs in Library Automation in Taiwan." Journal of Educational Media Science 19 (2): 119-136 (Winter 1982).

Lee outlines the purposes of the International Workshop on Chinese Library Automation, held in Taipei in 1981, and lists the papers delivered at the Workshop. He highlights the following major breakthroughs in Chinese library automation: the development of computer input and output devices for Chinese scripts, the design of a cross-reference index of various coding systems used in computer input of Chinese characters, the compilation of the Chinese Character Code for Information Interchange, the complete revision of Chinese cataloging rules, the adoption of the Chinese MARC format, and the development of a prototype online cataloging system.

685. Lee, Lucy Te-chu and others. "Chinese MARC Format for Books." Paper presented at the 47th Annual Conference of the International Federation of Library Associations, Leipzig, East Germany, August 17-22, 1981. 28 pp. (ED 214 508).

This paper examines the principle, purpose, and scope of designing a format for Chinese publications. This work has been done by the Chinese MARC Working Group, which was formed by the Library Automation Planning Committee of the Library Association of Taipei in 1980. The paper comments on present activities, accomplishments, and future development of the Working Group. It also discusses the ultimate objective of the Chinese MARC, outlines its characteristics, and compares the Chinese MARC and UNIMARC. The authors believe that the Chinese MARC not only succeeds in providing a uniform standard for processing publications in the Chinese language, but it also enables libraries to communicate with information service systems worldwide.

686. Lee, Lucy Te-chu; Hu, Nancy Ou-lan; Huang, Sophia Hong-chu; Huang, Jack Kai-tung; and Wu, Ming-ter. "Chinese MARC: Its Present Status and Future Development." Journal of Library and Information Science 7 (1): 1-18 (April 1981).

Presented at the International Workshop on Chinese Library Automation in Taipei on February, 14-19, 1981, this paper reports on the task of designing a Chinese MARC format, which was undertaken by the Chinese MARC Working Group of the Taiwan's Library Automation Planning Committee, established in 1980. It describes the guiding principle, purpose, and scope of the formation of the Chinese MARC, outlines the characteristics of the Chinese MARC format and compares the Chinese MARC and UNIMARC. It also highlights the present activities and accomplishments of the Working Group and discusses plans for its future development.

687. Li, Tze-chung. "The Current State of Bibliographical Services in Taiwan." Asian Pacific Quarterly of Cultural and Social Affairs 2 (4): 95-105 (1971).

Presented at the Library Seminars of the Twenty-eighth International Congress of Orientalists in Canberra in 1971, this paper reviews the current state of bibliographical services in Taiwan, covering three aspects: the development of bibliographical services, major bibliographical tools, and problems of bibliographical services. It provides descriptions of union catalogs, general bibliographies, trade bibliographies, subject bibliographies, lists of periodicals, general indexes, subject indexes, and government documents. It includes a selected list of works referred to in the paper.

688. Li, Weiming. "Status and Prospects of Computerized Information Retrieval in China." LASIE 17 (1): 2-14 (July/August 1986).

Discussing the development of computerized information retrieval in China since the late 1970's, this paper emphasizes the application of microcomputers and bibliographic data bases for information retrieval, domestic and international online retrieval, and Chinese character processing. It also discusses problems encountered and outlines possible strategies for improvement.

689. "Library Creates First Chinese Record Online in RLIN Data Base." Library of Congress Information Bulletin 42 (41): 347 (October 10, 1983).

This reports that the Library of Congress created the first online cataloging record in the RLIN data base to contain Chinese scripts on September 12, 1983. The event marked the first time East Asian language materials could be stored and retrieved at library terminals.

690. "The Library System of Chinese Academy of Sciences." United States Joint Publication Research Service No. 28136: 83-96 (January 1965).

This paper reviews the events surrounding the building of the library system of the Academy of Sciences, which has 124 libraries at the Academy, the branch academies, and various research institutions affiliated with the Academy. It summarizes attempts to promote better service to scientific research. It also outlines nine major tasks of the Academy: acting as purchasing agent, synchronizing purchases, planning international exchanges, transferring books, offering professional guidance, compiling and publishing materials, fostering cadres, arranging periodical visits, and convening conferences. Finally, it sums up, on the basis of fifteen years of experience, five necessary measures for building up a good library system: employing a common policy in running libraries, relying on Party leadership, setting up regional centers, establishing a professional management system and method, and further strengthening mutual ties and exchange of experiences.

691. Lin, Zixin. "China's Scientific and Technical Information Work and Application of New Information Technology." In The Challenge of Information Technology: Proceedings of the Forty-first FID Congress, Held in Hong Kong, 13-16 September 1982, edited by K. R. Brown, pp. 233-240. Amsterdam and New York: North-Holland Publishing Company, 1982. Also in International Forum on Information and Documentation 9 (1): 10-13 (1984).

Examining the current status of China's scientific and technical information work, this article characterizes principle types of information users in order to determine forms and methods of information service. It also outlines prospects for establishing a state computerized system for scientific and technical information. Finally, it summarizes preliminary views on formulating the policy and measures of developing scientific and technical information work.

692. "LITA Eyes Technology in China, UC, Dartmouth." Library Journal 105 (14): 1568 (April 1980).

These are brief notes on a forum on new developments in technology, which was sponsored by the Library Automation Discussion Group of the Library and Information Technology Association (LITA). Of particular interest was a report by Hank Epstein (Information Transform) on the current status of computer technology in China. He noted that China is five or more years away from its first operational system.

693. Liu, Zhaodong. "Planning the Future." In Computer Information Systems in the People's Republic of China, compiled and edited by Harry Campbell, pp. i-ii. Toronto: China Business Consulting, 1986.

This is an opening speech to the First International Chinese Symposium on Computerized Information

Retrieval held in Peking in 1985. It reports on various projects on computer information retrieval carried on by the Chinese since 1978 as well as plans for a nationwide information retrieval system.

694. Lu, Xiaocun. "The Development of Online Information Retrieval Services in the People's Republic of China." Online Review 10 (2): 127-133 (April 1986).

Lu traces the development of online information retrieval services in China since 1980, with emphasis on the last four years. In the beginning, China was not connected to international data communication networks, such as Tymnet and Telenet. Through the joint efforts of communications agencies in Peking and Rome, the communication line was finally extended to link with Tymnet and Telenet in 1984. As a result, users in China are able to access Dialog and SDC. The article discusses various cooperative networks in China as well as the problems of user-training and the lack of exchange with information specialists outside China. It also stresses the need for research on retrieval strategies, online systems, and their data bases.

695. Luo, Xingyun. "Libraries and Information Services in China." Journal of Information Science 6 (1): 21-31 (March 1983).

Based on the personal experience of the author, staff member of the Institute of Scientific and Technical Information of China (ISTIC), this article first describes the development and current status of library and information services in modern China. It then provides background on the establishment of the Chinese information network and discusses the basic policy and tasks of information service. Finally, it describes elements of the Chinese information system which is coordinated by the ISTIC, the structure of the library system, staff training, and the prospect of automation.

696. Ma, John T. "Library Automation for Chinese Collections in Western Europe: Potentials and Problems." Journal of Library and Information Science 7 (2): 161-175 (October 1981).

Presented at the International Workshop on Chinese Library Automation in Taipei on February 14-19, 1981, this article surveys the present situation of Chinese collections in Western Europe, including the United Kingdom, France, the Federal Republic of Germany, The Netherlands, Italy, the Scandinavian countries, Belgium, and Switzerland. It describes the present status of library automation in the United Kingdom and The Netherlands to demonstrate the technical, personnel, and financial problems facing these countries in automating their Chinese collections. The author believes that the potential for automation is good and hopes that international cooperation will result in development in this area in the near future.

697. Maier, John H. "Computer Science Education in the People's Republic of China." Honolulu: Pacific Telecommunications Council, 1986. 7 pp. (ED 274 311).

Although this paper concentrates on computer science education in China, it also discusses one of the critical campus needs, the automation of Chinese libraries. It points out that the dated library classification coding system, which also differs from other widely used systems in the world, and the lack of standardization are two major concerns in developing automation procedures in Chinese libraries.

698. Maier, John H. "Information Technology in China." Asian Survey 20 (8): 860-875 (August 1980).

The article first provides a general overview of today's information technology. It then analyzes the state of China's information technology, including domestic satellite and telecommunications capabilities. It also discusses the potential of selling computer technology to China and the social impact of technological advances upon China.

699. Maier, John H. "IR Progress in the People's Republic of China." Information Retrieval and Library Automation 22 (6): 4-6 (November 1986).

Based on the author's visit to sixteen top university libraries, various Chinese Academy of Sciences libraries, and the National Peking Library, this paper reports on information retrieval practice in China in 1984-85. It notes that online information storage and retrieval of the Chinese language is now possible, and that the first networking linkages of online information retrieval are now emerging and in rare instances have been implemented and are in use. The author predicts that linkages, both in China and internationally, are possible within the next decade.

700. Maier, John H. "Library Automation in the People's Republic of China." Information Technology and Libraries 5 (2): 106-111 (June 1986).

Based on the author's year of work, research, and lecturing in China, this article describes Chinese progress in and plans for automation of libraries, with a view towards China's entrance into the global age of information technology. It details the difficulties of automation and national networking in China in five areas: hardware inventory, software applications development, Chinese character automation, library classification system, and networking topology. It stresses compatibility of standards as the most important factor in global networking.

701. Management of Information Centres in China: Results of a Course Held in Kunming, Yunnan Province, People's Republic of China, 6-18 December 1982, edited by K. P. Broadbent. Ottawa, Ont.: International Development Research Centre, 1984. 470 pp.

Defined as an informal seminar in the management of information centers in China, this title represents a series of lectures. It is based on various experiences in the field and is designed to serve as a guide to help China in planning and organizing its own centers. It is offered as a means of promoting and stimulating knowledge in this field, which can contribute to China's modernization program and help information scientists increase their skills in order to achieve greater self-sufficiency in information services. It offers lectures in the areas of information systems, information centers, networking and cooperation, information sources, information services, and institutional management, as well as case studies.

702. Miller, W. George; Chan, Yim-sang; and Bishop, Enid. "Computer-Based Information Services in Asia: Some Comparative Searches on China and Indonesia." BACA 7 (5-6): 111-123 (1980).

This article describes a study conducted by the Asian Studies Division of the Australian National University Library to assess the quality, extent, and depth of coverage of the online, computer-based information services for research on Asia, particulary pertaining to China and Indonesia. Twelve data bases offered by the Lockheed Dialog service were selected for searching the social sciences and humanities to determine how well Asian Studies are covered by computer-based services in general. The article outlines the search technique, provides an analysis of the search results, and notes the availability, location, and languages of journals cited.

703. Murata, S. "The Information Processing of Chinese Characters and Problems about It in the People's Republic of China" (in Japanese). Joho Kanri [Journal of Information Processing and Management] 23 (7): 614-623 (October 1980).

704. Nie, Chunrong. "Chinese Scientific and Technical Information: Present Status and Future Prospects." UNESCO Journal of Information Science, Librarianship and Archives Administration 2 (2): 74-77 (April-June 1980).

Introducing the work of the Institute of Scientific and Technical Information of China (ISTIC), a national, comprehensive information center, this article outlines the principal tasks of ISTIC and highlights its accomplishments during the last few years. The major work of ISTIC includes acquisition, compiling, translating, and disseminating foreign scientific and technical literature. It also offers literature and consultation services and encourages the development of international relations with various countries.

705. Paricharak, M. P. "China: A Late Starter in Modern Information Science." Annals of Library Science and Documentation 29 (4): 143-152 (December 1982).

Paricharak presents a firsthand account of China's major institutions in science and technology, information centers, and libraries. He highlights the progress and programs of the following: the Institute of Scientific and Technical Information in Peking, the Institute of Scientific and Technical Information of Shanghai, Peking University, the Peking University Library, the Peking Library, the Nanking University Library, and the Chekiang University Library. He also predicts that China is likely to face an information explosion within a decade if the present rate of progress continues.

706. "People's Republic of China: Publication of a Standard Character Set for Information Interchange." International Cataloguing 10 (3): 28-29 (July/September 1981).

This is a note on the publication of Code of Chinese Graphic Character Set for Information Interchange: Primary Set (Peking: State Bureau of Standardization, 1981). It summarizes the distinguishing features of this national standard.

707. Shen, Tseng-chee. "The Science and Technology Information Center, National Science Council, Republic

of China." Journal of Library and Information Science 1 (2): 94-105 (October 1975).

Shen provides a general description of the Science and Technology Information Center (STIC), founded in 1973 in Taipei. He details its organization and functions, outlines its present activities, describes its information networks with some of the educational and research institutions and industries, and notes various services provided by the STIC. He also includes a list of STIC's free-of-charge publications, which are available for researchers as tools for information services.

708. Shi, Jian, and Yan, Lizhong. "The Development of the Library and Information System of the Chinese Academy of Sciences." Paper presented at the 48th Annual Conference of the International Federation of Library Associations, Montreal, Canada, August 22-28, 1982. 11 pp. (ED 229 042).

This paper presents an historical review of the establishment of the Library and Information System of the Chinese Academy of Sciences (LISCAS) in 1951. It reports that the system, based on the principles of centralization, unification, and cooperation, now includes more than 140 library and information units throughout China. The paper outlines the requirements of building a good library and information system according to professional practices. It identifies the following problem areas in LISCAS: links, layout, organization of the system, general management, and efficiency.

709. Strain, Paula M.; Metzger, Eva C.; and Fenichel, Carol H. The National Technical Information Service--Institute for Scientific and Technical Information in China Exchange of Information Specialists, July 1983. Washington, D.C.: National Technical Information Service, 1983. 50 pp.

This is a report by three special librarians who visited Peking, Wuhan, Chengtu, Sian, Shanghai, and Canton in July 1983 as members of an official exchange of information specialists between the National Technical Information Services and the Institute of Scientific and Technical Information for China. The report describes what they learned about the profession in China and the institutions visited. It includes reports on Chinese library services, their general impressions, a proposal for further cooperation advanced by the Szechuan Scientific and Technical Information Center, and visits to various institutions.

710. Sun, Xuechen, and Baark, Erik. Technology Policy Trends and Information Services in Sweden and China: A Comparison. Lund: Research Policy Studies, 1983. 50 pp.

Using macroscopic and qualitative methods, this comparative research project outlines the current trends in technology policy in China and Sweden and explores the role of information in formulating appropriate technology policy and information service. It pays particular attention to policy in order to minimize the difficulties which exist between China as a developing country and Sweden as one of the most industrialized countries.

711. Tai, Wen-lang. "Report on the Activities in the Field of Scientific and Technological Documentation in the Republic of China." In Training Course in Documentation Techniques in Asia (Tokyo, 20 July -- 21 August 1970): Final Report, pp. 30-32. Tokyo: Japanese National Commission for UNESCO, 1970. (ED 059 739).

This is an account of the acquisition of scientific documentation, available scientific documentation, and documentation service in Taiwan. The paper states that the academic and industrial circles have fully recognized the importance of science documentation to the nation's economic development. The government also has formulated a science information policy, established the Scientific Documentation and Instrumentation Center, and is prepared to cooperate with all interested information agencies.

712. Takahashi, Tokutaro. "A Proposal for a Standard Common Core Character Set (CCCS)." International Cataloguing 10 (2): 7-8 (January/March 1981).

This article discusses the characteristics of East Asian scripts, uniform coding of Chinese character sets for data processing, Chinese character sets in East Asian countries, and the development of UNIMARC for universal bibliographic control. It includes a proposed standard for East Asian scripts and format and authority control of East Asian bibliographic records in order to facilitate information interchange among libraries in the world.

713. Talbot, H. D. "The Indexing of Chinese Names." The Indexer 2 (3): 99-103 (Spring 1961).

Talbot outlines the main problems encountered in indexing Chinese names, such as Chinese personal names, imperial titles, Chinese titles and ranks, and place names. He also lists sources of information which may help solve the problems.

714. Tell, Bjorn V. "Government Responsibility for Scientific and Technical Information Provision." Baca 7 (3): 49-53 (1980).

Presented to the "Seminar Informasi Ilmu dan Teknologi untuk Menunjang Pembangunan" in Jakarta in 1980, this paper describes policy in Sweden, China, and Malaysia and summarizes the governments' responsibility in acquiring, processing, and disseminating scientific and technological information. It explores more fully recent developments in China.

715. Tell, Marianne. A Note about China's Scientific and Technological Information System. Stockholm: Royal Institute of Technology Library, 1980. 50 pp.

Based on the observations of a delegation from the Swedish Academy of Sciences to China, this report describes the development of various types of libraries in China. It explores library, documentation, and scholarly publications from an historical perspective. It also evaluates the present state-of-the-art in terms of the situation before and after the Cultural Revolution. It uses a bibliometric approach to evaluate how Chinese scientists utilize their information sources.

716. Wan, Jinkun. "Chinese Data Base On-Line Retrieval." In Computer Information Systems in the People's Republic of China, compiled and edited by Harry Campbell, pp. 2.1-2.7. Toronto: China Business Consulting, 1986.

This paper reports on the progress of the Chinese University Journals Abstracts Project (CUJA), which is an English machine-readable bibliographic data base for international information exchange and a domestic supplement to Chinese documents, since 1982. The Tsinghua University Library Computer Center was selected as the project's center, and 340 member universities participate in the project. Since CUJA is a comprehensive bibliographic data base, it includes all areas of the humanities, social sciences, technology, and life sciences. The paper explores CUJA's development, bibliographic description, personnel training, and centralized data processing.

717. Wang, Chi, and Dunn, Robert. "Chinese Character Computer Encoding Methods and Library Automation: A Bibliographical Survey." Library of Congress

<u>Information Bulletin</u> 41 (13): 95-100 (March 26, 1982).

This is a bibliographical survey of reports, articles, and other materials on the subject collected by the Library of Congress. The authors wish to share and disseminate these materials, which cover related activities in the People's Republic of China, Taiwan, Japan, Korea, Canada, Great Britain, and the U.S. The article concludes that much effort in developing Chinese character computer encoding methods and library automation is expended in individual and isolated projects, and it suggests increased communication and concerted endeavors to solve common problems.

718. Wang, Yongcheng. "Chinese Character Processing for Information Retrieval." In <u>Computer Information Systems in the People's Republic of China</u>, compiled and edited by Harry Campbell, pp. 8.1-[8.7]. Toronto: China Business Consulting, 1986.

Wang outlines the characteristics of Chinese words and sentences, and discusses problems in the automatic dividing of Chinese sentences by computer. He also describes in detail the method of Automatic Extraction of Keywords in Chinese Textural Data in order to popularize the retrieval of Chinese information by computer in the near future.

719. Wee, Lily K., and Tsen, Chao-pin. "Design Considerations for the ASIC MARC Bibliographic System." <u>Journal of Educational Media and Library Sciences</u> 21 (1): 70-85 (Autumn 1983).

This paper discusses the design considerations in setting up a bibliographic data base, the ASIC MARC Bibliographic System, by the Agricultural Science Information Center (ASIC) of Taiwan. The system uses the UNIMARC as a communication format and the AACRII as a cataloging standard to facilitate the international exchange of bibliographic data. The paper also outlines the projected subsystems which are being planned: serial control, interlibrary loan, SDI, acquisitions, and circulation.

720. Wittmann, A. "A Patent System for the People's Republic of China--Impressions from an Official Visit." <u>World Patent Information</u> 2 (4): 177-178 (1980).

Based on information acquired while the author was visiting China in 1980, the article discusses the state of patent information in China and plans for creating a patent system.

721. Wu, Wan-jiun. "Agricultural Science Information Center, Taiwan." International Association of Agricultural Libraries and Documentalists Quarterly Bulletin 25 (4): 65 (1980).

As the director of the Agricultural Science Information Center (ASIC), Wu briefly traces the history of the Center and its activities. Wu notes that ASIC's plan for networking the agricultural libraries in Taiwan to share cataloging, acquisition, and other information was to be finished by 1981.

722. Wu, Wan-jiun; Kao, Chiu-fang; Wang, Huan-hsin; and Hsu, Mei-chu. "Agri-thesaurus: A Chinese Thesaurus for the Agricultural Science and Technology Information Management System." Journal of Educational Media and Library Sciences 20 (2): 161-167 (Winter 1983). Also in Information Interaction: Proceedings of the American Society for Information Science Conference, Columbus, Ohio, 1982, vol. 19, pp. 342-344. White Plains, NY: Knowledge Industry Publications (for the American Society for Information Science), 1982.

This article describes three files of the Agricultural Science and Technology Information Management System which was developed by the Agricultural Science Information Center. The data bases are: Files for Agricultural Science and Technology Personnel; Files for Agricultural Science and Technology Projects; and Files for Agricultural Science and Technology Literature. The article discusses the scope, compilation process, contents and layout, functions, problems, and prospects of the Agri-thesaurus in Taiwan.

723. Wu, Wan-jiun; Shen, Hong-shyang; and Wu, Lily. "A Chinese Agricultural Information Management System." In Proceedings of the 44th ASIS Annual Meeting, Washington, D.C., Oct. 25-30, 1981, vol. 18, edited by Lois F. Lunin, Madeline Henderson, and Harold Wooster, pp. 62-64. White Plains, NY: Knowledge Industry Publications (for the American Society for Information Science), 1981.

This paper describes the Agricultural Science and Technology Information Management System, a national system created by the Agricultural Science Information Center in 1979 to maintain bibliographic control over the increasing volume of agricultural literature produced in Taiwan. It notes that as of

1980, five data bases were completed. The paper also discusses the system's problems and prospects.

724. Wu, Yuan-li, and Sheeks, Robert B. The Organization and Support of Scientific Research and Development in Mainland China. New York: Praeger Publishers, 1970. 592 pp.

This study provides a descriptive survey of the organization and support of science in China, relates trends in science activity to policy movements, and deduces some guidelines for narrowing the range of probable developments under future conditions. It covers the following topics: historical background of Chinese science, goals of research and development (R&D), evolution of science plans and their coordination with other plans, evolution of the organizational structure and the multiplication of R&D institutions, magnitude and sources of funds for science, use of these funds, development of scientific manpower for R&D, growth of R&D, and output indicators and management of R&D.

725. Xu, Wenxu. "Chinese Library Networks: Retrospect and Prospect." Paper presented at the International Federation of Library Associations 48th General Conference, August 22-28, Montreal, Canada, 1982. 7 pp. (ED 227 865).

Xu discusses library networks in China since 1958, when two National Central Libraries Committees and nine Central Libraries Committees at the regional level were established. The author describes coordinating book and periodical acquisition on a regional or national level, centralized cataloging, allocating and exchanging duplicates, compiling and publishing union catalogs, reporting new publications, training staff, issuing interlibrary readers cards, and a national standardization meeting on cataloging rules and subject retrieval systems for the preparation of a national network.

726. Yang, Chen-chau. "Application and Design Considerations CJK for Information Interchange Code." Journal of Library and Information Science 11 (1): 24-32 (April 1985).

This paper discusses the application requirements of the Chinese, Japanese, and Korean (CJK) information interchange code in library environments, identifies problems to be considered in designing an information interchange code for CJK applications in library use, and reviews the design of the Chinese Character Code for Information Interchange and the feasibility of adopting it as an international standard for the CJK information interchange code.

727. Yu, Jinfeng, and Xiao, Zhongyi. "Chinese in the Computer: Efficiency in Input and the Role of Nested Element Analysis." Information Processing and Management 19 (5): 321-340 (1983).

Originally written in Chinese and intended for a Chinese audience, the paper advocates automating Chinese characters for information retrieval. It analyzes and compares several proposed methods for inputting Chinese and discusses the relation between Chinese characters and automation. It also puts forward an ideal evaluation standard, criteria against which any proposed input plan can be evaluated, and describes an ideal method for inputting Chinese characters that satisfies all these criteria--the authors' Nested Element Analysis.

728. Yü, Jizheng. "Library System of the Academia Sinica." INSPEL 20 (3): 144-147 (1986).

The article discusses the Library of the Academia Sinica as the center for the system of libraries and information services at the Academia Sinica in the People's Republic of China. The discussion centers on the Library's supervisory role as well as its acquisition policy, cataloging activities, user services, publications, and staff training.

729. Zeng, Minzu. "English/Chinese Data Base Compatibility." In Computer Information Systems in the People's Republic of China, compiled and edited by Harry Campbell, pp. 4.1-4.9. Toronto: China Business Consulting, 1986.

The inception of the Beijing Document Service (BDS) in 1981 and the loading of the whole National Technical Information Service (NTIS) abridged bibliographic data base in 1983 are reported. Because of pressing demands from Chinese users, BDS is moving rapidly towards an operational system. The paper summarizes changes made to date, which include the creation of larger and new data bases, the introduction of the computer for use in Chinese characters information processing, the development of information retrieval application packages, the establishment of communication lines and terminals, and the experiment of data entry on a preliminary production scale. The paper also outlines the prospects for the BDS online information retrieval system and highlights possible new projects.

730. Zhang, Jiaxiang; Wang, Taihe; and Jin, Yanxia. "An International Online Information Retrieval Service in China." IFLA Journal 12 (4): 321-324 (1986).

This is an account of the establishment of the International Online Information Retrieval Service (IOIRS) in China in 1983 with the support of Unesco and the European Space Agency. It discusses users, training users of IOIRS, data base usage, and various problems.

731. Zhou, Dingheng. "On-Line Retrieval Systems Design." In Computer Information Systems in the People's Republic of China, compiled and edited by Harry Campbell, pp. 1.1-1.14. Toronto: China Business Consulting, 1986.

While discussing plans to build a national online retrieval system of scientific and technical information with Chinese features, this article suggests that a three-part strategy of "unified design, implementation by stages, and construction of a network" be adopted in planning the system for China. The article explores the details of the system's structure, its organizational structure, development of data bases, design lessons, problems, access to foreign data bases, and telecommunication and computer networks.

7

Education for Librarianship

732. Berninghausen, David K. "Education for Librarianship--Taiwan (Formosa)." Country fact sheet presented at the ALA Preconference Institute on International Library Manpower, Education and Placement in North America, Detroit, June 26-27, 1970. 2 pp. (ED 073 784).

Based on the author's observations in 1962-63, this paper discusses the general education system and education for librarianship in Taiwan. The author reports that at present there are two universities, National Taiwan University and Taiwan Normal University, which provide comprehensive library education at the undergraduate level. At the World College of Journalism, there also is a junior college program and an evening extension program designed to provide junior library staff. The paper also discusses the need to set up a graduate program for librarianship.

733. Berninghausen, David K. "Library Education in Taiwan and Recommendations for Advanced Library Education." China Today 6 (2): 26-30 (1963). Also appeared as "Library Education in Taiwan" in NTU Library Science Circular No. 1: 1-8 (January 1966).

Emphasizing the importance of librarian education for the future economic, educational, and cultural development of Taiwan, the author recommends a graduate library school as an essential step to fulfill these needs. He bases his recommendation on the conviction that librarians must be scholars if they are to provide the services necessary for the people of Taiwan. The author believes that a librarian must study one field of human knowledge thoroughly in order to be competent to select, organize, and administer the flow of literature produced by modern scholars. It includes "Recommendations for Advanced Library Education."

734. Boone University. Library School. _China's First Library School_. Wuchang: Boone Library School, 1928. 20 pp.

This report includes discussions on: (1) the Boone Library School, China's first library school, by Director Thomas Chin Sen Hu; and (2) the Boone Library and its forward developments, by Librarian Samuel T. Y. Seng. It presents figures on the students and graduates of the Boone Library School, and outlines plans of the library.

735. Bramley, Gerald. "The New Colonialists: U.S. Influence on Library Education in the Developing Countries." In _World Trends in Library Education_, pp. 151-157. Hamden, CT: Linnet Books, 1975. Also in (ED 116 677).

Containing information on American contributions to library education in Taiwan, this chapter describes U.S. aid and assistance, courses in librarianship, course content, teaching methods, the impact of the schools of librarianship, and future trends of library education in the developing countries. It especially notes the fellowship program and courses in librarianship offered in the library schools in Taiwan.

736. Campbell, Harry. "Modernizing Information Training in China." _Information Development_ 1 (1): 26-30 (January 1985).

This article explores the problems of existing library resources and personnel in light of China's modernization program, the growth of foreign literature collections, the expansion of publishing, and the increase in the educated population. It also describes training programs offered by over thirty university library science departments and training centers in Peking and Shanghai, as well as the activities of the new national information college at Wuhan University. Finally, it outlines opportunities for foreign assistance.

737. "Carl White Goes to China." _Library Journal_ 69 (18): 896 (October 15, 1944).

This is an announcement that Carl White, director of Columbia University libraries and dean of the School of Library Service, will be a visiting professor in the field of library administration and higher education in China.

738. Chen, Ching-chih. "Education and Training in Information Science in the People's Republic of China." Bulletin of the American Society for Information Science 6 (4): 16-18 (April 1980).

Focusing on the two model institutions for library science at Peking and Wuhan universities, the author outlines the curricula of the library science department of each institution. She indicates that the country's stance toward the individual and underdevelopment has had a significant influence on the education and training of library professionals in China. She also points out that China needs the help of American colleagues in training qualified information science educators in order to catch up with the new technology in libraries.

739. Chen, Shann-jye. "On the Arrangement of 'Curriculum of Library Science' in Several Colleges of Republic of China." Journal of Educational Media Science 18 (1): 113-127 (Autumn 1980).

This paper discusses the current trends and practices in library science. It examines five colleges and universities in Taiwan which offer library science curricula to determine if the arrangement of these curricula is proper and effective. It also explores the difficulty library science graduates are facing and recommends changes in the library science curricula in Taiwan. The text is in Chinese, with an abstract in English.

740. Chiang, Fu-tsung. "Education for Librarianship: Appraisal and Proposal." West and East 6 (2): 5-6 (February 1961).

Discussing the forty-year history of Chinese library education beginning in the 1920's, the author places his emphasis on Mainland China before 1949 and on Taiwan afterwards. He calls for general professional training at the undergraduate level and specialized professional training at the graduate level as the best way for librarians to become competent.

741. Chou, Tsin-fu; Wang, Chen-ku; Lan, Chien-chang; Fang, Tung-sheng; and Liu, Chung-jen. "Library Education in the Republic of China Today." Journal of Library and Information Science 2 (1): 45-73 (April 1976).

This is a collection of five reports prepared by department heads of five library science programs in colleges and universities in Taiwan. These colleges are the National Taiwan University, the National Taiwan Normal University, Fu-jen University, Tamkang

University, and the College of World Journalism. For each program, the following items are included: history, purpose, curriculum, teaching faculty, facilities, employment of graduates, and future prospects. All of the programs described are at the undergraduate level. The text is in Chinese.

742. Fan, Chu Shu. "Information Science Education in China." LASIE 14 (6): 2-6 (May/June 1984).

Fan outlines two ways of obtaining education in information science in China: (1) through formal education at universities and colleges specializing in scientific and technical information studies; and (2) through continuing education of practicing professionals. The author also briefly discusses the development of education programs in library and information science.

743. Hausrath, Donald C. "China Opens Doors on Library Education." American Libraries 11 (7): 451 (July 1981).

This is a report on the first two librarian training workshops held in Peking and Shanghai, which were sponsored by the China Society of Library Science and the U.S. International Communication Agency. It discusses the preservation of rare books, modern library buildings, international bibliographic standards, personnel training, and organizational design.

744. Hill, Ruth A. "The Training of Librarians in China." Library Journal 62 (3): 107-110 (February 12, 1937).

As a new instructor at the Boone Library School, Wuchang, China, Hill was impressed with the role America was playing in influencing the development of libraries there. She discusses in detail the Boone Library School, its curricula, staff, students, and Mary Elizabeth Wood, founder of the Boone Library in 1910 and the Boone Library School in 1919.

745. Hsu, Chia-lin; Huang, Tsung-chung; and Ch'en, Kuang-tso. "Library Cadres Training over the Past 15 Years." Selections from China Mainland Magazines No. 465: 3-12 (April 20, 1965).

This article examines the goals, curricula, and teaching methods of various part-time, in-service training courses for library cadres. It describes programs for training classes, research classes, correspondence courses, and spare-time universities. It also discusses full-time library education offered by colleges in China and provides detailed information on the library schools of Peking University and Wuhan University. Finally, it identifies some problems in library science education and their possible solutions.

746. Hu, Thomas Chin Sen. "China's First Library School." Library Journal 54: 153 (February 15, 1929).

Written by the director of the Boone Library School, the short article recounts the work of the School at the end of the eighth year of its operation.

747. Kaneko, Hideo. "Chinese Librarian Trains at Yale." Leads 25 (4): 2, 7 (Winter 1983).

This is a news item regarding a librarian from the Wuhan University Library who came for intensive in-service training at various units of the Yale Library system in 1983. Her training was sponsored by the Yale-China Association.

748. Kwei, John Chih-ber. "The Boone Library School." China Weekly Review 59 (6): 190 (January 9, 1932).

Kwei presents a brief historical account of the Boone Library School, the first library school in China, which was established in Wuchang in 1920 by Mary Elizabeth Wood. He also includes details of the curriculum and responsibilities of the School.

749. "LAC 1968 Summer Library Workshop." NTU Library Science Circular No. 6: 1-3 (September 1968).

This article describes the 1968 Summer Library Workshop sponsored by the Library Association of China, which was held in Taipei. The workshop offered in-service training to library workers in order to improve present library services through a better understanding of library aims and methods. The article includes a list of the courses offered, special lectures delivered, and field trips taken during the period.

750. Lai, Yung-hsiang. "Birth of the Graduate Library, National Taiwan University" (in Chinese). Bulletin of the Library Association of China 20 (8): 15-18 (December 1968).

751. Lai, Yung-hsiang. "Department of Library Science, National Taiwan University." Bibliotheca No. 1: 38-42 (April 1967).

This article describes the development, organization, and curriculum of the Department of Library Science at the National Taiwan University, established in 1961, and the Department's library.

752. Lai, Yung-hsiang. "Present Scene of Library Education in China (Taiwan)." In <u>Library Education and Training in Developing Countries</u>, edited by George S. Bonn, pp. 51-64. Honululu: East-West Center Press, 1966.

The author details the undergraduate programs in library science at the National Taiwan University and Taiwan Normal University, and the new plan to establish a two-year graduate library institute at National Taiwan University. He also discusses the junior college training program, summer library workshops, introductory library courses offered in various universities, and study abroad. He calls for professional librarian status, library training at all levels, and informal training.

753. Lai, Yung-hsiang. "The Present Status of Education for Librarianship in Taiwan." <u>Journal of Education for Librarianship</u> 6 (4): 274-280 (Spring 1966).

An abridged version of the article listed above (#752), this paper concentrates on the curricula offered by the National Taiwan University and Taiwan Normal University. It includes a discussion on the junior college training program, summer library workshops, and universities that offer introductory library science courses.

754. Lan, Chien-chang. "Bibliography and Its Influence on the Design of the Curriculum of Library Schools in China." In <u>Proceedings of the First Conference on Asian Library Cooperation</u>, edited by Tamkang College, pp. 396-430. Taipei: Tamkang College, 1974. Also in <u>Chinese Culture</u> 16 (3): 109-128 (September 1975).

Presented at the First Conference on Asian Library Cooperation held in Taipei, Taiwan in 1974, this paper is divided into two sections. It first traces the historical background of the organization of knowledge in China, including descriptive cataloging and subject cataloging. It then discusses, in some detail, the design of the curriculum of library schools, with an emphasis on present conditions in Taiwan.

755. Li, Tze-chung. "Library Science Education in the Republic of China: An Appraisal." <u>Journal of Education for Librarianship</u> 14 (1): 16-31 (Summer 1973).

Based on recent surveys, personal observation, and experience closely related to education, this excellent paper reviews and appraises library science education in Taiwan since 1955. The author points out that Taiwan has enough trained librarians and yet the library profession does not attract these people due to: (1) low job classifications, low scale of salaries, and low status of librarians; (2) an inadequate budget for library development; (3) a conservative concept of libraries; (4) professional complacency or apathy; (5) the Library Association of China's inactivity in promoting the importance of librarianship in the social fabric; and (6) the government's lack of attention to the development of librarianship. He believes that it would be impractical at this time to concentrate on graduate studies and to discontinue the present undergraduate program.

756. Li, Tze-chung. "A Proposal for a Sino-U.S. Cooperative Graduate Program in Library Science." In Proceedings of the First Conference on Asian Library Cooperation, edited by Tamkang College, pp. 433-443. Taipei: Tamkang College, 1974.

Reviewing current library education in Taiwan, this paper points out that based on a report there are two critical problems confronting the library field: (1) the limited outlet for trained librarians; and (2) the serious shortage of librarians with subject competence and professional training to meet the needs of scientific, technological, industrial, and educational developments. The author proposes a Sino-U.S. cooperative graduate program for library science as a possible solution. The program calls for an exchange of faculty and students, seminars or summer workshops, scholarships, etc.

757. Li, Weiming. "Library and Information Science Education." In Computer Information Systems in the People's Republic of China, compiled and edited by Harry Campbell, pp. 6.1-6.11. Toronto: China Business Consulting, 1986.

This paper traces the history and recent development of library and information science education (LIS) in China, with emphasis on development in the 1980's. It highlights important features of LIS programs and achievements in LIS research. It recommends proper use of qualified professionals, core courses for higher education, and increased user education. The core courses of LIS should include an introduction to LIS, classification and subject headings, cataloging in Chinese and foreign languages, bibliography, reference materials and services, information retrieval, management of library and information services, collection development and user services, library automation, and computerized information retrieval systems.

758. Lin, Sharon Chien. "Education for Librarianship in China after the Cultural Revolution." Journal of Education for Librarianship 24 (1): 17-29 (Summer 1983).

Emphasizing the present status of library education and libraries in China after the Cultural Revolution, the author describes the ways in which the government mobilizes limited resources to cope with the shortage of library personnel. She also discusses such topics as new trends in library modernization, the expansion of library and information science education, and possible future developments.

759. Lin, Sharon Chien. "Historical Development of Library Education in China." Journal of Library History 20 (4): 368-386 (Fall 1985).

The author provides an historical review of the modern library movement and the development of library education in China. She traces the history in three stages: (1) early development, 1905-49; (2) new ideology in librarianship, 1949-76; and (3) recovery and expansion, 1976-present. She concludes that since the essential role libraries play in the modernization process has been well recognized, the outlook for librarianship is very hopeful.

760. Lung, Ch'ien. "Library Cadres in Institutions of Higher Education Must Be Cultivated and Elevated." Survey of China Mainland Press No. 1448: 7-8 (January 11, 1957).

This article states that because of the increase in library collections in institutions of higher education, the professional standard of library cadres is inadequate to meet the needs of the libraries. It discusses methods of local recruitment and cultivation and suggests offering a short training course and correspondence classes for library cadres and placing apprentices under the supervision of experts to raise the standard of library personnel.

761. Mote, Frederick W. "Library Skills in the Chinese Field, a Proposal for Action." Committee on East Asian Libraries Newsletter No. 47: 75-76 (July 1975).

762. Ozolins, Karlis L. "The Role of the Library Science Education in the Development of the Public Libraries in Taiwan." Bibliotheca No. 1: 12-30 (April 1967).

This paper discusses the growth of the book industry and surveys the condition of public libraries in Taiwan. It outlines eight roles of library science education for the development of the libraries of Taiwan in general and public libraries in particular: training professional librarians, offering professional courses, promoting library standards and codes, bettering bibliographic controls, furnishing a forum for professional writers, providing qualified library staff, achieving professional status for librarians, and controlling not only the physical aspects of books but also their contents.

763. Phillips, Grace D. "The Boone Library School Through the Eyes of a Newcomer." Boone Library School Quarterly 7 (2): 315-318 (June 1935).

Written by an American faculty member at the Boone Library School, the first library school in China, the article comments favorably on the quality of the teaching faculty, their publications, the curriculum, the library building, and the achievements of the graduates.

764. "Pittsburgh to Train Librarians for China's First Hi-tech Library." Library Journal 109 (20): 2200 (December 1984).

This is a brief note about the training of three librarians from Shanghai Chiao Tung University at the library school of the University of Pittsburgh through a grant from the United States Information Agency.

765. Seng, Samuel T. Y. "Library Schools and Libraries in China." Library Journal 69 (1): 932-933 (November 1, 1944); 69 (1): 994+ (November 15, 1944).

This lengthy letter from Seng, director of the National Library of Peking, to Charles H. Brown, chairman of the American Library Association (ALA) Committee on the Orient and Southwest Pacific, describes library work at the Boone University Library and the contribution of the Boone Library School to the Chinese library movement. Seng also acknowledges what the ALA has done for Boone and for Chinese libraries in general.

766. Seng, Samuel T. Y. "Looking to the Future." Boone Library School Quarterly 7 (2): 313-314 (June 1935).

On the occasion of the seventh year of the Boone Library School Quarterly, the author notes the aims and purposes of the journal and various shortcomings of the title. He announces the decision to include English articles in future volumes.

767. Seng, Samuel T. Y. "Professional Training of Librarianship in China." In Libraries in China, pp. 59-65. Peking: Library Association of China, 1935.

This paper chronicles library development in China, with emphasis on the appearance of the modern public library since Mary Elizabeth Wood founded the Boone Library in 1910 and the Boone Library School in 1919. It also explores the problems both faculty and students face in professional library training.

768. Shaw, Estelle Fu. "A Study on the Continuing Education for Librarians." Journal of Educational Media and Library Sciences 22 (1): 53-64 (Autumn 1984).

Based on a questionnaire survey of 147 librarians, the article examines in-service training and continuing education of library personnel in Taiwan. It discusses the need for staff development and presents significant differences in findings according to types of personnel, sex, marital status, and age group. It also offers recommendations to the Library Association of China, library schools, and planners of continuing education activities. The text is in Chinese, with an abstract in English.

769. Stueart, Robert D. "A Personal Observation on Library and Information Science Education in the People's Republic of China." Journal of Education for Librarianship 22 (3): 207-211 (Winter 1982).

These comments on library and information science education in China are based on the author's observations, discussions, and readings during a seven week stay as lecturer and consultant on collection development and management techniques at four universities. Library education programs at Wuhan and Peking universities are especially noted.

770. Tees, Miriam. "1986 IFLA Post-Conference Seminar: Education and Research in Library and Information Science in the Information Age: Means of Modern Technology and Management, Beijing, China, 1-6 September, 1986." IFLA Journal 13 (1): 72-75 (1987).

This is a detailed news report on a conference held by the China Society of Library Science following the IFLA Tokyo Conference in 1986. There were twenty papers presented at this post-conference seminar, including a paper on planning education in library science for such an enormous country as China, a paper on in-service training in Chinese public libraries, and a paper on professional education in library and information science. Twelve foreign visitors from ten countries and thirty-one Chinese experts attended the seminar.

771. "Training Course on Computerized Information and On-line Systems, Peking, 1979." UNESCO Journal of Information Science 2 (1): 66 (January/March 1980).

This notes on the training course offered at the Institute of Scientific and Technical Information in Peking in 1979. The aim of the course was to introduce techniques of automatic information and the use of online systems to Chinese documentalists and information specialists.

772. Tsuneishi, Warren M. "Education of Chinese Librarians in the U.S." Leads 24 (2): 1+ (Summer 1982).

This reports on the training programs provided to Chinese librarians by U.S. institutions since the U.S. and China signed an educational and cultural exchange agreement in 1979. It notes that UC Berkeley, Simmons College, SUNY Geneseo, the Library of Congress, and Harvard are among the host institutions.

773. Whitbeck, George W. "Comparative Study of Education for Librarianship and Information Science in the Republic of China and North America: A Survey." Journal of Library and Information Science 10 (1): 40-62 (April 1984).

This study provides both a survey of library education in Taiwan and a comparative view from the West, and recommends steps for developing the field. It examines curricula of the schools providing education for librarianship and surveys library educators. It finds that the library education community of Taiwan has provided quality professional education for their students and practitioners.

774. Yan, Yimin. "Information Science Education in the People's Republic of China." In Proceedings of the 48th ASIS Annual Meeting, Las Vegas, Nevada, October 20-24, 1985, vol. 22, edited by Carol A. Parkhurst, pp. 377-380. White Plains, NY: Knowledge Industry

Publications (for the American Society for Information Science), 1985.

This paper traces the development and progress of information science education in the People's Republic of China since the first national information office was established in 1956. The author identifies the problems facing information science education today and suggests the following as possible solutions: (1) have a full understanding and appreciation of information science and its applications; (2) emphasize in-service training of information professionals; (3) encourage cooperation between schools and employers in providing training; and (4) accelerate reformation of the old educational system.

8

Publishing and Trade

775. Albert, Leo A. "More on Book Pirating in China." Publishers Weekly 214 (12): 75-76 (September 18, 1978).

In reply to Joseph J. Nerbonne's article entitled "Book Pirating Is Lively on Formosa but Authorized Reprints Are Making Gains" (see #845), Albert recounts his mission ten years ago in gaining support from the Taiwan government to reduce unauthorized reprints of U.S. publications.

776. "Albert Reports on Peking Visit, Coming Book Exhibit." Publishers Weekly 212 (16): 19-20 (October 17, 1977).

This is a summary of a report by Leo Albert, chairman of the board of Prentice-Hall International and the first American publisher to be officially invited to China, on his trip to Peking. It notes how China National Publications Import Corporation, the sole and official importer of books and periodicals for all of China, functions. It also urges American publishers to participate in the coming book exhibit in China.

777. Arboleda, Amadio A. "Scholarly Publishing in China." Scholarly Publishing 12 (4): 366-368 (July 1981).

The author examines what went on during the Cultural Revolution and discusses the present state of scholarly publishing in China. The author reports that from 1966 to 1976, publishing activities were pushed backwards and recovery began only in the late 1970's. By 1979, more than 1,000 journals were being published. Because much of China's scholarly and academic publishing is handled by specialized houses, there are still very few university presses.

778. Baark, Erik. "The Structure of Technological Information Dissemination in China: Publication of

Scientific and Technological Manuals, 1970-1977." China Quarterly No. 83: 510-534 (September 1980).

Largely drawn from an analysis of 282 technical manuals on electronics and metallurgy, the article describes the dissemination of scientific and technological information through the publication of manuals. It is mainly concerned with the structures involved in the dissemination process and the performance of the publications industry in relation to the industrial sectors covered. It concludes that during this phase of the dissemination process, the policies on decentralization and cooperation have a considerable effect. Publishing, however, reveals a pattern which points to much more centralization during this period.

779. Baker, J. B. "Klopfer, RH Chairman, Reports on China Visit." Publishers Weekly 206 (25): 10 (December 16, 1974).

Reporting on Random House Chairman Donald Klopfer's recent visit to China, Baker notes that the Chinese were not at all interested in any publishing association with the U.S., though they did express an interest in receiving American publishers' catalogs.

780. "Bamboo Curtain Falls on Export of Chinese Science Journal." Library Journal 86 (5): 968-970 (March 1, 1961).

The Chinese authorities' decision to place an embargo on science journals to the U.S. is discussed. As a consequence, translations of specialized Chinese materials in science became necessary.

781. "Benjamin Company Launches Books-to-China Program." Publishers Weekly 219 (15): 27 (April 10, 1981).

This relates discussions between Roy Benjamin, president of the Benjamin Company, and members of the Publishers Association of China in regard to marketing low-cost paperbacks to the libraries in Chinese schools, colleges, factories, communes, cooperatives, government agencies, and other booklending facilities.

782. Booher, Edward E. "In China: Western Publishers Sign Agreements for 20 Books." Publishers Weekly 217 (23): 10+ (June 13, 1980).

This is a report on Western publishers' visit to China in 1980, resulting in the signing of twenty transactions with the Chinese to supply books for Western markets.

783. "Book Market Flourishes." Beijing Review 26 (15): 28-29 (April 11, 1983).

A survey, conducted by the head office of Hsinhua Bookstore, is reported. The survey result indicates that there is an increased demand for books on political theories, law, business management, philosophy, political economics, child care, agritechniques, and decreased sales of low-quality novels and some other literature.

784. "Books and China." Publishers Weekly 209 (11): 44-46 (March 15, 1976).

This report of two visits to China by American publishers and managers discusses publishing and distribution of books in China, reviews problems and requirements related to importing American books into China, provides a broad overview of book exports and imports to and from China, and indicates that China could become a valuable market for American publishers. It is divided into three sections: how Chinese publishing and bookselling works, selling Chinese books in America, and the prospect for selling American books in China.

785. "Buying for China." Publishers Weekly 218 (12): 104-109 (September 19, 1980).

A visit to the China National Publications Import Corporation (CNPIC) by the staff of Publishers Weekly is reported. It notes that CNPIC imports some 600,000 books a year, and that importing books and periodicals from the U.S. amounted to close to $10 million in 1979. Topics include CNPIC's procedures for importing foreign books, selling for China, copyright questions, government regulations on unauthorized publishing, and the establishment of the Publishers Association of China.

786. Campbell, Harry. "The Present Revival of Scholarly Publishing in China." Scholarly Publishing 16 (3): 223-237 (April 1985).

On the basis of his personal experiences in training library and information staff in Anhui Province in 1984, the author analyzes the current status of scholarly publishing in China. He also discusses the impact of scholarship from abroad, some objectives of scholarly communication in China today, and the results achieved. He includes a list of agencies active in scholarly publishing.

787. Carnese, Paul J. "China Diary: U.S. Publishers, in Historic Visit, Discuss Copyright and Other Book-Related Matters." Publishers Weekly 215 (23): 27-34 (June 4, 1979).

This is a report of the first U.S. delegation of publishers ever to visit the People's Republic of China. They were invited in 1979 by the China National Publications Import Corporation. It discusses facts and figures about the Chinese publishing industry as well as the copyright question. It also notes impressions on libraries in China and a printing plant.

788. Ceadel, E. B. "The Far East." In Acquisition and Provision of Foreign Books by National and University Libraries in the United Kingdom, compiled with a foreword and an afterword by B. C. Bloomfield, pp. 3-11. London: Mansell Information Publishing, 1972.

Presented at the Morecambe Conference in 1972, this paper surveys the publishing and bookselling markets of the Far East, particularly in China, Taiwan, Hong Kong, Japan, and Korea. It comments on some specific aspects of the publishing output of the countries: printing, subjects, and the scholarly level of the current output. It also discusses demands for the Far Eastern materials in Great Britain and policies for accessions.

789. Chan, James. "Selling Books in China." Publishers Weekly 230 (6): 23-26 (August 8, 1986).

As a consultant on trade with China, the author offers his expert view on the current state of the Chinese market for Western books. In the past, the China National Publications Import and Export Corporation has had a monopoly on book imports; today, more direct import companies exist. The Chinese are acquiring a more diverse range of materials in order to keep up with the expansion of libraries. He urges American publishers to view China as a long-term market and to treat it that way.

790. Chan, Yim-sang. "Chinese Publishing in Transition, 1972-1979." Australian Academic and Research Libraries 12 (1): 26-34 (March 1981).

The author analyzes Chinese publishing activity by examining the national bibliography Ch'uan-kuo Hsin Shu-mu (New Books Catalog of the PRC) from 1972 to 1980, including subject divisions. He outlines the changed situation since 1972, noting particularly that the "Four Modernizations," the rehabilitation of disgraced scholars, and the denunciation of Mao Tse-tung's role in China have had a great impact on the Chinese publishing world. He also mentions problems of inflation and the lack of experience in distributing expensive works to foreign purchasers.

791. Chan, Yim-sang. "The New Era of Chinese Publishing and Its Implications for Chinese Book Acquisitions." Center for Chinese Research Materials Newsletter No. 25: 1-6 (March 1978).

Originally delivered at the First East Asian Library Seminar sponsored by the Australian National University Library in 1977, this paper describes publishing in China since the outbreak of the Cultural Revolution in 1966 and outlines its problems and their implications for library acquisitions.

792. Chang, Hsiao-nung. "Expand Sources of Books and Develop Book-Lending Services: A Letter from Chang Hsiao-nung from Anta City, Heilungkiang." Survey of China Mainland Press No. 2754: 15-16 (June 7, 1962).

This is a letter in appreciation of the effort made by the Hsinhua Bookstore to establish a booklending service which offers a great variety of books in a small city. Chang calls for the expansion of book sources to develop more booklending services.

793. Cheng, Heng-hsiung. "An Overview of Chinese Reference Publications." Journal of Educational Media Science 18 (1): 88-106 (Autumn 1980).

Cheng gives an overview of 3,312 items of Chinese reference publications identified in two guides of Chinese reference books edited by Do-yuan Ho (1938) and Tze-chung Li (1972). He discusses the type of reference works (i.e., bibliographies, indexes, dictionaries, thesauri, encyclopedias, etc.), their categories, quantities, and the merits and defects in their compilations. The text is in Chinese, with an abstract in English.

794. Cheng, Heng-hsiung. "Periodical Publications in the Republic of China, 1950-1971," translated and condensed by Teresa Wang Chang. National Central Library Newsletter 5 (2): 1-5 (July 1973).

This article presents a statistical analysis of periodical quantity, based on the "Statistical Abstract of Interior of the ROC," which indicates an increased rate during the period. It also provides a summary account of a survey of periodical quality based on the "Guide to Chinese Periodicals, 1972."

795. Cheng, Heng-hsiung. "Selected List of Reference Books Published in the R.O.C., 1976." Journal of Library and Information Science 3 (1): 55-72 (April 1977).

A classified and annotated list of sixty Chinese reference books published in Taiwan in 1976 is provided. It is divided into seven categories: bibliography, index, encyclopedia, dictionary, yearbook, handbook, and laws. It provides full bibliographic descriptions for each entry. It excludes reprints of old works and statistical reports issued by government departments. The text is in Chinese, with an abstract in English.

796. Cheng, Heng-hsiung. "Selected List of Reference Books Published in the R.O.C., 1977-78." Journal of Library and Information Science 5 (1): 111-126 (April 1979); 5 (2): 239-259 (October 1979).

Divided into ten categories, this is a classified and annotated list of 136 Chinese reference books published in Taiwan in 1977 and 1978: bibliography, index, abstract, encyclopedia, dictionary, biography, yearbook, chronology, handbook, and laws. It excludes reprints of old works, statistical reports issued by government departments, and periodical reference materials. The text is in Chinese, with an abstract in English.

797. Chien, Florence. "The Commercial Press and Modern Chinese Publishing: 1897-1949." M.A. thesis, Graduate Library School, University of Chicago, 1970. 143 leaves.

Tracing the origin and development of the Commercial Press, this study places special emphasis on its organization, management, personnel, and leadership. It notes its contributions to social and intellectual life in general and to the publishing industry in particular in modern China. It is chronologically divided into four periods: (1) the beginning of modern Chinese publishing and the establishment of the Commercial Press, 1897-1912; (2) the growth, disputes, and problems between 1912 and 1927; (3) the production, destruction, and restoration period of 1927-37; and (4) wartime operations and the post-war years, from 1937 to 1949.

798. "Chinese Books." Booklist, 1973-

This is an annual listing of selected Chinese titles with annotations for selection purposes.

799. "Chinese Children's Books." Booklist, 1977-

This is an annual listing of selected Chinese children's books with annotations for selection purposes.

800. "Chinese Periodical Boom." Leads 24 (2): 6 (Summer 1982).

This is news about the booming Chinese periodical publishing industry. Over 2,000 magazines were published in 1980, more than half of which were scientific and technical journals.

801. "Chinese Publishers Form Publishing Association." Publishers Weekly 217 (8): 76 (February 29, 1980).

A news brief on the establishment of a Chinese publishers' association and its first meeting is reported. The association will promote all aspects of publishing, sponsor academic activities, give prizes for outstanding work, uphold the legal rights of publishers, and organize welfare facilities for workers in the publishing industry.

802. "Chinese Publishers Impressed by U.S. Public Library." Library Journal 105 (15): 1684 (September 1, 1980).

These are notes about a fifteen-member delegation of Chinese book publishers, editors, and executives on tour in the U.S. They were particularly impressed by the Darien Library in Darien, Connecticut because of its size and its extensive services for children.

803. Chung, Ho. "Ten-Year Catalogue." Peking Review 2 (46): 22-23 (November 17, 1959).

Chung examines the major achievements of book publishing in China during the first decade of the People's Republic. A list of publications gives some idea of the range and variety of themes, subject matter, and forms of publications, as well as the main trends.

804. "Circulation of Books and Periodicals in the Countryside." Union Research Service 37 (13): 189-205 (November 13, 1964).

This is a collection of articles regarding rural supply and marketing cooperatives. Since 1955, the Chinese Communist state-run Hsin-hua Bookstore has been entrusted with the work of circulating books and periodicals in the countryside. In 1963, there were more than 10,000 selling points and a circulation of 120 million copies; however, the supply and marketing cooperatives have not met the full demands of the readers in the countryside. The articles discuss measures to strengthen the work of book circulation.

805. "Circulation of Books and Periodicals in the Countryside." Union Research Service 40 (23): 331-345 (September 17, 1965).

Consisting of four articles, this report describes recent activities by the state-run Hsin-hua Bookstore and its branches in distributing revolutionary reading materials in rural areas. It also reports on the establishment of libraries and reading rooms to enforce political-ideological education. The four articles are: "Send Revolutionary Books and Periodicals to the Countryside"; "Turn the Face of Book Circulation Work Toward Rural Villages and Serve the 500 Million Peasants"; "Travelling Far and Wide with a Carrying-Pole; See Happy Peasants Welcoming the Arrival of New Books"; and "Be Promoters of Cultural Revolution in the Countryside."

806. DeBlois, Diane. "Exploring China's Antiquarian Treasures." AB Bookman's Weekly 64 (24): 3995-3998 (December 10, 1979).

The author, who toured China as a partner of a bookselling firm, relates her attempts to seek out antiquarian book items. She found out, while visiting a university library, that the Chinese have little interest in rare, old materials, preferring to focus on contemporary matters.

807. "Delivering Publications for Revolution's Sake: An Editorial Postscript." Survey of China Mainland Press No. 3570: 10-11 (November 2, 1965).

This reports that although large numbers of books, newspapers, and periodicals are published, quite a few are stacked up behind the salescounters of the supply and marketing cooperatives and in libraries and really do not reach the readers for whom they are intended. It suggests ways to take the initiative in sending books to the countryside and to the readers, instead of waiting for readers to come to borrow books.

808. Dong, Stella. "Albert Sees 'Positive' Change on Second Visit to China." Publishers Weekly 214 (22): 21-22 (November 27, 1978).

Leo Albert, chairman of the board of Prentice-Hall International, reports on his second visit to China. He notes that Chinese publishers have a marked interest in increasing trade and cooperative ventures with the U.S.

809. Dong, Stella. "In the U.S.: Chinese and American Publishers Exchange Information." Publishers Weekly 217 (23): 10-12 (June 13, 1980).

The first official visit by Chinese publishers to the U.S. since the normalization is recorded. It points out that the Chinese stressed the importance of book exhibits and cultural exchanges in strengthening publishing ties between the two countries. Other topics discussed include upgrading of showrooms for foreign books, educational exchanges, and copyright questions.

810. Fan, Zhilong. "China's Best-Sellers and How They Are Made." China Reconstructs 30 (4): 19-23 (April 1981).

As a general survey on the book-publishing industry in China, this paper discusses who publishes what among the close to 200 publishing houses, old and new literature, works from abroad, enterprising local houses, specialized publishers, and joint publication.

811. Feldman, Gayle. "Beijing's First Book Fair." Publishers Weekly 230 (19): 24-29 (November 7, 1986).

The first Peking International Book Fair, which was sponsored by the China National Publications Import and Export Corporation in September 1986, is described. Representatives from more than 1,000 publishing houses from thirty-five countries and regions came to the event. They discussed problems of the devaluation of the Chinese currency, the bureaucratic bottlenecking of orders, and the mushrooming of book-importing agencies in China. Foreign exhibitors and Chinese publishers also exchanged opinions.

812. Fields, Howard. "AAP Scales Down Plans for Book Exhibit in China." Publishers Weekly 217 (25): 18 (June 27, 1980).

This reports that the Association of American Publishers cut its budget for a U.S. book exhibit scheduled in China in 1981. It trimmed the original $650,000 budget to $150,000 to make federal support from the International Communication Agency more likely.

813. Foo-Kune, Chinfon. "Periodicals From China and the Use of Pinyin." Interlending Review 7 (2): 59 (April 1979).

The author reports on periodical publications, which have gradually resumed since 1972, and on the 1979 decision to exclusively use the "Pinyin" system of transliteration.

814. Forman, Rose. "Notes on a Shanghai Bookstore." Publishers Weekly 216 (4): 85 (July 23, 1979).

While providing observations on the Shanghai Children's Publishing House and the Children's Bookshop in Shanghai, this article also comments on some aspects of the contents of Chinese children's books.

815. George, Brian. "Publishing and Politics in China." Scholarly Publishing 18 (1): 53-58 (October 1986).

Based on a trip to China in 1983 and the author's service at the New World Press from 1985 to 1986, this article provides an analysis of the history and institutional nature of the Chinese government's Foreign Languages Press and takes a look at its present editorial mechanisms. The article points out that although the Press has always directly reflected the policies of the Chinese government, today it is relatively free of political restrictions and is reaching out to foreign publishers for copublishing partners and effective distribution of its books.

816. Giblin, James Cross. "Three Months Every Year in the Countryside." School Library Journal 22 (9): 25-28 (May 1976).

This is an account of an interview between the author and the staff of the Tientsin People's Publishing House. It includes comments on the decentralization of the publishing industry, book distribution, and the contents and quantity of publications.

817. Giusto, Joann. "Cooperation Grows Between U.S. and Chinese Publishers." Publishers Weekly 215 (2): 23-24 (January 8, 1979).

Giusto reports on various contacts between U.S. and Chinese publishers in the wake of President Carter's announcement to normalize diplomatic relations between the two countries.

818. Herdan, Innes. "New Readers; New Writers." Assistant Librarian 67 (4): 58-60 (April 1974).

These are the author's impressions of a visit to China in 1972. Amazed by the crowds in bookstores everywhere, she points out that neither creative writing nor printing can keep pace with the demands of readers in China.

819. Hickey, Paul Christopher. "Chinese Periodicals and Political Change, 1895-1911." M.A. thesis, Cornell University, 1982. 72 pp.

This thesis focuses on the periodical press and its relationship to public opinion and the politicization process between the end of the Sino-Japanese War in 1895 and the 1911 Revolution. More specifically, it examines problems concerning the distribution and readership of Chinese journals.

820. Hoopes, Townsend. "Showing the Flag in China; A Recent Show of 18,000 U.S. Books in Six Chinese Cities--Without Censorship--Was a Big Boost to Publishing Relations." Publishers Weekly 220 (5): 27-29 (July 31, 1981).

The first large comprehensive exhibit of American books held concurrently in six Chinese cities in 1981 is noted. Supported by the U.S. government through the International Communications Agency, the exhibit was comprised of 18,000 titles divided into four sections: humanities and social sciences, technology and hard sciences, U.S. government publications, and a special composite called "America Through American Eyes." The author notes that as a result of the exhibit, the prospects for increased U.S.-China trade in books are good.

821. Houn, Franklin W. "Publications as a Propaganda Medium in Communist China." Far Eastern Survey 29 (12): 177-186 (December 1960).

Tracing the history of Chinese Communists' utilization of publications as a medium of propaganda since the formation of the party in 1921, this article discusses measures imposed by the Chinese government to exercise thought-control and to secure ideological conformity. It points out that as a result of censorship, various reading materials for public use have been eliminated.

822. Hsiung, Dun Seng. "The Book Industry in Taiwan." Proceedings of the Second Asian-Pacific Conference on Publications, pp. 53-65. Taipei: Publishers' Association of the Republic of China, 1978.

Presented at the Second Asian-Pacific Conference held in Taipei, Taiwan in 1978, this paper contains an introduction to recent conditions in the book industry in the Taiwan area of the Republic of China. Other topics included in the discussion are the expansion of the book market, the efficacy of book exhibitions, the protection of copyrights, contacts between publishers and libraries, the relationships between publishers and writers, awards for publications, and a self-examination in the publishing circles.

823. Hu, Ch'i-ming. "Strengthen Nationalities Publishing Work and Carry Out the 'Politics First and Quality First' Publishing Policy." Selections from China Mainland Magazines No. 354: 10-14 (March 4, 1963). The original article was in Chinese and appeared in Min-tsu T'uan-chieh [Nationalities Unity], (January 1963).

In commemoration of the tenth anniversary of the founding of the Nationalities Publishing House, the article reviews the current status of minority nationalities' publishing activities in China. It also urges workers to follow the policy of "politics first and quality first" to increase publications in the future.

824. Hu, Tseng-jo. "Book-Lending Service Welcomed." Survey of China Mainland Press No. 2754: 15 (June 7, 1962).

Originally appeared in Jen-min Jih-pao [People's Daily] on May 19, 1962, this translated letter describes the booklending services set up by Hsinhua Bookstores in over seventy cities and towns of Kiangsu Province.

825. "Indiana University Press to Co-Publish Chinese Titles." Publishers Weekly 218 (3): 12 (July 8, 1980).

This is a short note about the copublishing agreement signed by Indiana University Press and the Foreign Languages Press of China. It outlines their plan for exchanging personnel and publishing a joint imprint in North America on English-language translations of Chinese literary titles and scholarly books, especially in archaeology.

826. Jurist, Janet. "[Letter in Reply to D. DeBlois.]" AB Bookman's Weekly 65: 833-834 (February 4, 1980).

A brief account of the author's personal experience in hunting old books in China and Hong Kong is described. It also includes notes on book publishing in China.

827. Kapczynski, Helmut, and Field, Sandra. "Notes on a Book Industry Serving 800-million Readers."

Publishers Weekly 214 (11): 68-70+ (September 11, 1978).

This report on a visit to China in 1978 by a delegation of American booksellers provides an overall view of the book trade in China. It describes in detail the organization and function of Hsin-hua (New China) Bookstore, with its head office in Peking, 29 province bureaus, and 5,000 retail outlets throughout China.

828. Keightley, David N. "Bookstores in China." Early China No. 1: 4-6 (Fall 1975).

As one of the "Early Man" delegates, the author depicts his impression of bookstores during his visit to China. He comments on both regular and second-hand bookstores in Peking and Shanghai.

829. Koch, H. William. "People and Publishing in China." Physics Today 32 (8): 32-39 (August 1979).

830. Krader, Ruth. "Sinological Periodicals in Chinese and Japanese." Master of Librarianship, University of Washington, 1955.

This study provides a list of Sinological periodicals in Chinese and Japanese to guide the beginning Western student in the use of periodical literature published in these languages. The list is divided into two sections according to the periodicals' country of origin: China and Japan. Within each section, entries are arranged alphabetically by title.

831. Li, Maria Lien-hui. "A Study of Periodical Publishing in Mainland China, 1949-1966." M.A. thesis, University of Chicago, 1968. 117 pp.

832. Li, Tze-chung. "Publishing in the Republic of China." Journal of Library and Information Science 3 (2): 141-156 (October 1977).

The general publishing situation in Taiwan since 1949 is described. Using statistics, it discusses various types of publications: newspapers, books, magazines, and non-print materials. It also provides information on the import and export of both print and non-print materials and on bibliographical tools published in Taiwan. It includes suggestions for improving the publishing situation.

833. "Library Exhibit in China." Library Journal 54 (6): 265 (March 15, 1929).

This reports on the first elaborate library exhibit held in China in 1929, which was attended by more than 8,000 visitors. The exhibit was planned and supervised by a library specialist and was arranged in ten groups.

834. Lin, Ching-chang. "The Problems of Current Forged Books." Journal of Educational Media and Library Sciences 22 (2): 186-198 (Winter 1985).

Discussing the pirating problem in Taiwan during the past thirty years, this article investigates the causes of the problem and the methods used in producing pirated works authored by Mainland China writers. It also provides tips for identifying or authenticating these forged books. Finally, it proposes several tentative solutions to reduce the problems faced by researchers and librarians. The text is in Chinese, with an abstract in English.

835. Liu, Alan P. L. Book Publishing in Communist China. Cambridge, MA: Center for International Studies, Massachusetts Institute of Technology, 1965. 92 pp.

Liu presents a comprehensive study on the state of publishing in Communist China, which is one of a series of reports on systems of mass communication in Communist China. He examines the historical background of Chinese publishing, current publishing practices under the Communist regime, and the types of books and translations of foreign books published in Communist China.

836. Lo, Karl. "Impressions of the East Asian Antiquarian Book Market." Antiquarian Bookman 38 (1/2): 28-30 (July 4-11, 1966).

This is an account of an American librarian in search of second-hand book dealers in the East Asian countries, including Taiwan. He points out that because the second-hand book market in East Asia is complicated and fluid, it is difficult to work effectively with it from the distant U.S.

837. Lo, Karl. "Publication Trends in the People's Republic of China." Committee on East Asian Libraries Bulletin No. 59: 29-33 (June 1979).

Based on the author's experiences in acquiring Chinese books and his observations while visiting China in 1977, this article describes publishing activity in China after 1976. The author points out that the lack of comprehensive and dependable bibliographic sources providing information about current publications in

China and what kind of publications are available to American readers are major problems in acquiring books from China. He proposes recommendations for U.S. librarians.

838. Lottman, Herbert R. "China: The Inside Story." Publishers Weekly 218 (12): 101-127 (September 19, 1980).

Reporting on a survey of China's new book world, the author attempts to fill in some of the details of the Chinese publishing infrastructure and to update information on the fast-growing book industry. Topics include China's coming book trade, buying for China, selling for China, reaching the customer, the Hsin Hua Book Store, politics and freedom, Shanghai trade, and English in China.

839. Lottman, Herbert R. "China's Publishing Operations Reorganized." Publishers Weekly 221 (22): 16 (May 28, 1982).

Lottman reports on the reorganization of China's publishing operations, which includes the integration of China's National Publishing Administration into the Ministry of Culture. He points out that publishing houses will retain their autonomy and predicts an increase in publishing activities.

840. Lucas, Barbara. "China: Growing Toward the Year 2000." Publishers Weekly 216 (4): 83-86 (July 23, 1979).

This reports on the 1979 visit to the Children's Book Publishing House in Shanghai and the Kwangchow School for the Deaf in Canton by the author and members of the U.S. Readers and Booksellers Delegation. It briefly discusses various aspects of the publishing house.

841. "Marek Signs Trade Book Agreement with China." Publishers Weekly 217 (18): 13 (May 9, 1980).

This is a news announcement that on April 4, 1980 Richard Marek Publishers, Inc. became the first American publisher to sign a trade book agreement with the People's Republic of China.

842. Martinique, Edward. "The Availability of Publications from China Since the Fall of the 'Gang.'" A paper presented to the panel, "Asian Studies in the 1980's: An Overview of Research, Resources, and Computerized Bibliographic Access," at the Association for Asian

Studies/Southeastern Conference, Washington and Lee University, Lexington, VA, January 24, 1981.

843. Mitchell, Edna. "Children's Books from the People's Republic of China." Language Arts 59 (1): 30-37 (January 1980).

The author analyzes children's books from the People's Republic of China since 1965. She finds that although children's books are widely available and inexpensive and their use is encouraged at home and at school, the themes of these stories are limited. The majority of the books carry political messages and follow a party-line formula for teaching the specific values of revolutionary Communism.

844. Myers, Ramon H. "Government Statistics in China." Reference Services Review 10 (3): 91-93 (Fall 1982).

Presented as part of the GODORT International Documents Task Force's program, "Statistics on Developing Countries," at the 1981 American Library Association's Annual Conference in San Francisco, this paper explores how statistics are produced and used in China and when the first impulses for a modern statistical system arose. The author advises librarians to warn patrons about the problems with Chinese government statistics and recommends a remedy for the current situation.

845. Nerbonne, Joseph J. "Book Pirating Is Lively on Formosa but Authorized Reprints Are Making Gains." Publishers Weekly 214 (6): 28-30 (August 7, 1978).

This is an account of book pirating in Taiwan and the ongoing problems of gaining legitimization for authorized reprints. The author explains why piracy persists and traces the development of authorized reprints, mainly from the U.S. and England. He maintains that the problem of pirating is decreasing as more publishers seek authorized reprints.

846. "New Books from Shanghai." Peking Review 15 (21): 22 (May 26, 1972).

Commenting on new books published in Shanghai in the last few years, this short article notes that the most popular types of materials relate to socialist revolutions and construction, science and technology, and the study of Marxism-Leninism-Mao Tsetung thought.

847. "New Policy on Popular Books." Current Scene 9 (12): 19-21 (December 1971).

This comments on an article entitled "Publish More and Better Popular Reading Material," which appeared in Red Flag. It urges a relaxation of restrictions on non-political publications and the publication of more novels, reading materials for young people, and popular readings on science and technology.

848. Nunn, G. Raymond. Chinese Publishing Statistics, 1949-1959. Ann Arbor: Committee on American Library Resources on the Far East, Association for Asian Studies, 1960, unpaged.

Supported by a grant from the National Science Foundation to the Association for Asian Studies, this paper presents a statistical tabulation of Mainland China's publishing activities in the social, natural, and applied sciences, 1949-59. The data in this paper have been compiled from the Chinese National Bibliography in its editions covering publishing for the years 1949-58. It is arranged by subject.

849. Nunn, G. Raymond. "Mainland China." In Trans-Pacific Scholarly Publishing: A Symposium, edited by Thomas Nickerson, pp. 98-103. Honululu: East-West Center Press, 1963.

Largely based on Mainland China sources, this study considers book publishing and the possibilities of involving China in the general development of scholarly publishing. It also is concerned with publishing as a channel for distributing social, natural, and applied scientific information within and from Mainland China.

850. Nunn, G. Raymond. Publishing in Mainland China. Cambridge, MA: MIT Press, 1966. 83 pp.

This study analyzes the organization of book and periodical publishing in China from 1949 to 1964, with special emphasis on the natural, applied, and social sciences. It discusses the flow of information from outside China and its development in China, publication of books and periodicals, distribution, and libraries.

851. Nwafor, B. U. "Problems of the Book Trade Infrastructure in Developing Countries in Relation to University Library Objectives." IFLA Journal 10 (4): 357-369 (1984).

This paper explores the variety and magnitude of the infrastructural problems of the book industry in Nigeria, Argentina, and the People's Republic of China, particularly in relation to university library objectives. It discusses such topics as authorship, printing, publishing, and distribution. It singles out the Chinese New China Bookstore as a model for bookstores in developing countries.

852. Peterson, Olga M. "So You're Celebrating China Book Week!" American Library Association Bulletin 38 (1): 11-13 (January 1944).

In 1944, the Office of War Information organized an information program on China, with emphasis on its libraries and bookstores operations. In cooperation, the American Library Association (ALA) designated March 25-31 as China Book Week. Peterson, chief of ALA Public Relations Division, describes ways and means of celebrating it.

853. "Reaching the Customer: Xin Hua Book Store." Publishers Weekly 218 (12): 110-112 (September 19, 1980).

Describing the network of Hsin Hua distribution centers, this article indicates that there is one center in each of the twenty-nine metropolitan districts, provinces, and autonomous regions and one in each of China's 2,470 counties, serving all of the country's 5,000 retail outlets. The article also mentions the publishing process in the book industry in China.

854. Richter, Harald. Publishing in the People's Republic of China: Personal Observations by a Foreign Student, 1975-1977. Hamburg: Institut für Asienkunde, 1978. 114 pp.

Based on the author's personal experiences and the material and information collected during his 18-month stay in China as an exchange student, this book deals with the organization of bookstores and major centers of the book trade. It then discusses access to bibliographies, the classification of printed materials, the situation in the market for periodicals, the export of books, and customs control. It includes bibliographical notes on selected groups of publications.

855. "Shanghai Bookstores Run Lending Libraries." Survey of China Mainland Press No. 5622: 22-23 (May 28, 1974).

This is a description of ten branch stores of the Hsinhua Bookstore in Shanghai which started lending books to supplement the existing network of facilities for the reading public.

856. Shu, Hsin-ch'eng. "Current Problems of Publishing." Survey of China Mainland Press No. 1587: 17-28 (August 9, 1957).

The author outlines the achievements of the publication business and identifies its principal problems, including a shortage of books and raw materials for publications, problems with the cadres, problems of organization and leadership, and problems with woodblocks. He also recommends ways to solve the problems by calling a national publishing conference, training cadres by various means, putting in order and reprinting old books, preserving old woodblocks, developing the production of handmade paper for printing old books, establishing a state editorial bureau to work on a Chinese encyclopedia, and strengthening leadership at key points.

857. Soong, James Chu-yul. "Chinese Publications in Early 1973." Journal of Asian Studies 33 (2): 289-293 (February 1974).

The article attempts to discuss recent developments in Chinese publishing by examining the first five issues of the Ch'üan-kuo hsin shu-mu [the National Bibliography], published in 1973. It gives special attention to a number of the important works listed.

858. Šťovíčková-Heroldová, Dana. "Chinese Books." Eastern Horizon 4 (8): 50-52 (August 1965).

Based on the author's experience in buying books in China, the article comments on Chinese booksellers, bookbinding, and the popularity of books in the 1960's.

859. Ting, Lee-hsia Hsu. Government Control of the Press in Modern China, 1900-1949. Cambridge, MA: East Asian Research Center, Harvard University, 1974. 318 pp.

Based on the author's Ph.D. dissertation from the University of Chicago in 1969, this study traces the development of publication laws and regulations, presents many censorship cases, and discusses various problems, emphasizing the suppression of "dangerous" publications between 1900 and 1949. It is chiefly concerned with books, newspapers, and magazines. The materials are presented chronologically according to five political eras in Chinese history: (1) the last years of the Ch'ing Dynasty, 1900-11; (2) the first fifteen years of the new republic, 1912-27; (3) the pre-war years under the Kuomintang rule, 1927-37; (4)

the war of resistance, 1937-45; and (5) the post-war years, 1945-49.

860. Tsai, David Wu-hsiung. "A Study of Modern Chinese Government Publications, 1912-1949." Ph.D. thesis, University of Chicago, 1979. 429 pp.

Based on a bibliographical survey of forty bibliographies and catalogs containing Chinese government publications, the study attempts to investigate the background and history of government publishing during the Republican Period, from 1912 to 1949. It discusses in detail the organization of modern Chinese government publishing, the pattern of government publishing in terms of centralization or decentralization, the degree to which the Chinese government is involved in printing and publishing, and the types and distribution of government publications.

861. Ts'ui, Yueh-hsien. "Deliver Books to the Peasants." Selections from China Mainland Magazines No. 510: 36-41 (February 7, 1966). Originally published in Hung-ch'i [Red Flag] (No. 1, January 1, 1966).

Ts'ui outlines the achievements of a book distributor in the Hsinhua Bookstore's Sungking Retail Department in Kirin Province.

862. "U.S. Ambassador Denies Aid for Book Exhibit in China." Publishers Weekly 217 (20): 14+ (May 23, 1980).

This reports on U.S. Ambassador Leonard Woodcock's refusal to endorse an American book exhibit, designed to introduce 25,000 titles to millions of Chinese people in six major cities and requested by the Chinese government.

863. Wang, Chi. "Increases in Periodical, Newspaper Publishing Reported in China." Library of Congress Information Bulletin 40 (8): 62-63 (February 20, 1981).

Wang reports on the hugh increase in the publication of periodicals and newspapers in the People's Republic of China. The author observes the total number amounts to between 7,000 and 8,000 items in recent years.

864. Wang, Sing-wu. "Chinese Periodicals and Newspapers." East Asian Librarians' Group of Australia Newsletter No. 5: 1-6 (June 1981).

Based on a 1980 visit to ten libraries in Peking, Shanghai, Hangchou, and Canton, this article provides a recent history and current survey of periodicals and newspapers published in China. The author concludes, with the support of five statistical tables, that China has published more journals on science and technology than on other areas and that the humanities and social sciences have not been treated as seriously as science and technology.

865. Wu, Eugene. "Recent Developments in Chinese Publishing." China Quarterly No. 53: 134-138 (January/March 1973).

This is a research note on the current state of publishing in China and the acquisition of Chinese language materials by American libraries, with reference to the factors which are likely to influence the future flow of materials from China. It also compares publications before and after the Cultural Revolution.

866. Wu, K. T., and Wang, Chi. "China." Library of Congress Quarterly Journal 26 (2): 92-96 (April 1969).

Describing reference publications from Mainland China, Taiwan, Hong Kong, and the U.S. that are essential to libraries, this article provides a detailed annotation for each item. Important titles include the National Catalog of New Books, Cumulative National Bibliography, The Monthly List of Chinese Books, and Contemporary China.

867. Yang, Yu. "A Visit to the China Youth Publishing House." Chinese Literature No. 8: 107-112 (1964).

This article presents the author's impressions of a visit to the Literary Section of the China Youth Publishing House, one of China's best known publishers serving young people. It also notes some of the popular titles produced by the Publishing House.

868. Yen, Marianne. "American Books in China: The First Shanghai International Book Fair." Publishers Weekly 227 (22): 25-29 (May 31, 1985).

Yen provides a detailed description of the First Shanghai International Book Fair, held in 1985. She mentions problems and suggestions for the future book fair. She also introduces the operations of the China National Publications Import and Export Corporation and the China Book Import Center.

869. Yen, Marianne. "China Offers U.S. Books 'Exciting Opportunities.'" Publishers Weekly 227 (16): 13 (April 19, 1985).

This article reports comments by Henry Noyes, founder of China Books and Periodicals, on his visit to China. Noyes points out that the Chinese are interested in importing and exporting general Western titles and are willing to copublish or sell manuscripts to the West. However, he cautions about the copyright problem and other difficulties of copublishing.

870. Yu, P. K. "Bibliographic Control in the People's Republic of China, 1949-1972." Paper presented at the 28th Annual Meeting of the Association for Asian Studies, Chicago, 1973; Conference report of the International Federation of Library Associations' 39th session, Grenoble, France, 1973. 31 leaves.

Divided into five sections, this paper includes: (1) statistics on publications in China, 1949-66, by geographical distribution and by field; (2) a discussion of the most important bibliographical tools published in Communist China, the National Bibliography and the Cumulative National Bibliography; (3) an exploration of the bibliographic control of newspapers and periodicals; (4) lists of known titles of bibliographies and indexes in chronological order and grouped by subjects; and (5) an examination of future developments in bibliographic control in China.

871. Yu, P. K. "Bibliographic Control in the People's Republic of China, 1949-1973." In Studies Presented to Dr. Chien Mu on His Eightieth Birthday, pp. 1-19. Hong Kong: New Asia Research Institute, 1974.

This is a revision of the paper presented at the International Federation of Library Associations' thirty-ninth session at Grenoble, France in 1973. For annotation, see #870.

9

General Works

872. "ARL Chinese Import Center Funded for Two More Years." Library Journal 98 (22): 3593 (December 15, 1973).

This reports on the two-year extension of a grant to the Center for Chinese Materials from the National Endowment for the Humanities. It also notes recent acquisitions from Mainland China and Taiwan.

873. "Association of Research Libraries Announced the Establishment of a Center for Chinese Research Materials." Wilson Library Bulletin 43 (2): 103 (October 1968).

A news item on the Association's establishment of a Center for Chinese Research Materials in Washington, D.C., supported by a Ford Foundation grant. The Center is expected to increase the availability of publications in Chinese on contemporary China.

874. Bell, Lynda S., and Chauncey, Helen R. "Republican Period Library and Archival Research in Contemporary China." China Exchange News 12 (3): 12-15 (September 1984).

The authors recount their experience in using library and archival materials during 1979-1981 to conduct research on the Republican period in China. Despite the frustrations encountered in securing materials at libraries and archives, they found research in contemporary China well worth the effort. They hope that in the future there will be more access to some of the richest materials currently off-limits to foreign scholars.

875. Berninghausen, David K. "Research in Librarianship." Bibliotheca No. 1: 1-10 (April 1967).

This article discusses the need for research in librarianship in Taiwan in general, and at the National Taiwan University in particular. It concludes that library education in Taiwan, with emphasis on research, is the key to the future of librarianship.

876. Bishop, Enid. "Aspects of Chinese Librarianship in Australia: Three Decades at the Australian National University." In Essays in Commemoration of the Golden Jubilee of the Fung Ping Shan Library (1932-1982): Studies in Chinese Librarianship, Literature, Language, History and Arts, edited by Chan Ping-leung and others, pp. 58-79. Hong Kong: Fung Ping Shan Library, University of Hong Kong, 1982.

Divided into three periods, this paper retraces the events, conditions, and influences which have shaped the history of the Australian National University's Chinese collection since 1950: (1) the first decade, 1950-60; (2) amalgamation, planning, and growth, 1960-70; and (3) achieving maturity, 1970-80. In addition, it discusses the technical problems of processing Chinese materials and professional development. It also briefly mentions the 1980's and beyond. "Rationalization Scheme for Cooperative Acquisitions of Chinese Materials," agreed to at a conference between the Australian National University and the National Library of Australia in 1973, is appended.

877. Bixler, Paul, ed. "Libraries in the Far East: An Inquiry into the State of the Library Art in Burma, Taiwan, Communist China, Korea, Indonesia, and East Pakistan." Library Journal 87 (20): 4123-4151+ (November 15, 1962).

This is a selection of six papers on libraries in the Far East, two of which concern China: (1) "Taiwan: Continuation of New Patterns," by Pearl Wu (pp. 4129-4132); and (2) "Communist China: Restoration and Expansion," by Leslie T. C. Kuo (pp. 4137-4142). See annotations #318 and #225 respectively.

878. Cha, Lincoln H. "Library Legislation in China." In Libraries in China, pp. 67-72. Peking: Library Association of China, 1935.

Cha describes in detail the contents of the first library law in China, codified by the Ministry of Education and sanctioned by the ex-emperor in 1908. He also surveys subsequent regulations governing various aspects of library operation which were promulgated between 1915 and 1932.

879. Chang, Chin-lang. "The Origin and Usage of Chinese Encyclopedias." Journal of Educational Media Science 19 (4): 394-409 (Summer 1982).

This article explores the historical background and origin of Chinese encyclopedias and discusses their usage. It especially explains the arrangement, identification, and classification of the tool used. It also introduces the special features and usage of some important Chinese encyclopedias. The text is in Chinese, with an abstract in English.

880. Chang, Yih-der. "How to Study Bibliography: A Personal Point of View." Journal of Educational Media and Library Sciences 20 (4): 385-395 (Summer 1983).

Based on personal experience and profound learning, this article provides an interesting and useful account in the study of Chinese bibliography. It also lists and reviews ten most commonly used bibliographies and remarks on their merits and defects for reference purposes.

881. Chen, Eunice. "A Study of the Chinese Library Association." M.A. thesis, Kent State University, 1962. 104 leaves.

This study first describes Chinese libraries in Taiwan and then elaborates upon the history, organization, and location of the Chinese Library Association, which was founded in 1953 in Taipei. Finally, it analyzes the data by examining such characteristics as sex distribution, status by age, sex by age, sex of members, and educational levels of members.

882. Ch'iao, Yen-kuan. "About Biographical Materials: A Review in Guide to Chinese Reference Books." Journal of Educational Media and Library Sciences 21 (3): 321-328 (Spring 1984).

Citing Chapter 7 of Chin-lang Chang's Guide to Chinese Reference Books, this article elaborates upon the classification, function, layout, coverage, and merits and defects of the biographical materials. The guide intends to facilitate users' access to biographical materials by systematically introducing reference books. The text is in Chinese, with an abstract in English.

883. "China and Korea." In History of Libraries: Ancient and Mediaeval, edited by D. N. Marshall, pp. 119-128. New Delhi: Oxford and IBH Publishing Company, 1983.

Surveying the course of learning and libraries in China, this chapter provides an account of the important role China has played in the history of libraries, from oracle bones to paper writing, and from the building of imperial libraries to their contribution to world culture.

884. "China Expected to Move on Copyright Statute." AB Bookman's Weekly 74 (10): 1290 (September 3, 1984).

Reported by David Ladd, U.S. Register of Copyrights, this describes his trip to Shanghai and Peking for the Patent, Trademark and Copyright Law Section of the American Bar Association. Ladd predicts the enactment of copyright statutes by the People's Republic of China but cautions that the Chinese be allowed to develop their own copyright regime according to their needs.

885. "China Sets Up Library Society." IFLA Journal 5 (4): 349 (1979).

Announcing the formation and aims of the China Society of Libraries, this news item also provides information about China's first National Forum on Library Science, held in Peking in 1979.

886. "China Society for Scientific and Technical Information." Journal of Information Science 9 (1): 29-30 (August 1984).

An organizational profile of the China Society for Scientific and Technical Information (CSSTI), a professional organization under the China Science Association, is described. Established in 1978, the Society has 36 corporate and more than 10,000 individual members. This article states the aims, objectives, organizational structure, academic activities, international activities, financial sources, and address of CSSTI.

887. "The China Society of Library Science." Committee on East Asian Libraries Bulletin No. 64: 12-16 (February 1981).

This describes the establishment of the Society in 1979, outlines the professional qualifications for membership, and lists its chief officers and publications. It also describes the activities carried on by twenty-eight library societies in China.

888. "Chinese Honor A.L.A." Library Journal 66 (15): 723 (September 1, 1941).

This is a news item on a gift received by the American Library Association from librarians in war-torn China as a token of their appreciation for services rendered by American libraries. Over twenty thousand books were sent to Chinese colleges and universities which were destroyed by the war.

889. "Chinese LA." Library Association Record 81 (10): 470 (October 1979).

Reporting the formation of the China Society of Libraries, the first library association in China, this news item outlines its aims, activities, and publications.

890. "Chinese Research Center Established by ARL." Library Journal 93 (15): 2950 (September 1, 1968).

This is an announcement about the establishment of a Center for Chinese Research Materials by the Association of Research Libraries. The Center will serve American libraries by acquiring and distributing important publications from Mainland China.

891. "Chinese Society of Librarianship." East Asian Librarians' Group of Australia Newsletter No. 4: 3-6 (June 1980).

Translated by S. W. Wang, this is the Constitution of the Chinese Society of Librarianship adopted at the General Meeting of Representatives of the Society on July 13, 1979.

892. Chou, Nelson. "Information, Library and Library Education." Journal of Library and Information Science 10 (1): 33-39 (April 1984).

The author attempts to define the following terms in order to clarify misconceptions created by the news media about their use in Taiwan: information and computer, information system and computer system, information science and computer science, and information industry and computer industry. He also discusses the relationship between information, libraries, and library education in Taiwan.

893. Clift, D. H. "Association of Research Libraries Announced the Establishment of the Center for Chinese Research Materials." American Library Association Bulletin 62 (7): 804 (July/August 1968).

This is a news item on the establishment of the Center for Chinese Research Materials to be located in the headquarters of the Association of Research Libraries in Washington, D.C. The new Center is supported by a grant from the Ford Foundation to promote research on Chinese publications.

894. Cooper, Douglas W. "Library Literature in Mainland China: A Content Analysis." College and Research Libraries 48 (3): 194-202 (May 1987). An earlier version of the article in somewhat different form under the authorship of T. H. Chow and D. W. Cooper appeared in Papers of the Library Cooperation and Development Seminar, August 17-18, 1986, pp. 11.1-11.20. Taipei: National Central Library, [1987].

Presented at the 1986 Library Cooperation and Development Seminar in Taiwan, this paper analyzes the library literature published in 1985 in three of Mainland China's journals: Bulletin of the China Society of Library Science, Library and Information Services, and Library Journal. It also compares these writings with reports regarding the current library science literature on China published in the West. It concludes that much remains to be done in the library science field in the People's Republic of China.

895. "Copyright Delegation Reports Impressions of Visit to China." Library of Congress Information Bulletin 40 (30): 241-242 (July 24, 1981).

This reports on a copyright delegation's visit to Peking and Shanghai at the invitation of the National Publishing Administration and the Publishers Association of China in 1981. The delegate notes that the Chinese are willing to share their problems and concerns about copyright and are serious about developing an internal copyright structure.

896. "Copyright Publications Presented to People's Republic of China." Library of Congress Information Bulletin 41 (27): 197-198 (July 2, 1982).

This is a news item about the shipment of forty-seven titles on basic copyright publications to China which were requested by the Chinese Copyright Working Group. It points out that these books will help speed up the process of drafting copyright laws in China.

897. Essays in Commemoration of the Golden Jubilee of the Fung Ping Shan Library (1932-1982): Studies in Chinese Librarianship, Literature, Language, History and Arts, edited by Chan Ping-leung and others. Hong Kong: Fung Ping Shan Library, University of Hong Kong, 1982. 439 pp.

A collection of articles on the subjects mentioned in the title of the book, including five articles on library science: Sing-wu Wang's "Recent Development of Library and Information Services in China" (#259); Tung-king Ng's "The Chinese Collections in Canada: A

Review of Their Development and Status in Academic Libraries" (#609); Enid Bishop's "Aspects of Chinese Librarianship in Australia: Three Decades at the Australian National University" (#876); Nelson Chou's "Information Retrieval and the Chinese Language" (#653); and Karl K. Lo's "The Chinese Vernacular Presses in North America, 1900-1950: Their Role in Social Cohesion."

898. "The Fight Against Piracy." Publishers Weekly 218 (12): 107-108 (September 19, 1980).

While describing the discovery of pirated editions of Western books in the back rooms of a distribution center in Peking, this article also summarizes the provisions of a government regulation to stamp out the practice.

899. "Focus on Library and Archival Research." China Exchange News 12 (3): 1-20 (September 1984).

This is a collection of firsthand accounts by historians who used Chinese archives and libraries during their research in China. The articles include: "An Overview of Libraries in the People's Republic of China," by Chi Wang (#258); "Doing Library and Archival Research on Local History: A Study of Huizhou Prefecture during the Ming and Qing Periods," by Harriet Zurndorfer (#943); "Working at the First Historical Archives in Beijing," by Yeh-chien Wang (#511); "Library Resources for Qing Studies in Nanjing," by Barry Keenan (#387); "Republican Period Library and Archival Research in Contemporary China," by Lynda S. Bell and Helen R. Chauncey (#874); "Foreign Student Use of Libraries in Shanghai," by Ernst Schwintzer (#404); and "The Shanghai Municipal Archives," by Bryna Goodman (#503).

900. Foo-Kune, Chinfon, and Helliwell, D. J. "China Library Group." In SCONUL Group of Orientalist Libraries: Report of the Annual Conference Held at the University of Durham, 6-7, January 1977, p. 33. London: The Group of Orientalist Libraries of the Standing Conference of National and University Libraries, 1977.

Reporting on the formation of the new China Library Group in London in 1976, this note outlines its scheduled activities and immediate projects.

901. Fu, Tina C. "Chinese Women Library Workers." WLW Journal 7 (3): 2-3 (July/September 1982). Reprinted from Feminist Collections 3 (2): 7-8 (Spring 1982).

Recording a two-hour meeting with ten Chinese women library workers in 1981, this article discusses salaries, the sex ratio in key library administrative positions, equality in promotions and salary increases, and Women's Studies collections.

902. Fung, Margaret C. On Library and Information Science. Taipei: Student Book Company, 1982. 227 pp.

This is a collection of sixteen articles, either in Chinese or in English, published by the author during the past two years. Some of the titles are concerned with the development, services, and automation of libraries in Taiwan.

903. Harvey, John F. "Critique of Seven Asian-English Language Library Serials." The Serials Librarian 7 (2): 61-73 (Winter 1982).

Harvey reviews five periodicals and two continuations according to a set of about sixty criteria which are arranged under three headings: journal information, circulation information, and paper information. One of the titles reviewed, the Journal of Library and Information Science, is from Taiwan.

904. Hays, Florence C. "Another Letter from China." Public Libraries 28 (7): 358 (July, 1923).

Addressed to public libraries in the U.S., this letter reports on a meeting held in Kuling, China in 1922 by five Chinese librarians who discussed the possibilities of cooperation among libraries and the formation of an organization of librarians in East China.

905. Hsia, Tao-tai, and Haun, Kathryn. "Communist Chinese Legislation on Publications and Libraries." Quarterly Journal of the Library of Congress 27 (1): 20-33 (January 1970).

This article summarizes in chronological order seventeen of the most important provisions in the laws and decrees pertaining to publications and library services in China. The authors divide the discussion into two periods: (1) the Pre-Constitutional Enactments period, when measures to provide and to control publishing enterprises were established; and (2) the Post-1954 Enactments period, when the Chinese government enforced policies concerning the legal deposit of publications and promoted library services.

906. Hsia, Tao-tai. Guide to Selected Legal Sources of Mainland China: A Listing of Laws and Regulations and

Periodical Legal Literature with a Brief Survey of the Administration of Justice. Washington, D.C.: Library of Congress, 1967. 357 pp.

This guide lists translated titles of laws and regulations in Mainland China from 1949 to 1963 and articles relating to legal matters selected from Chinese periodicals. The laws are arranged in chronological order and subdivided by subjects. Specific laws and regulations governing libraries and publications can be accessed through the use of the subject index.

907. Hsia, Tao-tai. "National Report: People's Republic of China--the Legal System and Literature of the People's Republic of China." International Journal of Law Libraries 2 (2): 74-84 (July 1974).

Offering an overview of the Chinese legal system, this paper emphasizes its most basic and distinctive features, and makes some general remarks about Chinese legal literature. For discussion purposes, the article divides the development of law in China into six periods since the founding of the People's Republic in 1949. It also gives an idea of the unique problems Chinese law poses for American law librarians.

908. Hsu, Chia-pi. "An Inquiry into the Chinese National Library Act Relating to Public Libraries: An Historic-Analytic Study with Practical Suggestions for Its Future Development." Master's thesis, School of Library Science, Columbia University, 1949. 135 leaves.

The study explores the field and discovers the merits and weaknesses of the library act. It deals with the area of national library legislation in China relating to public libraries, with emphasis on an examination of the national library act of April 1947. It considers whether there is a need for its immediate revision.

909. Hung, Y. F. "Chinese Librarians in Conference." Library Journal 47 (16): 770 (September 15, 1922).

This is a news item about the meeting of the Library Section during the annual conference of the National Association for the Promotion of Education in 1922, where eight proposals were formulated and ways of carrying them out were suggested.

910. "ICLG China Seminar." Focus on International Comparative Librarianship 12 (1): 11-12 (1981).

Reporting on the Library Association International Comparative Librarianship Group's seminar on the People's Republic of China in 1981, this article presents information on cultural relations between Great Britain and China, publishing in China, the British Council and China, Chinese librarianship in the twentieth century, and information services and current library development in China.

911. Koh, Thong-ngee. "The Beginning of Chinese Bibliography: A Study of the Record of Literature in the History of Former Han Dynasty (206 B.C.--A.D. 8)." The Repository No. 7/8: 26-41 (Spring/Summer 1964); No. 9/10: 1-26 (Fall/Winter 1964).

Based on the author's M.A. thesis at the University of Chicago in 1963, this lengthy two-part article, analyzes the principles of classification and cataloging demonstrated in the bibliography, the Record of Literature. The study also investigates the events which led to its production and the work of bibliographers who contributed to it.

912. Kwei, John Chih-ber. "A Chinese Library Meeting." Libraries 31 (2): 88 (February 1926).

This reports on a library section held in connection with the Second Biennial Conference of the China Association for Christian Higher Education in 1926. It includes a list of suggested topics for the library sectional meetings.

913. "Ladd Predicts Chinese Copyright Law in 3-5 Years." Copyright Notices 32 (8): 1+ (August 1984).

914. Lai, Yung-hsiang. "Oriental Research Resources in Taiwan." NTU Library Science Booklet No. 3: 1-35 (August 1967).

Prepared for the panel on "Library Resources in Asian Studies" of the Twenty-seventh International Congress of Orientalists held in Ann Arbor, Michigan in 1967, this paper describes the libraries and archives which hold some notable oriental resources in Taiwan, including the National Central Library, Academia Sinica, National Palace Museum, National Museum of History, Kuomintang Party Archives, Academia Historica, Provincial Taipei Library, Provincial Taiwan Museum, Historical Research Commission of Taiwan Province, and college and university libraries. It also notes various union catalogs, bibliographies, and periodical holdings for further consultation and identification of the holding institutions.

915. "LC's Chinese Periodical Microfilming Project." Library of Congress Information Bulletin 25 (26): 343-370 (June 30, 1966).

This provides information on the microfilming of 109 periodical titles in the social sciences and the humanities published in Mainland China between October 1959 and December 1963. It also includes a list of titles with price and ordering information.

916. Lee, Chang C. "Institution Building for Library Services Development in Taiwan." Journal of Educational Media Science 18 (2): 53-64 (Winter 1980).

Based on the concepts of the institution building model designed by Milton J. Esman, this paper examines the current status of Taiwan's library services and makes a feasible and realistic suggestion for their reform. It recommends that the Ministry of Education build an institution called the Office of Library Services to serve as a central governing body of libraries in Taiwan in order to induce changes and to improve the poor library services.

917. Lee, Hwa-wei. "Challenges for the Library and Information Profession." Journal of Educational Media and Library Sciences 21 (3): 248-265 (Spring 1984). Also published in the commemorative volume of the Bulletin of the Library Association of China No. 35: 235-246 (December 18, 1983).

Dedicated to the Library Association of China on its thirteenth anniversary, this essay identifies five important challenges for the library and information profession in the coming years, and discusses them in terms of their relevance to Taiwan: (1) the information explosion and information pollution; (2) new information technology; (3) the changing roles of libraries and information centers; (4) requirements for new professional competencies; and (5) global interdependence. It also focuses on ways in which the profession can relate to and cope with the challenge of the "information age."

918. Library Association of China. Libraries in China: Papers Prepared on the Occasion of the Tenth Anniversary of the Library Association of China. Peking: Library Association of China, 1935. 132 pp.

This is a collection of nine articles reviewing the progress made by Chinese libraries between 1925 and 1935. The articles include: "Modern Library Movement in China," by A. Kaiming Chiu (#142); "Ten Years of

Classification and Cataloguing in China," by K. T. Wu (#587); "Professional Training of Librarianship in China," by Samuel T. Y. Sneg (#767); "Library Legislation in China," by Lincoln H. Cha (#878); "Co-operation Between Chinese Libraries," by W. Y. Yen (#209); "National Libraries in China," by Fu-tsung Chiang (#324); "The Provincial Libraries in China," by I-cheng Liu (#439); "Medical Libraries in China," by Julie Rummelhoff Tai (#483); and "Public Libraries and Adult Education in China," by Ding U Doo (#429).

919. Liu, Chao-yu. "Academic Research and Reference Tools." Journal of Educational Media and Library Sciences 22 (3): 250-255 (Spring 1985).

Examining the close relationship between an author's originality and the success of academic research, this article points out the importance and effective use of reference tools in doing research, with a particular focus on Chinese reference materials. It urges researchers to pay more attention to the acquisition and use of reference tools in the library. The text is in Chinese, with an abstract in English.

920. Liu, Songfu. "A Proposed Model for Interlibrary Lending in China." Interlending and Document Delivery: IATUL Proceedings, edited by Nancy Fjällbrant, vol. 16, pp. 73-89. Gothenburg, Sweden: International Association of Technical University Libraries, 1984. (ED 256 374).

Providing an overview of interlending and document delivery in China, this paper notes the population distribution, administration divisions, transportation, and library and information centers in China. It also describes the roles of four institutions in the national library and information field. It discusses the existing pattern of interlibray loan and its problems, and proposes a model for interlending in science and technology.

921. Luo, Xingyun. "Management Development and Its Practice in Chinese Library and Information Services." International Library Review 17 (2): 129-149 (April 1985).

Tracing the development of business and library management in Western countries, this article deals with management approaches in China in general and in Chinese library and information services in particular. It discusses suggestions for improving Chinese library services, such as greater geographic distribution, regional cooperation, national referral services, open access, a publicity and users' survey, library education, personnel management, and a library act.

922. "National Bibliography of China: Retrospect and Prospect." International Cataloguing 15 (1): 5-8 (January/March 1986).

Prepared by the National Bibliography Section, National Library of China, Peking, for the Fifty-first IFLA Council and General Conference in Chicago, this paper provides historical background on the bibliography in China and the organization of ancient bibliographies. It discusses modern bibliographies, with emphasis on the Chinese national bibliography. It outlines the actual scope of the Chinese National Bibliography, which is scheduled for publication in 1987 and will be available in three different forms: book form, card form, and machine-readable tapes.

923. National Central Library. Proceedings of the 1980 Library Development Seminar, December 1-7, 1980, Taipei. Taipei: National Central Library, 1981. 547 pp.

The proceedings include thirty-four papers presented at four sessions of the meeting held in Taipei in 1980. The majority of the papers are concerned with Chinese libraries and librarianship, library automation, and information retrieval systems being developed in Taiwan.

924. Nelson, Dale. "China Moves Toward Copyright Law." Wilson Library Bulletin 57 (9): 758-759 (May 1983).

This is a short note on the current status of China's copyright law and the process of drafting such laws in the near future.

925. Otness, Harold M. "Bibliography of the Far Eastern Tropics: Taiwan's Pioneer Union List." Journal of Educational Media Science 19 (3): 284-291 (Spring 1982).

Otness describes a published union catalog compiled in Taiwan in 1938: the Bibliography of the Far Eastern Tropics. The catalog, which includes the Western language holdings of the Southeast Asian materials of eight Taiwan research libraries, is considered the first interlibrary cooperation effort and a valuable historical record of library development in Taiwan.

926. "Peking Library Association." Library Journal 44 (8): 553 (August 1919).

The establishment of the Peking Library Association is announced in this news item. It notes that any institution which possesses a library and maintains the services of a regular librarian is eligible for institutional membership.

927. "Post-Conference China Study Tour." Library of Congress Information Bulletin 39 (48): 468 (November 28, 1980).

This is a news item on the post-IFLA China study tour, sponsored by the American Library Association, which twenty-six librarians went on in 1980. It notes that the two most interesting topics for the Chinese librarians were the second edition of the Anglo-American Cataloguing Rules (AACR2) and automation.

928. "PRC Establishes Library Association." Library of Congress Information Bulletin 38: 369 (September 7, 1979).

While reporting on the establishment of the Chinese Library Association and China's first national meeting on library science in 1979, this also announces the publication of the first issue of the Association's Library Science Bulletin.

929. "Priorities and Troublespots in Chinese Studies Pegged." Library Journal 99 (19): 2789 (November 1, 1974).

This is a news item about a Chinese Studies conference held in 1973. Among the topics discussed which should be of interest to librarians involved in Chinese Studies are: the role of the Library of Congress as a national center for Chinese research, competition among libraries for meager funding, the role of major libraries, the Center for Chinese Research Materials as a model national institution, field development priorities, professional development, and the establishment of an ad hoc committee on library problems in Chinese Studies.

930. Seng, Harris B. H. "Research in Librarianship in the Republic of China." Research Librarianship 3 (17): 133-136 (May 1971).

Citing three reasons for the productive research activities, this paper reports on the research situation in Taiwan after 1948: (1) there are more opportunities for the publication of research papers; (2) reading materials are better organized for research work; and (3) there has been a change away from the American method. The paper also identifies problems of research.

931. "Some Notes on the Library Association of China." NTU Library Science Circular No. 9: 1-4 (December 1968).

Highlighting the main contributions of the Library Association of China between 1953 and 1968, this article discusses its constitution, name, purpose, location, activities, membership, organization, honorary directors, membership dues, and annual meeting. The program of its sixteenth annual conference is appended.

932. Swann, Nancy Lee. "Seven Intimate Library Owners." Harvard Journal of Asiatic Studies 1: 363-390 (1936).

This is an account of seven bibliophiles and their large private libraries, which are located within the metropolitan area of Hangchou, the provincial capital of Chekiang. The intimate human relationships which existed within this group of library owners enabled them to carry on a private practice of interlibrary loan without any known formal organization; they were for all practical purposes a library association. They often discussed methods of preserving their books and scholarly research. The author maintains that their contribution to the library movement in China can not be ignored.

933. Tam, Kwok-kan, and Lee, Kuang-hua. "Library Developments in the PRC: A Bibliographic Survey." Chinese-American Librarians' Association Midwest Chapter Newsletter, pp. 5-8 (April 1984).

Covering the period from 1976 to 1983, this article surveys library literature that concerns the development of Chinese libraries. A total of twenty-four articles, written in English, are cited according to the following categories: first-hand empirical experience with Chinese libraries, theoretical aspects of the library system, technical problems, historical development, and encyclopedic information.

934. Tsien, Tsuen-hsuin. "China, Library Association of." In Encyclopedia of Library and Information Science, vol. 4, edited by Allen Kent and Harold Lancour, pp. 656-657. New York: Marcel Dekker, 1970.

Tracing the history of the Library Association of China from its founding in 1925 to the present, this short article touches upon its contributions as well as its organization, publications, and activities.

935. "U.S. Librarians Go to China." Library Journal 104 (18): 2153 (October 15, 1979).

This is a news item on a delegation of U.S. librarians representing the Library of Congress, the American Library Association, the Association for Research Libraries, and the Association for Asian Studies, who were invited to China by the National Library of Peking. The invitation was in response to the hospitality shown a delegation of Chinese librarians who visited the U.S. in 1973.

936. Van der Sprenkel, Otto Berkelbach. "Chinese Bibliography: A Personal View of Some Basic Problems." Australian Academic and Research Libraries 1 (4): 127-133 (December 1970).

Based on the author's personal experiences in Australia, the article describes the difficulties a bibliographer confronts in compiling a subject bibliography on China. It highlights the problems of collecting materials and devising an appropriate subject classification.

937. Wong, Wensan. "The Development of Library Buildings in China." Library Journal 64 (8): 295-298 (April 15, 1939).

Divided into four periods, this is an historical survey, with illustrations, of the development of library buildings in China: the conventional period, the transformation period, the transplantation period, and the creative period. It outlines suggestions for future expansion.

938. Wong, William Sheh. "Chinese Literature and Bibliography." In Encyclopedia of Library and Information Science, vol. 21, edited by Allen Kent and Jay E. Daily, pp. 36-131. New York: Marcel Dekker, 1977.

This lengthy article is a part of a longer work entitled, "Oriental Literature and Bibliography." It examines the origin and development of the Chinese language, the history of the Chinese book, the unique features of Chinese books, the history of libraries in China, the intellectual foundations of China, bibliographical controls for Chinese Studies, classification and cataloging of Chinese books, and the current state of Chinese publications. It includes a selected, briefly annotated list of basic reference works for Chinese Studies.

939. Wu, Eugene. "China Materials Development Center of the Association of Research Libraries." In Library Resources on East Asia, pp. 47-50. Zug, Switzerland: Inter Documentation, 1967.

Wu describes the establishment of the China Materials Development Center (the name was later changed to the Center for Chinese Research Materials), which was recommended by some 120 institutions engaged in China Studies. The Center, in cooperation with academic libraries, was designed to improve the availability and bibliographical control of the research materials on China.

940. Wu, K. T. "The National Government and the Library Movement." China Critic 3 (34): 797-798 (August 21, 1930).

Listing fourteen library regulations revised by the Ministry of Education and promulgated on May 10, 1930, this article also discusses the role taken by the central government in the development of public libraries in China.

941. Yuan, T'ung-li. "American Cultural Influence on China in the Field of Libraries." Chinese Culture 4 (1): 144-146 (March 1962).

This paper deals with two major aspects of Chinese library development which have been influenced by American methods and techniques: (1) the professional training of librarianship; and (2) library organization and administration. Mary Elizabeth Wood, founder of the first Chinese library school, is cited as a representative of American influence in library education. American organizational and administrative influence can be seen in library organization, cooperation, and microfilm reproduction of journals during the war.

942. Yuan, Yongqiu. "Window of Chinese Libraries--a Brief Sketch of Bulletin of China Society of Library Science, the Learned Journal of Chinese Libraries." Paper presented at the International Federation of Library Associations 50th General Conference, Nairobi, Kenya, August 19-25, 1984. 21 pp. (ED 259 736).

This paper presents the historical development of the Bulletin of China Society of Library Science, beginning in 1979 when the Society was established. The paper outlines the responsibilities of the Bulletin, which concentrates on library science, bibliography, library/information science, and documentation. The paper also includes two reprints which highlight Chinese libraries: "Major Events in China's Library Today, 1978-1981" and "Major Events in China's Library Today, 1982-1983."

943. Zurndorfer, Harriet. "Doing Library and Archival Research on Local History: A Study of Huizhou Prefecture during the Ming and Qing Periods." China Exchange News 12 (3): 5-8 (September 1984).

The author spent more than seven months in China in 1983 doing library and archival research on the Huizhou prefecture. She recounts her experience at various libraries, archives, and museums in Peking, Nanning, and Hefei. She advises researchers to come with a well-defined project and a realistic expectation of what might be accomplished in a relatively short period of time.

10

International Exchange and Activities

944. "ALA Chinese Exhibit Given to Ohio University." Library Journal 106 (14): 1468 (August 1981).

This is a short note on the collection of 634 volumes of Chinese books, valued at over $10,000, which was displayed at the American Library Association's (ALA) annual meeting in San Francisco and donated to the Chinese collection of Ohio University by the Chinese government.

945. Beeston, A. F. L. "The Earliest Donation of Chinese Books to Bodleian." Bodleian Library Record 4 (6): 304-313 (December 1953).

Beeston describes a surprise discovery of Chinese books donated to the Bodleian Library in England which bear the donors' names and date back to the early seventeenth century. He includes lists of the works and present shelfmarks as well as donors.

946. "Chinese Delegation Visits LC." Library of Congress Information Bulletin 41 (42): 332-333 (October 15, 1982).

This describes the highlights of a trip by four librarians, representing the National Library of China and the China Society of Library Science, who visited the Library of Congress on August 11 and August 13, 1982.

947. "Chinese Librarians Visit LC." Library of Congress Information Bulletin 32 (42): 359-361 (October 19, 1973).

This is a news item on a visit to the Library of Congress on October 1-2, 1973 by a delegation of librarians from the People's Republic of China, led by the director of the National Library of Peking.

948. "Chinese Library to Columbia." Wilson Library Bulletin 92 (10): 963-965 (June 1968).

The presentation of 6,000 rare books by China's former Minister of the Interior, General Han-hun Li, to Columbia University is reported. The collection is from General Li's personal library and is one of the most comprehensive collections on Chinese civilization and culture in existence outside China.

949. Day, Dorothy A. "The Exchange of Publications: China and the United States." M.A. thesis, University of Chicago, 1969.

950. "Distinguished Chinese Librarian Touring U.S. Libraries." Library Journal 72 (17): 1348 (October 1, 1947).

This is a brief note about Wen-yu Yen, of China's National Roosevelt Library, on tour in the U.S. to seek books and aid for the library established in memory of the late President Roosevelt.

951. Exchange of Ideas: East and West Meet the Challenge; Final Report of the Seminar on the International Exchange of Publications in the Indo-Pacific Area, November 4-11, 1957, Tokyo. Tokyo: The National Diet Library, 1958, pp. 29-40.

Chapter I (First Session: Australia, Republic of China, U.S.A., Thailand) of Part One (First Meeting: Experiences in International Exchange of Publications) of the proceedings gives summary minutes of the proceeding by the rapporteur and verbatim proceedings of the discussion regarding the four countries' international exchange of publications.

952. Library of Congress. Exchange and Gift Division. "Current Status of the Exchange Program with China." Mimeograph. September 11, 1981.

953. "Ohio U. and Taiwan National Library Trade Books for Training." Library Journal 109 (15): 1708-1710 (September 15, 1984).

The new exchange program between Ohio University and the National Central Library of Taiwan is noted. The agreement specifies that Ohio University will train Chinese middle librarians in library management and automation. In exchange, the National Central Library of Taiwan will donate 600 Chinese books and 212 non-print items, which were on exhibit at the American Library Association conference in Dallas, to Ohio University's Chinese collection.

954. "Ohio University Hosts Librarian from Peking University." Chinese-American Librarians Association Newsletter No. 33: 8 (May 1985).

This is a news report regarding the international internship program offered by Ohio University librarians. The program hosts its latest intern, a librarian from Peking University, for training in online cataloging with the Online Computer Library Center (OCLC) system and other library operations.

955. "Ohio University Receives Chinese Material." Wilson Library Bulletin 56 (1): 9 (September 1981).

This is a short note on the Ohio University Library, which received 634 gift books from the National Central Library of the Republic of China.

956. Perushek, Diane. "Investigating Exchanges with Chinese Libraries." Committee on East Asian Libraries Bulletin No. 66: 31-36 (October 1981).

Describing the trip the author took in 1981, this article highlights the academic and national libraries, the Academy of Social Sciences Literature Research Section in Peking, the Number Two Archives in Nanking, and the Nanking University Library. It also discusses materials for purchase and exchange between Cornell University Library and Chinese libraries.

957. "Rutgers University Accepts Two Library Interns from Jiaotong University, Shanghai, in February 1985." Chinese-American Librarians Association Newsletter No. 31: 15 (December 1984).

This is a news item on the acceptance of two librarians from China to be trained at Rutgers University Library.

958. "Seton Hall and Chinese Library Initiate Staff Exchange." Library Journal 108 (4): 328 (February 15, 1983).

The exchange of staff agreed upon by the Seton Hall University Library and the Library of Academia Sinica in the People's Republic of China is recorded in this news item.

959. "Sino-American Book Exchange." National Central Library Newsletter 15 (2): 34-39 (August 1983).

This special report chronicles the history of U.S.-China book exchange, dating back to 1868. Various statistics are provided to show the latest exchange between the U.S. and the National Central Library in Taiwan.

960. "Sino-Pak. Cooperation in Libraries." Pakistan Library Bulletin 17 (2): 27-28 (June 1986).

Reporting on a 1986 visit to China by the Director of Libraries in Pakistan, this article explores the possibilities of cooperation between Pakistan and China, particularly with respect to an exchange of books between libraries.

961. "Taiwan and Ohio Libraries Barter Books for Service." American Libraries 15 (8): 550-551 (September 1984).

An exchange program between the National Central Library of Taiwan and Ohio University is reported. In exchange for the training of two librarians from the National Central Library in library management and automation, Ohio University will receive 600 Chinese books and 212 nonprint items.

962. Tsien, Tsuen-hsuin. "First Chinese-American Exchange of Publications." Harvard Journal of Asiatic Studies 25: 19-30 (1964-1965).

Tsien provides background information on the first Chinese-American exchange of publications, which was initiated by the Smithsonian Institution in 1867. Two years later, with the consent of the Emperor, the Chinese responded positively by sending some Chinese materials to the U.S. government. A list of the ten publications from the Chinese government, running to 934 volumes and wrapped in 130 t'ao, is appended, with annotations reproduced verbatim.

963. Tsuneishi, Warren M. "East Asia: The Flow of Books and Librarians: Report of the IRRT Area Chairperson for East Asia." Leads 23 (3): 1+ (Fall 1981).

This reports on the flow of books and librarians since the U.S.-People's Republic of China Cultural Exchange Program was instituted in 1979. The exchange programs with the National Library of Peking and with major university and national academy libraries are conducted by major East Asian libraries in the U.S. The personnel exchanges involving librarians and major book exhibits are also underway.

964. Tsuneishi, Warren M. "East Asian News." Leads 23 (1): 10-11 (Spring 1981).

This presents various reports on the Asia Foundation's activities in China, Japan, and Korea; the United

Board for Christian Higher Education in China; the faculty exchange for library educators in China; and the library development programs in China.

965. Tsuneishi, Warren M. "U.S.-China Exchanges of Librarians." In _ALA Yearbook of Library and Information Services_, vol. 10, edited by Robert Wedgeworth, pp. 161-163. Chicago: American Library Association, 1985.

Reporting on library-related exchange programs between the U.S. and China since the establishment of diplomatic relations in 1979, this article presents the results of a 1984 survey of Chinese students and faculty in North American institutions which requested names, home institutions, and sources of funding. It elaborates upon various individual and group exchanges as well as special institutional programs.

966. Wan, Weiying. "International Co-operation Concerning Chinese Materials." In _Library Resources on East Asia_, pp. 65-70. Zug, Switzerland: Inter Documentation, 1968.

Reviewing the existing relationship between American libraries and the libraries in Mainland China, Taiwan, Hong Kong, and Japan, this article provides some samples of projects to indicate what can be achieved with minimum additional effort. The samples cited include a Union Catalog of Rare Chinese Books, a Union Catalog of Fang chih, and an Index to Chinese Periodical Literature on Archaeology.

967. Yu, Priscilla C. "International Exchange and Chinese Library Development." In _Advances in Library Administration and Organization_, vol 3, edited by Gerard B. McCabe and Bernard Kreissman, pp. 1-24. Greenwich, CT: Jai Press, 1983.

The study is divided into three sections. First, it examines the historical development of Chinese libraries, particularly research and university libraries, from 1949 to 1981. It then considers contemporary Chinese attitudes and practices concerning exchange. Based on the Chinese experience, the study concludes with some thoughts on how to further international exchange and improve library services. It includes valuable bibliographic notes.

968. Yu, Priscilla C. "International Gift and Exchange: The Asian Experience." _The Journal of Academic Librarianship_ 6 (6): 333-338 (January 1981).

This article is based on a survey conducted among a select group of American academic and research libraries known for their third world collections and field research conducted in East Asia and supplemented by a questionnaire to a major research library of an Asian country. The study examines whether gifts and exchanges provide American academic and research libraries with effective methods for the acquisition of materials from the third world. The author reports that the field research in Taiwan and Hong Kong was designed to identify problems facing their libraries, measure the value these libraries assign to international gifts and exchanges, and ascertain the needs of third world libraries within the context of gifts and exchanges.

969. Zhai, Zongshu. "International Exchange of Publications in the Library and Information System of the Chinese Academy of Sciences." Paper presented at the 49th Annual Conference of the International Federation of Library Associations, Munich, West Germany, August 21-27, 1983. 13 pp. (ED 239 629).

Tracing the history and development of the library and information system of the Chinese Academy of Sciences, this article notes that the Academy consists of four regional libraries and more than 140 libraries belonging to different institutes affiliated with the Academy. It also recognizes that the Academy's international exchange of publications has grown enormously, from initially receiving 3,760 volumes from fifteen countries to receiving 600,000 volumes from eighty countries in 1983. The author summarizes the Academy's thirty years of experience in the exchange of publications and cooperation in the field of literature.

11

Librarians

970. Bostwick, Arthur E. "Liang Chi-chao, Chinese Librarian." Library Journal 54: 152-153 (February 15, 1929).

This is a biographical sketch in memory of Liang Chi-chao, the first librarian of the Metropolitan Library in Peking and founder of the Sung Po Memorial Library. It also includes notes on Liang's Memorial Library, which consists of his private collection of 300,000 volumes in Chinese.

971. Chen, Tsu-lung. "Nécrologie: Yuan T'ung-li." T'oung Pao 52 (1/3): 154-157 (1965).

In memory of Yuan T'ung-li, the article sketches his life and career in library and Chinese Studies.

972. Cheng, Heng-hsiung. "Mr. Ting-yo Tu: A Pioneer in Library Career in the Republic of China." Journal of Educational Media and Library Sciences 20 (2): 185-187 (Winter 1983).

Cheng presents a biographical study of Ting-yo Tu, a pioneer in the field of library science in early twentieth-century China. Tu's contributions in promoting library education, organizing the Library Association of China, and designing classification schemes for cataloging library materials are especially recognized. The text is in Chinese, with an abstract in English.

973. Cheng, James K. M. "Fifty Years Embracing the Wall of Books: The Life and Career of Dr. Tsuen-hsuin Tsien." Committee on East Asian Libraries Bulletin No. 82: 29-38 (September 1987).

974. Chiu, A. Kaiming. "Reminiscences of a Librarian." Harvard Journal of Asiatic Studies 25: 7-15 (1964-1965).

An abridged version of a speech delivered before the Board of Overseers' Visiting Committee on East Asian Civilizations in 1963, this article is an autobiographical sketch of the author up to 1939. It especially notes Chiu's contributions in devising a classification scheme and cataloging system for Harvard, establishing the romanized catalogs of the Harvard-Yenching Library, acquiring books for the Library, and reorganizing the cataloging and classification system for the Yenching Library in China.

975. Chiu, A. Kaiming. "Wood, Mary Elizabeth." In Notable American Women, 1607-1950, vol. 3, edited by Edward T. James, pp. 647-648. Cambridge, MA: Belknap Press, 1971.

This is a biographical entry on Mary Elizabeth Wood. It especially notes her contribution to the public library movement in China and to Chinese librarianship.

976. Huang, George W. "Miss Mary Elizabeth Wood: Pioneer of the Library Movement in China." Library History Review 1 (4): 42-54 (December 1974). Also in Journal of Library and Information Science 1 (1): 67-78 (April 1975).

Huang provides a biographical essay of Mary Elizabeth Wood, the founder of China's library system. The author especially notes her contribution in the establishment of the Boone Library and the Boone Library School. He also points out Wood's effort in gaining the support of the U.S. Congress to approve the remission of the Boxer Indemnity Fund to be used for libraries.

977. "In Memoriam: Alfred Kaiming Chiu." Committee on East Asian Libraries Bulletin No. 55: 2-20 (March 1978).

978. Kirkes, Stephanie. "Mao as Library User and Worker: How Early Experiences in Traditional Chinese Libraries Contributed to Mao's Revolutionary Ideas." American Libraries 7 (10): 628-631 (November 1976).

This is a biographical study of Mao Tse-tung from 1912, when he was eighteen until 1919, when he turned twenty-five. Between 1912 and 1918, Mao attended Changsha Normal College, where he spent most of his time studying in the library. After 1918 he moved to Peking, where he worked in the library and was greatly influenced by the library's director, Li Ta-chao, founder of the Chinese Communist Party. The article describes how his political ideas were formed and developed and how intellectual life in Peking had a profound effect on Mao's future.

979. "A Light Under a Bushel." Literary Digest 109 (13): 22 (June 27, 1931).

In memory of Mary Elizabeth Wood, founder of the Boone University Library and Boone Library School, this short note recognizes her contribution to the library movement in China.

980. Nelson, Diane M., and Nelson, Robert B. "Li Ta-chao (1888-1927)." In ALA World Encyclopedia of Library and Information Services, edited by Robert Wedgeworth, pp. 333-334. Chicago: American Library Association, 1980. Also in 2nd ed., p. 501. Chicago: American Library Association, 1986.

This is a biographical entry of Li Ta-chao, a founder of the Chinese Communist Party and the father of modern Chinese librarianship. It notes that Li's brief career as the head Librarian at Peking University from 1918 to the mid-1920's had a tremendous impact on modern Chinese history and the political activism of Chinese libraries in the decades following the founding of the People's Republic in 1949.

981. Nelson, Diane M., and Nelson, Robert B. "'The Red Chamber': Li Ta-chao and Sources of Radicalism in Modern Chinese Librarianship." Journal of Library History 14 (2): 121-128 (Spring 1979).

Presenting a biographical study of Li Ta-chao, the individual most responsible for the radical foundation of modern Chinese librarianship, this article examines the role of the library in the promulgation of Marxism in modern China. It points out that Li's position as the chief librarian of Peking University enabled him to involve the library in the dissemination of his political views and that his role in the May Fourth Movement is regarded as significant in the development of modern librarianship in China.

982. Seng, Samuel T. Y. "Miss Mary Elizabeth Wood: The Queen of the Modern Library Movement." Boone Library School Quarterly 3 (3): 8-13 (September 1931).

In memory of Wood's death, this article describes her thirty-two years of services to the modern Chinese library movement as founder of both the Boone Library and the Boone Library School in Wuhan, China. It outlines her accomplishments in chronological order:

establishing university extension lectures, setting up traveling libraries, sending students to be trained in the U.S., founding the first library school for training young men in China, lobbying in Washington to use the remitted indemnity fund for introducing public libraries in China, launching a national library movement, establishing the National Library Association, opening the National Library of Peking, and forming the China Foundation for the Promotion of Education and Culture.

983. Teng, S. Y. "Cheng Ch'iao, A Great Chinese Bibliographer." Committee on East Asian Libraries Newsletter No. 44: 47-48 (July 1974).

This is a biographical sketch of Cheng Ch'iao (1104-62), a great systematic bibliographer and a pioneer librarian in medieval China.

984. Wang, C. T. "Miss Wood as China's Friend." Boone Library School Quarterly 3 (3): 2-3 (September 1931).

Wang, Minister of Foreign Affairs in the Republic of China, praises Mary Elizabeth Wood's outstanding contributions to library work in China and her valuable services to the Chinese people. He divides her achievements into three periods: (1) her thirty years' service as an educator; (2) her twenty years' labor in building up the Boone Library; and (3) her ten years' effort in founding the Boone Library School in Wuhan.

985. Wang, Chi. "Yuan, T'ung-li (1895-1965)." In ALA World Encyclopedia of Library and Information Services, 2nd ed., edited by Robert Wedgeworth, pp. 863-864. Chicago: American Library Association, 1986.

This is a biographical entry of Yuan T'ung-li, Chinese librarian, educator, library administrator, and a pioneer of the modern library movement in China.

986. Ward, Marion DeConway. "Tribute to Miss Wood." Library Journal 56: 499 (June 1, 1931).

In memory of Mary Elizabeth Wood, the article notes her work in the development of libraries in China. It points out that her efforts in gaining the Boxer Indemnity money to be used for cultural and educational purposes were especially important to public library development in China.

987. Winkelman, John H. "Mary Elizabeth Wood (1861-1931): American Missionary-Librarian to Modern China." Journal of Library and Information Science 8 (1): 62-76 (April 1982).

Combining a biographical study of Mary Elizabeth Wood and the development of public library services in China during the first quarter of the twentieth century, this article chronicles Wood's early life, her Episcopal mission in Central China, her promoting public library service, and her training librarians in China. It especially recognizes her contribution to modern Chinese librarianship through her establishment of Boone University Library and the Boone Library School in Wuhan.

988. Wong, William Sheh. "Alfred Kaiming Chiu and Chinese American Librarianship." College and Research Libraries 39 (5): 384-388 (September 1978).

Offering a biographical description of the life of Alfred Kaiming Chiu and his activities in librarianship, this article focuses on his contribution in devising a classification scheme for Chinese and Japanese books, building three libraries, and training librarians and researchers.

989. Wu, Eugene. "A. Kaiming Chiu and the Harvard-Yenching Library." Committee on East Asian Libraries Bulletin No. 74: 2-6 (June 1984).

Providing a biographical sketch of Chiu, this article especially notes his dedicated services to the Harvard-Yenching Library and his contributions in devising a classification scheme suitable for Chinese and Japanese books in an American libraries, establishing the use of romanization for the author and title on a library card, and encouraging interlibrary cooperation.

990. Wu, K. T. "Cheng Ch'iao, a Pioneer in Library Methods." T'ien Hsia Monthly 10 (1): 129-141 (January 1940).

Presenting a biographical study of Cheng Ch'iao (1104-1162), the first Chinese to systematize and popularize library technique, this article examines his contribution to library science. It points out that the techniques of acquisition, classification, and cataloging are summarized in his work, General History. It mentions Cheng's own classification scheme, which was arranged in twelve classes and further subdivided into 100 sections and 422 subsections.

991. Wu, K. T. "Yüan T'ung-li and the Modern Library Movement in China." Midwest Chinese Student and Alumni Services Newsletter 9 (3/4): 4-5 (July 1966).

This is an abstract of an article written by Wu for the Modern China Project of Columbia University. The abstract gives a biographical sketch of Yüan and his role in the modern library movement in China. It especially notes his wartime activities and work in the U.S. The abstract also includes a short bibliography by Yüan.

Author Index

Numbers below refer to entry, not page, numbers

Subject Index

Numbers below refer to entry, not page, numbers

About the Compiler

KAREN T. WEI is Associate Professor of Library Administration and Chinese Librarian at the University of Illinois. In addition to articles on topics in library science and studies of library automation, she is the author of *Women in China: A Selected and Annotated Bibliography* (Greenwood Press, 1984).

www.ingramcontent.com/pod-product-compliance
Ingram Content Group UK Ltd.
Pitfield, Milton Keynes, MK11 3LW, UK
UKHW041640031026
15587UKWH00001B/396

9 780313 255489